More Praise for

DON'T MAKE ME PULL OVER!

"A book with a title as good as *Don't Make Me Pull Over!* has a lot to live up to, and somehow Richard Ratay manages to deliver. It's a memoir, a work of popular history, and a love letter all in one. Books this wise are seldom so funny; books this funny are rarely so wise."

—Andrew Ferguson, former White House speechwriter and author of *Land of Lincoln* and *Crazy U*

"With smartphones and rear-seat entertainment systems, the family road-trip experience has changed dramatically, writes Ratay in this enjoyable reminiscence on what [these trips] used to be. . . . [His] informative, often hilarious family narrative perfectly captures the love-hate relationship many have with road trips."

—*Publishers Weekly*

"Richard Ratay's impressively researched book isn't just a road trip across America—it's a trip back in time. Suddenly I was eight years old again and bouncing around seatbelt free in the back of a Ford Country Squire station wagon."

—Ken Jennings, *New York Times* bestselling author of *Maphead* and record-breaking *Jeopardy!* champion

"Artfully entertaining and informative at once, Ratay's book will interest all those who look back fondly on days spent fighting with siblings in the backseat of a station wagon, on the road to somewhere."

—*Booklist*

"A wonderful revelation, filled with unexpected—and frequently amusing—insights into how so much of our culture was built . . . Like any great road trip, *Don't Make Me Pull Over!* is a journey full of unexpected detours, curious surprises, and plenty of reminders that our destinations in life aren't nearly as fascinating as the miles spent getting there."

—Rob Erwin, author of *Lost with Directions: Ambling Around America*

"An amiable guide . . . fun and informative."

—*New York Newsday*

"As an expert on the 1970s (I was there), I encourage you to climb in, wait for that sweet Toronado engine to purr, and let Rich Ratay take you on his wonderful ride through the great American pastime known as the family road trip. I was laughing the whole way."

—Tom Shillue, Fox News host, former *The Daily Show* correspondent, and author of *Mean Dads for a Better America: The Generous Rewards of an Old-Fashioned Childhood*

"Much of the narrative will find favor with older readers who can readily recall their own experiences riding in the car while Dad drove and Mom navigated. . . . A lighthearted, entertaining trip down Memory Lane."

—*Kirkus Reviews*

"Entertaining social history spiced with funny family memories. The characters include the first man to drive a car around the world, in 1906 (before fast food!). And America's first highway czar, who served under seven presidents until Eisenhower fired him. And then there's Ratay himself, as a ten-year-old, on the

CB radio: 'Blue Thunder here, gobbling up the zipper dashes like PacMan rollin' for a power pill.' Great stuff."

—Paul Ingrassia, Pulitzer Prize–winning
author of *Engines of Change*

"Smooth prose that entertains and enlightens . . . For anyone who has ever been on a road trip, or is planning to take one, this book is a *must-read*. . . . The book's clever title—a mantra for legions of weary and nerve-frayed drivers at the helm of a fully loaded family vehicle—fits as well as a snug lug nut. Enjoy the journey!"

—Michael Wallis, *Route 66: The Mother Road*

"Ratay has perfectly captured the essence of what it was like to embark on a road trip in the golden days of family vacations. Combining spot-on history and a great sense of humor, *Don't Make Me Pull Over!* feels so authentic I got carsick reading it."

—Jane Stern, *New York Times*–bestselling coauthor of *Roadfood*

"*Don't Make Me Pull Over!* takes us back to the once-popular family road trips of vacationing Americans in the 1970s. Stuffed into a station wagon filled with luggage and provisions, back-seat-bound Rich typically set off on adventures that possessed all the idiosyncratic melodrama of family life but played out in a confined space. And the journeys were frequent. As he says, 'My family alone was responsible for approximately one trillion of the miles logged by seventies travelers.' In chronicling the rise and fall of family vacations, this book is both witty and poignant."

—Anthony Sammarco, bestselling
author of *A History of Howard Johnson's*

"Are we there yet? In this unputdownable book, Richard Ratay takes you on a nostalgic tour of the great American road trip and proves that the ride really is more important than the destination. You can almost feel mom slapping you from the front seat and smell dad's pipe tobacco as the miles roll by and a kaleidoscope of motels, greasy spoon diners, tourist traps, and other icons of twentieth-century travel plays on the windshield's movie screen."

—Mike Witzel, coauthor of *The Sparkling Story of Coca-Cola*

"Richard Ratay has given us a fast-moving narrative of what it was like to travel the interstates in the 1970s. The pages of this book fly by as if they were mile markers."

—Henry Petroski, author of *The Road Taken: The History and Future of America's Infrastructure*

"A smart review of twentieth-century US highway and travel history, from the first paved roads to the rise of airport parking lots as travel by air substantially diminished vacation travel by automobile. An engaging read."

—John A. Jakle, coauthor of *Remembering Roadside America: Preserving the Recent Past as Landscape and Place*

DON'T MAKE ME PULL OVER!

An Informal History
of the Family Road Trip

Richard Ratay

SCRIBNER
New York   London   Toronto   Sydney   New Delhi

Scribner
An Imprint of Simon & Schuster, Inc.
1230 Avenue of the Americas
New York, NY 10020

First Scribner paperback edition May 2019

SCRIBNER and design are registered trademarks of The Gale Group, Inc.,
used under license by Simon & Schuster, Inc., the publisher of this work.

For information about special discounts for bulk purchases,
please contact Simon & Schuster Special Sales at 1-866-506-1949
or business@simonandschuster.com.

The Simon & Schuster Speakers Bureau can bring authors to your live event.
For more information or to book an event contact the Simon & Schuster Speakers Bureau
at 1-866-248-3049 or visit our website at www.simonspeakers.com.

Interior design by Erich Hobbing

Manufactured in the United States of America

3   5   7   9   10   8   6   4   2

Library of Congress Control Number: 2018000125

ISBN 978-1-5011-8874-9
ISBN 978-1-5011-8875-6 (pbk)
ISBN 978-1-5011-8876-3 (ebook)

For Terri—
I couldn't have asked
for a better copilot in life.

CONTENTS

CONTENTS

DON'T MAKE ME PULL OVER!

CHAPTER 1

Swerving through the Seventies

A Family Boldly Leaves Its Driveway

One winter evening in 1976, when I was seven years old, I went to sleep in my bed in Wisconsin and woke up in a snowdrift in Indiana. I had little idea how I'd gotten there.

I dimly recall my father's arms cradling me as I looked up through eyelids heavy with sleep. I watched the white ceiling of the hallway turn into the shadowy pine rafters of our garage, then the fuzzy tan fabric of our family car's interior. I remember being tossed across the laps of my older brothers in the backseat, a pillow pushed under my head, and a blanket thrown over my body. Then I drifted off again into blackness.

Next came a startled yelp. I opened my eyes to find myself tumbling in a blur of stuffed animals, eight-track tape cartridges, Styrofoam coffee cups, and issues of *Dynamite* magazine. I landed on the car's floor with a *thud*, the round hump of the transmission housing pressed into my belly, my chin burning from sliding on the shag carpet.

I had no idea where we were. But I knew where we *weren't*—anywhere near the sunny beach in Florida that I'd been listening to my mom tell us about for weeks. All I could surmise was that I was in our car and it was cold and dark and eerily quiet. Even the engine was still. Finally, my dad's voice cut the silence.

"Jeez, Louise! Everyone okay? Anyone hurt?" my dad asked, his head swiveling around from my mom and sister beside him in the front seat to my brothers and me in the rear.

"Wha-what happened?" my mom replied, dazed. Like me, she'd just been roused from a deep sleep to find herself on a whirling carnival ride.

"Whoa! We did at least three three-sixties!" gushed my thirteen-year-old brother, Bruce, a little too enthusiastically for the rest of us.

"The highway just became a hockey rink!" my dad explained. "Cars spinning everywhere! It's a wonder we didn't smack into anyone!"

My twelve-year-old sister, Leslie, who got motion sickness from riding escalators at the mall, didn't say a word. She just stared straight ahead in her usual position between my parents in the front seat, trying not to barf all over the dashboard.

After counting heads to make sure none of us had been launched into orbit, my parents quickly assessed our situation. The car was upright, though pitched at an unnerving angle. Good. No one had any obvious fractures or gushing head wounds. Good. Not a single window showed a crack. Also good. The worst that could be said was that all of the loose contents inside our car—maps, Thermoses, shoes, me—were scattered about as though our vehicle had been picked up and shaken like a snow globe. But then that was how the inside of our car generally looked while on a road trip anyway. What was unusual was how dark it was. The only light inside our car streamed in shafts through gaps of thick snow caked on every window.

Dad turned the ignition key. To our surprise, the engine roared to life, pressing the windshield wipers suddenly back into action.

As they labored to push the clumps of snow aside, we got a better view of our predicament. Our car had come to rest well off the interstate, halfway down a broad slope that served as one side of a wide V-shaped highway median. Since I was only seven years old, I didn't dwell on the delicate nature of our predicament; instead, I thought about what a great sledding hill this would make—had we been on Dad's prized wood toboggan and not inside our 1975 Lincoln Continental Town Car. We weren't alone. As far as we could see, ahead of us and behind, vehicles were scattered about the interstate like toy cars dropped by a cranky toddler.

Dad pulled his door handle, allowing a ferocious blast of frigid air to swirl inside. The door barely budged, blocked by a mound of thigh-high snow outside. Dad's blood pressure instantly redlined. "Cripes Jiminy!" It was one of many colorfully benign phrases he kept ready to avoid blurting out a real ear burner in front of us kids. Others included: "Gee willikers!" "For crying out loud!" and his ever reliable go-to nonexpletive, "Criminently!" That they made no sense wasn't important. It was enough that they kept him out of the doghouse with my mom and the Catholic Church.

Dad slammed the door back and forth against the snow-drift like a battering ram. This took no small effort. The door of a mid-seventies Lincoln was only a slightly smaller version of the one guarding the entrance to a NORAD command bunker. Eventually he cleared enough space to slip outside, and my mom turned off the engine.

"There's no sense wasting gas," she said. "We may be here a while, and we'll need the heater." My mother was nothing if not practical. "Now did any of you happen to pack candy bars or anything else to eat?"

We hadn't been stuck in the ditch five minutes, and my mom was already formulating a rationing scheme to improve our chances of survival. If raising four kids had taught her anything, it was to always prepare for the worst.

Mom and my brothers also began to piece together the morning's events. As usual, we'd left our home in suburban Milwaukee hours before daybreak. Getting an early start was critical—we had to get through Chicago before rush hour or we'd lose two hours just crawling from one side of the city to the other. Dad's strategy was to pack the car the day before our departure. Then, promptly at 3:00 a.m. the following morning, he'd storm through the house, flipping on lights and hollering orders like a drill sergeant at reveille. As the baby of the family, and the one most likely to cause a delay, I was simply scooped from my bed, still clutching my beloved blankey, and carried out. Dad would deposit me in the backseat, jump behind the wheel, and we'd be off in a cloud of leaded gas fumes. We'd be a hundred miles from home before any of us were really conscious enough to grasp what had happened.

However, that morning my oldest brother, fifteen-year-old Mark, had remained awake. He recounted for the rest of us how the miles had passed uneventfully at first and how we'd even made it through Chicago in record time. But as we crossed Illinois into Indiana, it had begun to snow, and the light flurry quickly whipped into a raging squall. As we reached an exposed stretch of interstate south of Gary, Indiana, whiteout conditions slowed traffic to a crawl—but not slow enough, it turned out. Whipping winds had polished the moist pavement into a sheet of black ice, and without warning, a car ahead of us went into a spin. Trying to avoid a collision, trailing drivers hit their brakes, sending them into swirls of their own. Almost miraculously, Mark continued, no vehicles collided. Instead, each found its way into the snowy sloping median on one side of the interstate or down the steep embankment on the other. Of course, he couldn't be sure. We'd been busy spiraling into a ditch of our own.

The driver's door popped open, and my dad clamored inside, his face red with cold. "I talked to a trucker with a CB down the road. He said a fleet of wreckers are on the way. With any luck, we'll be back on the road in a couple hours!"

So we waited. Six of us huddled in a jumbo road barge beached on a highway median waist deep with snow. We'd all just been nearly killed in a horrible crash in Nowhere, Indiana. We'd have to endure hours of delay before reaching our hotel (and its pool and game room) that evening. We had no smartphones, no DVD players, no iPods to keep us entertained. Those were all years, even decades, from invention. In our remote location, we couldn't even find a radio station signal strong enough to get the local news. Really, we had nothing except each other.

Years later, we'd all agree it was the best start to a family road trip ever.

If there was ever a time Americans needed a vacation, it was the 1970s. Nearly everyone had a good reason to pack up their station wagon or VW minibus and leave it all behind.

The gloomy conclusion to the war in Vietnam had sent morale plummeting, while race riots taking place across the country kept tensions high. Unemployment and inflation skyrocketed and remained elevated so long that economists had to coin a whole new term for the phenomenon: *stagflation*. All the term really meant was that although the seventies also gave us great new things like backyard hot tubs, home VCRs, and countertop microwave ovens, fewer people could afford them. The pressure of making ends meet also helped push the traditional nuclear family into meltdown. The number of divorces filed in 1975 doubled that of a decade earlier. Couples who did stay together had fewer children. The U.S. birthrate plunged to its lowest level since the Great Depression—half that of the baby boom years. Even the government appeared to be falling apart. Just years into the decade, first a vice president and then a president were forced to resign amid allegations of corruption—and hardly anyone placed much faith in the officials who remained.

Not even a night at the movies offered much escape. In keeping with the sour mood, many popular movies of the seventies centered on disasters, demons, and dark conspiracies. Audiences were trapped in *The Towering Inferno* or booked on a doomed flight in any of three *Airport* movies. If you avoided being swallowed up by the ground in an *Earthquake*, you might be devoured by the *Jaws* of a great white shark. *The Exorcist* offered a hell of a fright. And if the devil didn't get you, the government would, even if it took *All the President's Men*. If you somehow managed to avoid all that, you could still be subjected to Linda Blair shaking her booty in *Roller Boogie*. It's hard to say which fate was most horrifying.

Things got so bad that Americans tried just about anything to find relief, from joining the Moonies (a controversial religious movement blending teachings of many faiths nicknamed for its founder, Sun Myung Moon) to disco dancing to learning to macramé. They were desperate times indeed.

All things considered, it isn't surprising that many people, including my parents, decided the best plan was simply to sit out as much of the seventies as possible at some distant beach, historic battlefield, or theme park. Anywhere but home.

Despite the flagging economy, Americans continued taking vacations throughout the seventies in record numbers, just as they had since the close of World War II. Thanks to two decades of prosperity, increasingly generous terms of employment, and broader acceptance of the benefits of taking time off from work, more Americans than ever before were able to escape the daily grind, if only for a couple of weeks each year. In fact, 80 percent of working Americans took vacations in 1970, compared to just 60 percent two decades earlier. As a result, attendance at national parks, historic sites, and other attractions surged 20 to 30 percent every year until 1976. Only then did the decade's second major fuel crisis force many families to pull the plug on their trip to see Old Faithful or halt their march to the Gettysburg Battlefield.

To reach these far-off places, my family, like most others, traveled by car. It wasn't that we enjoyed spending endless hours imprisoned together in a velour-upholstered cell, squabbling over radio stations and inhaling each other's farts. It was that we had no other choice.

Air travel had always been too expensive for anyone not named Rockefeller or traveling on the company dime, much less a pair of middle-class parents taking four kids to the beach. Adjusted for inflation, a domestic plane ticket in the seventies cost two to three times the price of the same ticket today. Given the cost, it shouldn't be too surprising—and yet still is—that as late as 1975, four in five Americans had never traveled by plane. Not for a weekend getaway to Las Vegas, not to head off to college, not for a once-in-a-lifetime honeymoon in Paris. Never.

Although ordinary Joes couldn't afford a plane ticket, nearly every family could afford a car, often two. If there was one thing America was very good at, it was producing automobiles. Following World War II, American car factories needed only to do some quick retooling to go from churning out airplanes and tanks to cranking out cars faster than ever. And thanks to a booming economy, Americans could afford to buy all those shiny new cars as fast as they rolled off assembly lines. By 1972, the number of cars on the nation's roads exceeded the number of licensed drivers (inviting the troubling thought that many cars were simply driving themselves around). What's more, Americans loved to get behind the wheel. During the 1970s alone, Americans logged 14.4 trillion highway miles—enough to travel from Earth to Pluto and back 2,500 times. To be sure, most travelers selected closer destinations, as there are so few decent hotel options along that route even today.

My family alone was responsible for approximately 1 trillion of the miles logged by travelers in the seventies. At least that's how it seemed to me: as the youngest of four kids, I was the one relegated to the backseat, rear window shelf, or rear cargo compartment of a series of fine American automobiles purchased by my father over the course of the decade. Together, we toured the country (well, half of it, anyway—we rarely traveled west of the Mississippi) in week-long journeys taken two and sometimes three times a year.

We were hardly pioneers, of course. By the time we got rolling on our family road trips, Americans had already been beating a well-worn path to the Grand Canyon and sunny beaches of Florida for more than half a century. But for much of that time and in many areas of the country, the routes those motorists took were often little more than dirt tracks. Even in populated areas, drivers often had to pick their way through a confusing maze of privately owned turnpikes and poorly constructed two-lane highways built simply to connect one town to the next.

It wasn't until well after World War II that America got serious about making long-distance road travel fast, safe, and convenient. That's when the country began rolling out the first of its mighty interstates, the so-called superhighways. The interstates were marvels of a modern era, unlike any roads Americans had traveled before. These high-speed highways weren't narrow and hemmed in by trees and tall buildings. They were wide and broad-shouldered, with huge swaths cleared on both sides to invite in sunshine and blue sky. What's more, they were elevated well above the surrounding terrain, affording drivers and passengers a panoramic view of the landscape. Perhaps the most remarkable thing about the interstates was the way they instantly made the country seem so much smaller. Suddenly it was possible to travel from one state to the next and even one coast to the other in a fraction of the time it once took. Places many Americans could once only read about in newspapers or see pictures of in magazines were now all within reach, given a reliable car and enough cash for fuel. What's more, the whole family could come along. In an automobile, four or five people could travel nearly as cheaply as one.

Making things even nicer for my family, many of the interstates had been around long enough by the 1970s for an ample number of restaurants, gas stations, motels, and other conveniences to sprout up along their sides. By and large, we could count on exits with such services at regular intervals, allowing us the opportunity to fill our tank, grab a bite to eat, or rush in to take a quick potty as needed. At the time, my siblings and I took all of these things for granted. It seemed like they'd been around forever. Of course, we were young. Compared to us, it all *had* been around forever. The reality couldn't have been further from the truth.

Like any destination worth reaching, it took considerable time and effort to make everything that went into those great road trips possible. It took the relentless determination of a long list of pioneers to plan and build the roads, highways, and interstates that allowed my family—and maybe yours too—to motor across the expanse of our country and go anywhere we pleased. It took the raw courage of a handful of daredevils to blaze the trails those road builders would follow. And it took the boundless ingenuity and quirky ideas of a long list of clever innovators and dogged entrepreneurs to create what we remember and think of today as the Great American Road Trip experience.

After all, *somebody* had to be crazy enough to be the first to try to drive a car across the country. *Somebody* had to chart the first road maps, open the first motel chains, and cut the first drive-through window into the side of a hamburger joint. *Somebody* had to come up with nifty gadgets like the police radar gun (boo!), the Fuzzbuster (yay!), the CB, cruise control, and the eight-track tape deck. *Somebody* had to decide it was just fine for precocious seven-year-olds like me to roam around the car—and even sprawl out across the rear window shelf—completely unrestrained. *Somebody* had to create the first station wagon; then *somebody else* had to come along years later, look at a perfectly fine brand-new design, and say, "You know what that model needs? Some fake wood paneling on the sides!"

So who were these *somebodies*? Where did they find the inspiration for all these ideas? How did everything we remember and love about those great road trips come to be? And why don't many families seem to take those long road trips together anymore?

Make yourself comfy. We've got some serious ground to cover along the seldom-traveled back roads of America's history. Fascinating stories await.

CHAPTER 2

Pioneers of the Pavement

The Long Road to the Interstates

Like Stonehenge, the pyramids of Giza, and Mick Jagger, the U.S. interstate highway system is one of those marvels that seems to have been around forever. The reality is quite the contrary. In fact, a short list of the notable items that have been around longer than our first interstate includes electronic computers, the Burger King Whopper, optic fiber, videotape recorders, wireless TV remote controls, microwave ovens, Disneyland, nuclear submarines, diet soft drinks, Ritalin, credit cards, the Chevy Corvette, NBC's *Today Show*, ultrasound, color TV, the reign of Queen Elizabeth II, *Playboy* magazine, marshmallow Peeps, and actor/singer/lifeguard David Hasselhoff. Even police radar guns have been around longer than our interstate system, which just goes to show that the odds have been stacked against drivers from the very beginning.

In fact, at the time my family was spinning off into medians in the 1970s, most superhighways were scarcely more than a decade old. That's not to say America didn't have plenty of roads. Depending on how loosely one defines the term, roads had been around since the first colonial settlements. But because our country is so young, so huge, and so generously endowed with every

11

type of obstacle to road construction—perilous mountain ranges, mighty forests, yawning canyons, baking deserts, boundless plains, impenetrable swamps, and rampaging rivers—America would lag far behind other nations in the development of a coordinated system of high-speed highways to connect its sprawling expanse.

As one might expect, the tale of how our modern highway system came to be is long, winding, and fraught with detours, potholes, and dead ends. But to understand why things are the way they are is a trip well worth taking.

The path to America's superhighways began with exactly that—paths—or, rather, narrow Indian trails trampled down by foot and horse traffic. As cities started to be built in the new colonies, farmers and lumbermen in outlying areas clamored for local governments to fund "King's highways" wide enough to accommodate wagons so they could more easily bring their goods to market. But the French and Indian War and then the American Revolution brought road building to a halt. There was no money or workers to spare for anything but the war efforts.

It wasn't until 1795 that Americans were able to set foot, horse hoof, or carriage wheel on anything truly resembling a paved long-distance road. Stretching sixty-two miles between the cities for which it is named, the Philadelphia and Lancaster Turnpike was the country's first major engineered road. The "engineering" consisted of leveling the ground and covering the surface with a layer of crushed gravel. In exchange for a toll, a turnpike keeper would rotate a spiked gate, or "pike," allowing the paying traveler passage to the next turnpike down the road. Because the road was constructed by private investors hoping to make a profit, the state of Pennsylvania avoided the burden of financing a major project. However, provisions in the turnpike's charter gave the state the right to oversee its operation. The arrangement worked well enough that more private companies began building similar toll roads in other populated areas of the country.

Public road building took far longer to gain traction. At the turn of the nineteenth century, America was a young country with many needs: schools, government buildings, prisons, public health facilities, and a military, to name just a few, and government was hard-pressed to fund it all. And roads were expensive. It cost between $1,500 and $2,000 per mile to construct a road at a time when a skilled craftsman might make $1.50 a day and a laborer half as much.

Federal funding of roads faced an additional obstacle: the US Constitution. The founding document merely granted government the power to "regulate Commerce . . . among the several States, and . . . establish Post Offices and Post Roads." Exactly what constituted a "post road" had yet to be determined.

For these reasons, few public roads were constructed, and even fewer remained passable in all but ideal conditions. Rainstorms regularly turned roads to knee-deep mud. As the roads dried out, passing horses and carriages left deep ruts that the sun baked into treacherously jagged surfaces. It made for a rough and dangerous ride.

One of the most notorious of these roads was the fifty-three-mile route from Fredericksburg, Virginia, to Washington, DC, the route Thomas Jefferson traveled on his frequent commute from Monticello. Following one particularly bone-jarring ride, an exasperated Jefferson declared the road "the worst in the world" and vowed to get Congress to commit federal money to improve public thoroughfares. The fact that he was the sitting president of the United States considerably helped his chances.

At Jefferson's prodding, Congress passed the Enabling Act of 1802. Along with establishing the state of Ohio, the act provided a faster way for aspiring settlers to get there. For the first time, federal money was spent constructing a highway, setting an important precedent. The route would be known first as the Cumberland Road and, later, the National Road. Hundreds of immigrant workers were hired to dig a bed sixty feet wide and up to eighteen inches deep, which was filled with crushed rock to form a level surface. The highway offered fast and reliable travel for wagon and horse traffic. In so doing, the National Road opened a gateway to the West for thousands of prospective settlers. Their journeys could very well be considered America's first road trips.

However, the momentum to build better roads would stall. In 1812, America found itself in another war with Great Britain, consuming the country's limited resources. After the conflict, the nation devoted itself to more promising means to expedite trade with its western reaches: canals to connect its many segregated waterways and railroads. With the success of the Baltimore & Ohio line (the B&O of Monopoly game board fame) and the first transcontinental railroad, America became obsessed with building railways, and road construction fell by the wayside. Even funds to maintain existing roads dried up. By the mid-1800s, even the National Road, once America's mighty highway to the West, had fallen into disuse and disrepair.

It would be nearly a century before America would resume rolling out roads with any resolve. The catalyst would be a wheeled conveyance, though not the one you likely expect. It was the bicycle, not the automobile, that would spur demand for better roads.

By the late 1800s, bicycles were nothing new. In fact, they'd been around in some form for centuries; it just took a while for them to evolve into anything resembling a practical means of transportation. It wasn't until 1864 that anyone even got around to attaching pedals. Before then, riders powered their contraptions by running their feet along the ground while seated, the same way Fred Flintstone propelled his engineless car.

The introduction of the "safety bicycle" in the late 1880s changed everything. The bicycle's revolutionary design shifted the position of the pedals from the front wheel to beneath the rider, which permitted riders to power the rear wheel instead of the front, using a treadle and, later, a chain. The modification eliminated the need for the huge front wheel of the "penny farthing" (so named because the model's tiny rear wheel resembled the small penny and farthing coins of the day), allowing riders to sit much lower, between two equal-size wheels, with their feet in easy reach of the ground. This configuration made riding a bicycle much safer—hence its name.

At a stroke, safety bicycles transformed bicycling from a risky sport for daring young men to a practical form of transportation and leisure activity for riders of all ages and both genders. People bought bikes in droves. By 1895, Americans owned nearly 10 million bicycles—one for every seven people. The only problem was that there weren't enough good roads on which to ride them.

With the sport's popularity booming, bicycling clubs such as the League of American Wheelmen popped up across the country. A main goal of these clubs was to promote construction of new and better roads on which bicyclists could ride their contraptions. Bicycle enthusiasts who had been across the Atlantic shared stories with fellow club members of the endless number of smoothly paved roads in and around major European cities— roads built by public funding. American bicyclists wanted the same for their own country. To press their case, they allied themselves with other groups seeking better roads, including farmers (who still wanted better roads for their produce wagons), engineers, journalists, and health advocates.* The good roads movement was off and running.

To enlist public support, good roads groups held conventions and demonstrations and published books and magazines promoting roads. By the late 1890s, the movement had tallied significant victories. New Jersey became the first state to invest in road construction, and others followed. Soon the federal government was pushed into exploring ways to improve and expand the nation's highway system.

But just as the bicycle was helping the good roads movement gain traction, another conveyance was about to shift the effort into a higher gear.

Brothers Charles and Frank Duryea weren't your ordinary bicycle makers. Charles, the older of the two, was known for producing bikes of peculiar design. One of his early creations featured a huge wheel in back and a much smaller one in front, which the rider moved to steer using levers beside his seat. Duryea called it the "Sylph." A bemused colleague called it "freak."

Soon the brothers began disappearing into a garage in Spring-

---

*What bonded better roads and better health? Manure. In turn-of-the-century America, horses and horse-drawn conveyances were the primary means of transportation. Cities were packed with horses—200,000 were stabled in New York City alone. On average, a horse produces 24 pounds of manure each day. That means horses were dropping nearly 5 million pounds of manure on New York City streets every day, creating dreadfully unsanitary conditions. Health professionals supported the construction of paved roads because it encouraged wider use of bicycles, and later automobiles, replacing horses that filled streets with piles of filth. Also, consider that people who work in the health field wear a lot of white clothing.

field, Massachusetts, to tinker with a new idea. Inspired by the recent invention of the internal combustion engine, Charles fixed on the idea of using the device to power a modified horse buggy. Frank, the more talented engineer of the two, went to work on making it a reality. Toiling away ten-hour days, he worked through various problems with ignition, carburetion, and transmission. After a year's labor, the pair parted the doors of the garage to reveal their revolutionary "motor wagon," the first American gasoline-powered vehicle. A newspaper account of the machine's demonstration in September 1893 enthralled the public. It was the beginning of America's long love affair with the automobile.

The Duryea brothers founded the first company to commercially produce automobiles in the United States and rolled thirteen gleaming motor wagons out of their garage in 1896. That same year, a thirty-three-year-old engineer working for Thomas Edison in Detroit unveiled his own self-propelled vehicle, which he dubbed the "Quadricycle." His name was Henry Ford. Encouraged by Edison, Ford tinkered with ways to improve his design and soon started his own company. A decade later, Ford began mass producing the Model T, the car that brought automobile ownership within reach of the common man.

It's worth noting that the world's first automobile accident also occurred in 1896. While zipping through the streets of New York City in his Duryea motor wagon, a driver named Henry Wells slammed into a bicyclist, who suffered a broken leg. The incident was all too symbolic: the golden era of bicycling was about to be broadsided by the age of the automobile.

So as America entered the twentieth century, it would be auto enthusiasts, not bicyclists, who would drive the campaign for better roads. Like bicyclists, they formed clubs and rallied public support. The American Automobile Association (AAA) was formed in 1902, in large part to organize efforts promoting better roads and highways. But the organization faced an uphill climb. Mass production had yet to bring down the price of automobiles, meaning that car ownership was still limited to the well-to-do. Also, most Americans felt government shouldn't involve itself in building roads. Something more was needed to capture the imagination of the public and stir the demand for better roads. That *something* would be a series of daring attempts to cross America by car, from coast to coast, sea to shining sea. The nation had no shortage of daredevils ready for the challenge. But a cross-country road trip through a land without roads? Things were about to get interesting.

The first noteworthy attempt to take a road trip across America began as many ill-advised feats do: on a bet. While visiting California in 1903, a thirty-one-year-old physician named Horatio Jackson accepted a friend's invitation to join him for a drink at San Francisco's University Club. It was there, over a cocktail, or likely several, that Jackson found himself embroiled in debate with another gentleman on the topic of whether automobiles were the future of transportation or merely a passing fad, with Jackson arguing vehemently in their favor. As the discussion grew livelier, Jackson boldly asserted that automobiles were already so rugged and reliable he could drive a car clear across the country back to his home in Vermont. Predictably, Jackson was challenged to prove his contention and a wager was set: $50, about $1,200 in today's money. Jackson wasn't fazed by the amount; he was wealthy. Nor was he dissuaded by the fact that he didn't own a car, had barely ever driven one, or that scarcely any roads existed west of the Mississippi. But he may have regretted having to explain the bet to his young wife the following morning. Rather than joining her husband on his adventure, she opted to take a train home instead.

Undaunted, Jackson made his preparations. He hired a young mechanic, Sewall Crocker, to serve as his backup driver and traveling companion. On Crocker's advice, Jackson purchased a two-cylinder, 20-horsepower Winton touring car. Jackson named the car "Vermont," after his home state and the destination he hoped to reach. Together, Jackson and Crocker planned a route heading north before proceeding east along the Oregon Trail. Their aim was to avoid the treacherous Rocky Mountains and baking deserts of the Southwest that had doomed earlier attempts to cross the country by car. The pair then loaded the Winton with all manner of gear: sleeping bags, blankets, canteens, overcoats, watertight rubber suits, water bag, ax, shovel, telescope, tools, spare parts, cans for extra gasoline and oil, rifle, shotgun, pistols, and a pulley system they could use to extricate themselves should they get stuck in mud. On May 23, 1903, Jackson kissed his bemused wife goodbye, and he and Crocker set off.

Things didn't start smoothly. Only 15 miles into their journey, the car blew a tire. On the second night, the men realized the Winton's side lanterns weren't nearly bright enough to light their way after dark, so they purchased a large spotlight to mount on the hood. Near Sacramento, they were given bad directions—on purpose—by a woman because she wanted her family to get their first look at an automobile. The detour added 108 miles to their route. In Oregon, the pair suffered two more flats. Lacking spares, they wound thick rope around the wheels as a makeshift substitute until they could find new tires. Not long afterward, they ran out of fuel. Jackson rented a bicycle and pedaled 25 miles to purchase gas, then rode back with four heavy cans strapped to his back. Along the way, the bicycle blew a tire. And all this was before the twosome had even departed the West Coast.

By the time Jackson and Crocker reached Idaho, news of their quest was beginning to spread. Their fame was bolstered by Jackson's decision to pick up another traveling companion, a spunky pit bull named Bud. While driving across the arid salt flats of Utah, the dog's eyes became so irritated by dust that Jackson had Bud fitted for his own driving goggles. The press ate it up, taking pictures of the three travelers and interviewing them at every stop. Jackson, Crocker, and Bud became national celebrities.

After reaching Nebraska, the quality of the roads improved, and so did the adventurers' luck. Finally, on July 26, 1903, after sixty-three days on the road (and off it), the "Vermont" and its exhausted crew rolled into New York City, completing the first successful crossing of the North American continent by automobile.

Yet even as Jackson and his companions were completing their historic feat, a man named Charles Glidden was preparing to top it. Glidden's goal wasn't merely to cross America; it was to encircle the globe. By car. At a time when even developed countries offered few reliable roads.

It was, to say the least, an outrageously ambitious proposition. But then Glidden was an outrageously ambitious man. By the time he was just twenty years old, he was already a rising star in the telegraph industry. When he saw a demonstration of Alexander Graham Bell's new telephone, he immediately recognized its potential. Striking up a partnership, Glidden and Bell developed technology that allowed existing telegraph lines to carry voice transmissions. His investment of his life's savings in the construction of new telephone lines and exchanges made him millions.

When the automobile came along, Glidden quickly jumped aboard it as well. He believed the automobile would fundamentally change the way people traveled in the same way the telephone had changed the way they communicated. As Glidden saw it, just two things were needed: public confidence in the reliability of cars and a network of good roads. He hatched a plan to inspire both. In 1901, he sold his telephone business and set off to drive a car around the world.

Of course, Glidden's plan had to account for certain practical realities—oceans, for one thing. He couldn't drive over them, so he shipped his automobile over water where necessary. He also realized that the rainy season in certain regions would make many roads impassable, so Glidden decided to travel in stages over several years, from 1902 to 1906. He'd conquer one continent or region one season, return home to wait out the bad weather, then pick up the following year where he had left off. Finally, Glidden promised to send the *Boston Globe* and other major newspapers regular updates and photos, allowing millions of readers to join him on his adventure.

With much ballyhoo, Glidden set off from London in a British-made Napier with his wife, Lucy, and Charles Thomas, a skilled engineer. Thomas's grandson, Andrew M. Jepson, provides a thoroughly entertaining account of the intrepid motorists' journey in his 2013 book *Around the World in a Napier: The Story of Two Motoring Pioneers*. Over the course of their travels, Glidden and his companions drove past the pyramids of Giza and through the gates of Jerusalem. They summited Afghanistan's Khyber Pass and penetrated the Arctic Circle. They scaled grades as steep as 20 percent in Japan and encountered cannibals in Fiji. They traveled into areas where the natives had never seen a car, much less even fathomed such a machine. Where there were passable roads, Glidden drove them. Where there weren't, Charles Thomas swapped out the vehicle's standard wheels for special flanged designs that allowed the car to drive on railroad tracks.* Throughout the expedition, Glidden remained dressed impeccably, in suit and tie, knowing the eyes of the world (and the press) were always on him. The trip was, of course, one giant publicity stunt. Being the brilliant promoter he was, Glidden did something even more amazing when he completed his journey: he circled the world again! In total, Glidden's epic road trip covered 46,528 miles (nearly twice the equatorial circumference of the Earth) and passed through thirty-nine countries—all without benefit of a single drive-through where he could pick up a quick burger and fries.

Back in the States, car companies and drivers began a prolonged competition to set new records for crossing America by automobile. In 1909, Maxwell-Briscoe sponsored the first cross-country attempt by a woman. The company believed that if Americans saw that even a woman (gasp!) could accomplish the feat in a Maxwell automobile, it would prove its product's reliability beyond a doubt.† To attempt the feat, the company chose Alice Ramsey, the mechanically inclined twenty-two-year-old daughter of a ship's captain. At one point, the scrappy Ms. Ramsey jerry-rigged a fix for a broken axle well enough to drive several miles to a town where a new one could be installed. She completed the journey in fifty-nine days, improving on Jackson and Crocker's mark by more than a week. A short time later, Bobby Hammond made the

---

*Interestingly, Glidden was forced to drive on rails through most of the western United States, which he deemed one of the largest areas in the world without good roads. In 1904, he traveled from Minneapolis to Vancouver entirely by rail.

†The idea of a woman even riding in a car was controversial at the time. One physician went so far as to declare that automobile travel could result in dire health consequences for women, writing, "A speed of 15 to 20 miles per hour in a motor car causes [women] acute mental suffering, nervous excitement and circulatory disturbances." This might be true. My wife tells me she has experienced all these symptoms in a car I'm driving.

same trek from San Francisco to New York in a record-smashing six days—yet even his record didn't survive the year. Each daring crossing generated loads of publicity. And with it, the campaign for improved roads gained momentum.

With good roads in America in short supply, it's hardly surprising there was also a scarcity of good road maps, or even a reliable system for numbering and marking roads. Even in the populated eastern states, the only guide to help drivers navigate the tangled web of dirt roads and trails was a series of dubious guides, called Blue Books, that offered brief descriptions or photographs of landmarks for drivers to look for along their route to direct them where to make turns. "Head north until you cross the trickling creek and look for a trail leading into a sunny prairie," read one entry. Another advised, "To travel in the direction of Baltimore, turn left at the fork with the fallen pine." In other words, if the landscape changed in even some small way due to a drought or ambitious beaver, drivers could become hopelessly lost.

A decade into the new century, the good roads movement was picking up speed. The bicycle craze had gotten things rolling, the automobile accelerated support, and the success of a handful of intrepid drivers in crossing the country—even circling the world—by automobile demonstrated the potential for long-distance travel by car. America was ready to start building a system of roads and highways to connect its distant ends.

All that was needed was someone to help pave the way.

Carl Fisher hardly seemed destined for success. He was the second of three sons born to a hard-drinking country lawyer and his long-suffering wife in tiny Greensburg, Indiana, in 1874. Fisher's mother, Ida, soon decided she'd had enough. Taking the children, she moved forty miles to Indianapolis in hopes of finding work that would allow her to support the family on her own. Fisher wasn't much of a student. He suffered from astigmatism so severe it prevented him from reading the blackboard. Eventually he gave up trying. Fisher quit school at the age of twelve, taking a job packing groceries to supplement the family's income.

Work taught Fisher more than he ever learned in school, especially when he took a job as a "news butcher" hawking newspapers, tobacco, and candy at the Indianapolis train station. He learned he had a natural gift for convincing people to buy whatever he had to sell. Soon he'd squirreled away $600, a substantial sum. At the same time, he became swept up in the bicycling wave enthralling the country. Resolved to marry his talent for sales and passion for cycling, Fisher, at just seventeen years old, convinced his brothers to join him in opening a bicycle shop in 1891.

Things were tough at first. The Fisher brothers couldn't afford much inventory. They kept the doors open repairing flats at 25 cents a pop (literally). But Fisher was as driven to succeed as he was fanatical about bike racing. As a member of the local Zig-Zag Cycling Club, Fisher's competitive streak stood out even among his teammates. They took to calling him "Crip," short for cripple, because Fisher's risky maneuvers often resulted in spectacular crashes leaving him battered and bloodied but always ready for more. Using that same determination, Fisher somehow convinced Ohio's leading bicycle manufacturer to supply him a substantial amount of merchandise solely on credit.

Still, Fisher had no money for advertising, so he embarked on a series of increasingly outlandish stunts to capture attention and draw customers into his shop. He built a twenty-foot-tall high-wheel bicycle to ride through the streets of downtown Indianapolis. He released a thousand balloons into the skies over the city, a hundred of them containing certificates for free bicycles. He even strung a tightrope between two downtown buildings and rode a bicycle between them as a thrilled crowd, twelve stories below, watched. The stunts worked, and Fisher's shop thrived. By the age of nineteen, he owned the largest bicycle store in the city.

But Fisher realized that bicycles were being overtaken in popularity by faster and more thrilling machines: automobiles. Fisher himself purchased what was likely the first automobile in Indianapolis, a French-made 2.5-horsepower De Dion-Bouton. He transformed his bicycle shop into an automobile dealership—possibly the first in America—and began selling cars using the same wild promotional tactics he had used so successfully selling bikes. Once, he showcased the durability of the automobiles he sold by pushing a seven-passenger car off the top of a tall city building. When the car came to rest on the street below, one of Fisher's brothers hopped in the driver's seat and drove off as an amazed crowd of onlookers cheered and followed along back to Fisher's dealership. At least that's what many believed happened. Considering Fisher's considerable flair for showmanship, it's likely a little chicanery (and an identical second car) was involved.

Bigger things lay in store for Fisher. In 1904, he was approached to help market a patented process that used compressed gas to illuminate automobile headlamps. The new system offered a substantial improvement over the dim kerosene lamps in current use (the same kind that had frustrated Horatio Jackson and Sewall Crocker). With a friend, Fisher founded Prest-O-Lite, a company that would become the leading supplier of headlamps in the United States. As head of Prest-O-Lite, Fisher made millions and developed friendships with top auto executives and politicians.

Joining a handful of other Indianapolis businessmen, Fisher invested in another project, a grand racetrack constructed just outside the city. Intended to test and showcase the auto industry's newest and fastest cars, the track eventually became known as the Indianapolis Motor Speedway. However, the legendary venue's 1909 debut would be marked by tragedy rather than cheers. The problem was the track's surface of loose gravel and tar. During that first race, the inferior material crumbled under the stress of the cars' maneuvering. Large chunks of rock were hurled in every direction. Before the race could be halted, dozens of onlookers were injured, and six people, including two drivers, were killed. Fisher and his partners were devastated. The decision was made to repave the track with 3.2 million 10-pound bricks, improving safety for drivers and spectators alike. In so doing, they also provided the Speedway with its famous nickname: "The Brickyard."

The tragedy also got Fisher thinking about the poorly constructed roads people traveled on every day. He understood that the continued growth of automobile sales—and the headlamps he manufactured—depended on the public's confidence in the safety of motorized travel. He also knew automobile owners longed to drive far beyond the limits of their home cities to far-off destinations. Never one to think small, Fisher conceived his most outrageous idea yet: he would build a paved highway spanning the country from coast to coast.

Fisher had nowhere near the means necessary to undertake such a monumental project alone. By his own estimate, construction would cost $10 million, about $260 million in today's money. The projection would prove to be laughably miscalculated. Still, Fisher hoped the project could be financed entirely by the automobile industry and private contributions. To that end, he called together a large group of his prominent friends to unveil his idea at a dinner party in Indianapolis in 1912. Fisher's plan called for a highway of crushed rock stretching from New York City's Times

Square to San Francisco's Lincoln Park. Its purpose, in Fisher's words, was to "stimulate as nothing else could the building of enduring highways everywhere that will not only be a credit to the American people but will also mean much to American agriculture and American commerce." His goal was to complete the highway in time for San Francisco's 1915 World's Fair.

As testament to Fisher's sales skills, the reception to his idea was overwhelmingly positive. Goodyear's Frank A. Seiberling wrote a check for $300,000 on the spot. Others pledged smaller amounts. Fisher also received checks from friends Thomas Edison, Theodore Roosevelt, and Woodrow Wilson. Notable for his absence of support was Henry Ford, who steadfastly declared that it was solely government's responsibility to build better roads. Packard Motor Company's president, Henry Joy, sent Fisher a check for $150,000, requesting the highway be named for a man both he and Fisher regarded as a hero. Fisher agreed. The project would be called "The Lincoln Highway," after the president who had preserved the Union. Joy was elected president of the Lincoln Highway Association (LHA), the organization responsible for overseeing construction, with Fisher serving as vice president.

Still, funding for the Lincoln Highway fell far short of what was needed. A month after presenting his idea, Fisher had collected just $1 million toward his $10 million goal. He needed another strategy and devised a scheme that was both simple and brilliant: the LHA would sponsor the construction of "seedling miles" along the highway's planned route. Fisher reasoned that when motorists traveled the route and could compare the paved and unimproved sections side by side, they would lobby local officials to finish the dirt portions and connect the whole. The plan worked—at least in areas where taxpayers lived. In sparsely populated areas of the country, particularly out West, there wouldn't be funds to construct vast stretches of the Lincoln Highway for years.

There was also the matter of determining the route itself. East of the Mississippi River, the task was easy. Planners could include a number of existing roads that needed only to be widened, paved, and connected. But the western United States was another story. In order to scout the best course, the LHA assembled a team of what were called Trail-Blazers. Their mission was to trek across the vast expanse and identify the most feasible path. The team spent months wandering the countryside and diligently surveying the landscape. Wherever they went, they were greeted by cheering residents and smiling public officials well aware of the potential economic rewards of their town's being included on the route. In the end, LHA leaders did as leaders often do: they largely ignored the recommendations of their subordinates and simply chose the most direct path possible. Stretching 3,389 miles, the route of America's first transcontinental highway traced the length of the original Lancaster Turnpike; crossed the Mississippi at tiny Clinton, Iowa; folded in sections of the Mormon Trail; and snaked up and over the Sierra Nevada at the Donner Pass before terminating in San Francisco.

Merely marking the official route was no small feat. That task fell largely to the Boy Scouts, who trudged through dense forests, across yawning plains, and up steep mountainsides to post signs bearing the distinctive Lincoln Highway emblem: a vertical rectangle bordered with red on top, blue on the bottom, and bearing a large blue *L* against white in the middle. A series of bronze statues of Abraham Lincoln was also commissioned to serve as landmarks in key locations.

Considering the common delays of road projects today, it should come as no surprise that Fisher's goal for completing the first Great American Highway was, in a word, optimistic. Vast sections of the Lincoln Highway would remain unconstructed for well over two decades. Yet the highway's signs remained posted, nailed into trees in remote forests and mounted on poles in the middle of empty prairies, no doubt to the considerable befuddlement of passing hikers and horseback riders.

Despite its incomplete state, the Lincoln Highway opened for motorists as work progressed. Suffice it to say, the situation set the stage for some interesting travel experiences. Even the LHA's own 1916 *Official Road Guide* described a cross-country trip along the Lincoln Highway as "something of a sporting proposition." Motorists were advised to plan for a journey of twenty to thirty days and to top off their gas tanks at every opportunity. More revealing, drivers were warned to get out of their cars and wade into any pools of water they encountered to determine the depth before attempting to drive through them. The guide also listed recommended travel accessories: shovel, ax, chains, jacks, cans of spare fuel, tire casings, inner tubes, and a complete set of tools. Firearms were deemed unnecessary, but travelers heading west of Omaha were advised to pack camping equipment. The guide also informed readers that in certain areas private citizens could be called on for help. Around Fish Springs, Utah, for instance, stranded travelers were instructed to "build a sagebrush fire. Mr. Thomas will come with a team. He can see you 20 miles off." Finally, the guide offered this last bit of advice: "Don't wear new shoes."

Still, intrepid motorists were not to be dissuaded. Among this group was Beatrice Massey, who in 1919 recorded her cross-country adventure both on and off the Lincoln Highway in a journal as her husband drove. She published their experiences in a book splendidly titled *It Might Have Been Worse: A Motor Trip from*

Coast to Coast. In the final chapter, Massey advises other would-be Lincoln Highway travelers: "You will get tired, and your bones will cry out for a rest cure; but I promise you one thing—you will never be bored! No two days are the same, no two views similar, no two cups of coffee tasted alike. . . . My advice to timid motorists is, 'Go.'" She made this declaration despite never completing the road trip herself. After covering more than 4,100 miles over seven weeks on their looping journey beginning on the East Coast, the Masseys encountered terrain they deemed impassable around the Great Salt Lake. So they simply loaded their car onto a train and made the rest of the journey to the West Coast by rail.

Once the country got rolling on road construction, not even the Great Depression could stop it. In fact, the dismal economy of the 1930s only encouraged it. With unemployment running as high as 25 percent, President Franklin D. Roosevelt viewed road building as an ideal way to put Americans back to work. Through passage of various New Deal emergency relief programs, FDR and Congress pumped a staggering $1 billion into road projects between 1933 and 1938. The spending spree funded the construction of 54,000 miles of improved roads. Just how "improved" they were, however, varied considerably. There simply weren't enough well-trained engineers and managers to supervise all the projects. In many cases, men were simply trucked off to worksites, handed shovels, and told to get going. The quality of the resulting roads was often correspondingly shoddy. (Of course, anyone who has recently lost a rim to a pothole might suggest things haven't changed much.)

The good roads movement began the push for better roads. Congress found ways to fund them, and Franklin Roosevelt made their construction a national priority. But it took the inimitable Thomas H. MacDonald to get them built. MacDonald, one of the more colorful characters in the history of American bureaucracy, was as fanatical about building paved roads as he was domineering, pedantic, and egotistical. As Earl Swift vividly described him in his book *The Big Roads: The Untold Story of the Engineers, Visionaries, and Trailblazers Who Created the American Superhighways*, MacDonald was the sort of man who "insisted that his brothers and sisters called him sir, his wife called him Mr. MacDonald, all of his friends called him chief. No one ever called him Tom."

MacDonald's mission in life was made clear to him while growing up in rural Iowa, where his family ran a lumber business. On countless journeys to haul their inventory to market, the youthful MacDonald and his father fought an ongoing battle with the area's dreadful roads. Often they spent as much time digging the wheels of their heavily loaded wagons out of waist-deep muck as they did advancing toward their destination. It drove MacDonald crazy. So when the time came, he headed off to Iowa State College to improve matters by studying civil engineering.

After graduating, MacDonald took a job with the Iowa State Highway Commission. He quickly rose up the ranks and was named president of the American Association of State Highway Officials. By 1921, MacDonald was appointed to head the US Bureau of Public Roads. He was just thirty-eight years old.

MacDonald ran the bureau in the same heavy-handed manner that J. Edgar Hoover ran the FBI. Among his first actions was to demand a 30 percent raise. He made himself the focus of any meeting, controlling those around him with his icy stare. Subordinates learned never to speak unless MacDonald addressed them first. One longtime assistant compared him to royalty, and he was often treated as such. Whenever he toured the country assessing

potential new highway routes, town officials and business owners would fall over themselves to ply MacDonald with the finest
accommodations, food, and drink.* Eventually MacDonald even
convinced Congress to give him personal authority to sign con-
tracts. He'd reach agreements with states and simply hand the bill
to the feds.

But MacDonald's tyrannical approach and industry connections also made him incredibly effective in getting roads built.
He was able to solicit support for road projects from dozens of
key organizations, including the Portland Cement Association,
American Automobile Association, and the American Road
Builders Association. He rallied public support for projects with
fanatical zeal, making the audacious argument that good roads
were a human right, akin to life, liberty, and the pursuit of hap-
piness. MacDonald once wrote that "next to the education of the
child, [road building] is the greatest public responsibility." Above
all, he had the ability to steamroll projects through all opposition
by sheer force of will. By his career's end in 1953, MacDonald
had directed the construction of more than 3.5 million miles of
paved highways.

MacDonald also laid out the blueprint for the US interstate
highway system. In a 1939 report to Congress, *Toll Roads and Free
Roads*, MacDonald and his assistant, Herbert Fairbank, set forth
their ideas for the creation of an interregional system of toll-free
superhighways. In part, the report was a response to President
Roosevelt's favored plan that called for charging tolls. MacDonald argued that no driver would pay to drive on a toll road if a free

---

*This didn't go unnoticed. One enterprising individual impersonated Mac-
Donald on a visit to Blackwell, Oklahoma, and received the royal treatment typically bestowed on "The Chief." It was only after merchants tried to cash bad
checks the man had written that they realized they had been played for suckers.

road was nearby. He predicted the soon-to-be-completed Pennsylvania Turnpike would be a flop, attracting no more than 715 cars daily. No one is perfect.

As part of his plan, MacDonald devised the numbering system for highways we still use today. East-west routes were assigned even numbers, and north-south routes were given odd numbers. The lowest numbers for north-south routes are in the western United States, and the lowest numbers for east-west routes are in the South. Later, beltways skirting large cities were given three-digit numbers that included the number of their associated interstate (hence, I-495, the famous beltway around Washington, DC, connects with I-95). Interchanges and exits were also assigned numbers, either in sequence or according to distance from a designated point. For drivers, the system offered a dramatic improvement over the previous patchwork of randomly chosen signs, numbers, and names.

A final note on MacDonald: he ended his tenure at the Bureau of Public Roads as memorably as he ran it. By 1953, MacDonald was seventy-one years old, widowed seventeen years, and had run the bureau for thirty-four years under seven presidents. His brusque manner had made him bitter enemies all over Washington. Newly elected President Dwight D. Eisenhower, who had big plans for highways that would require a more cooperative approach, decided he needed fresh blood to lead the effort and informed "The Chief" that his appointment would not be renewed. MacDonald immediately returned to his office, summoned his longtime secretary, and told her, "Miss Fuller, I've just been fired, so we might as well get married." And they did, living out their remaining days in College Station, Texas.

• • •

Just when it appeared that America was finally ready to begin building interstate highways in the early 1940s, the plan was sunk along with four U.S. Navy battleships when the Japanese bombed Pearl Harbor. With the nation drawn into World War II, highway construction was put on hold. The war initially put the brakes on the interstates, but it ultimately helped accelerate their construction.

The war effort pulled millions of men and women off farms and out of urban neighborhoods all over America. First, they were sent off for training at distant forts around the country. Then they were dispatched to fight across Europe and the South Pacific. For many, it was their first taste of travel and adventure. Except for the obvious drawbacks of armed conflict, most GIs decided they liked it. After the war ended and they returned home to start families, these former soldiers longed to see and experience new places, even if only in their own country.

What's more, American factories that had been busy producing Jeeps and airplanes for the military made an easy transition to making automobiles for consumers. It's hard to say if production inspired demand or vice versa, but car companies produced dramatically more cars each successive year following the war, from fewer than 1 million cars in 1945 to more than 9 million ten years later. It added up to scores of eager motorists driving a record number of cars looking for new places to go and a faster way to get there.

But when it came to building America's interstates, the war may have provided no bigger catalyst than Dwight D. Eisenhower. America's most famous general at the war's conclusion, Ike had become the country's president in 1952. He entered office with a healthy respect for roads. As a younger man, he'd made the treacherous journey across the Lincoln Highway as part of a famous highway-promoting, military-vehicle testing expedition, the 1919 Motor Transport Corps convoy. And his experience directing America's armies only strengthened his belief in the value of good roads. In particular, he observed how Germany's thoughtfully planned and well-engineered autobahn highway system allowed fast and easy transportation across the country.

As the Cold War with the Soviet Union heated up and the prospect grew that an atomic attack would focus on large cities, Eisenhower felt compelled to provide urbanites speedy evacuation routes. He'd also noted the obvious: owing to postwar prosperity, the nation's roads were becoming flooded with automobiles, making congestion a headache for civilians and raising doubts about whether the military would be able to maneuver through traffic in the event of war. Between 1945 and 1955, the number of cars on American roads doubled from 26 to 52 million.

In 1954, Eisenhower presented his solution. At a meeting of state governors, Eisenhower's vice president, Richard Nixon,* proposed a grand plan to create an articulated network of roads across America. At the heart of his plan was a national system of interstate highways to enable "safe, speedy, transcontinental travel and intercity communication." Ike argued that such a system would reduce congestion, increase economic efficiency, and improve the country's ability "to meet the demands of catastrophe or defense, should an atomic war come." The plan's estimated cost was as lofty as its goals: Eisenhower was proposing the most expensive peacetime project in history.

Approval of the project would, of course, hinge on determining who would pay for it. State governors didn't want to con-

---

*It wasn't that Eisenhower was afraid to present the proposal himself. He sent Nixon because he was he was, sadly, attending the funeral of his sister-in-law.

tribute any more toward highways than they already were, and Eisenhower didn't want the project to add to the national debt. The dilemma reinforced one of the great maxims of road building: everybody wants good roads, but nobody wants to pay for them. Eventually Eisenhower conceded that because the project promoted national interests, the federal government should bear the brunt of the cost. The feds would pay 90 percent of the costs of the new superhighways, with most of the money coming from an increased tax on gas.

With agreement reached on how to pay for the project, the Federal-Aid Highway Act of 1956 was passed, providing for the construction and purchase of 41,000 miles of interstate highways. While many existing roads would be folded into the system, the vast majority of the highways would be brand new. These superhighways would be far superior to the narrow two-lane highways motorists were accustomed to. The new interstates would be specifically designed for high-speed driving, with the vast majority of the system's mileage offering four-lane divided highways and broad shoulders to accommodate breakdowns or pullovers. At-grade crossings would be eliminated, with intersections replaced by overpasses and underpasses to keep traffic moving in all directions. Access to the interstates would be limited to on-ramps in select locations. Finally, the new high-speed highways would be elevated well above the surrounding terrain to prevent flooding and promote quick drainage.

America's superhighways were estimated to cost $30 billion and be completed in 1966. In what may be the single least surprising fact in this book, I must now inform you that the projections were a trifle off. I'll let Thomas L. Karnes deliver the grim details, as he summarizes so well in his book *Asphalt and Politics: A History of the American Highway System*:

Land costs, inflation and upgrading of standards forced Congress to amend the laws regularly after 1956 to raise more revenue. Taxes were increased in 1958, 1959, and 1961, pushing the interstate appropriation up to $41 billion. The Federal-Aid Highway Act of 1968 added 1,500 miles to the interstate system. At the end of 1974, 36,500 miles were completed, and 2,800 more were under construction. The bicentennial date of 1976 became the new target date. That proved naive. In 1981, approximately 5 percent of the network was still unfinished, and the federal bill now exceeded $130 billion.

Eisenhower and Congress didn't just miscalculate the cost of building the interstates. At the time of their construction, the interstate highways were engineered to last just twenty to thirty years. In other words, well before the last stretches of the interstates were completed, the first sections were already crumbling. If you've ever had the feeling that road construction never ends, you now know why: it doesn't. Today's road crews are engaged in a never-ending battle to patch and rebuild highways that have been falling apart since the late 1970s.

When construction of the national interstate highway system finally concluded in the 1980s, America was a much different place. It was crisscrossed from coast to coast and north to south in ribbons of thick concrete—enough to form seven hundred mounds the size of Egypt's Giza pyramid. It was also a fundamentally much smaller, more accessible country. Connected by smooth, multilane, high-speed expressways, America's distant ends didn't seem quite so distant. What's more, the land's treacherous mountain ranges, impenetrable swamps, and forbidding deserts no longer blocked the way in between. Suddenly the

Windy City was just a couple of days' drive from the Sunshine State. The hot springs of Arkansas lay just down the road from the snowcapped peaks of Colorado. A person could chow down a cheesesteak in Philly one day and a deep dish pizza in Chicago the next. All that was required was a car and gas money.

With the ability to explore more of their country than ever before, where did Americans want to go? Where would they stay along the way? And why did so many people suddenly have so much more time, money, and desire to take vacations than ever before? To learn the answers, we need to circle back just a bit.

CHAPTER 3

Hey, Where's Everybody Going?

Americans Set Off to Discover America

The early exploits of transcontinental drivers like Horatio Jackson and Charles Glidden had left a lasting impression on Americans. The completion of the Lincoln Highway and other major roads soon after made the prospect of exploring the country more enticing. And Henry Ford's Model T design made cars affordable, causing automobile ownership to explode. As America entered the 1920s, millions of motorists were ready to put the pedal to the metal.

It was also during the boom years of the 1920s that Thomas "The Chief" MacDonald began constructing highways in earnest. As new highways appeared, so did many businesses catering to motorists. Gas stations sprouted up almost overnight along well-traveled roads, giving drivers confidence they'd be able to refill their tanks when needed. Many of these gas stations also offered garages and mechanics ready to assist motorists with repairs. Farmers and merchants scrambled to set up roadside stands to hawk fresh produce and other goods.

However, outside cities and tourist destinations, hotels were nowhere to be found. Unable to find shelter, traveling motorists brought their own. Autocamping became a national phenomenon. The concept worked just as the name implies. After a long day's driving, travelers simply pulled off the road wherever they chanced upon an inviting trout stream or farm field. Once parked, they'd pop a tent out of the trunk and pitch it right beside the road, or sprawl out in their backseat and fall asleep under the stars. One estimate indicated that by 1924, as many as 15 million Americans had tried autocamping. As author James J. Flink writes in *The Automobile Age*, an account of early-American automobile culture, the autocamping craze inspired "an avalanche of tourists who never before had traveled more than a few miles from home . . . to descend on distant national parks, forests, and points of historic interest."

Of course, autocamping was really just trespassing with a car. Property owners along highways quickly wearied of "tin can tourists" squatting on their land at night and squatting in their bushes in the morning, leaving behind all manner of waste. Soon communities had to address the problem.

Realizing that autocampers spent money in their towns on groceries and gas, many local officials decided that rather than drive off the trespassers, they'd instead provide a public place for them to camp nearby. These municipal-sponsored campsites typically featured a central pavilion with a fireplace, picnic tables, gas stoves, and pumps for drinking water. Some offered stands at which campers could rent tents and recreational equipment. By the mid-1920s, more than five thousand municipal campsites dotted America's highways.

Observing the success of the public campsites, private entrepreneurs speculated that money might be made offering travelers better accommodations. Soon, private cabin camps popped up alongside autocamps, featuring enclosed wood huts with bedding, electricity, heat, and kitchens. Typically arranged in a U or L shape around a central courtyard where guests parked, these collections of huts came to be known as motor courts. For a fee of $2 or $3 per night, motor courts offered travelers better accommodations than a campsite at rates hotels in the cities couldn't match. As competition increased, owners added one amenity after another and adopted catchy—or, rather, kitschy—names like U Like Em Cabins, Kozy Kourt, and Pair-A-Dice Inn. Before long, motor courts were just a truckload of drywall, a case of Gideon's Bibles, and a tacky piece of neon or two from becoming full-fledged "motels," a portmanteau combining "motor" and "hotel." Technically, a motel is a lodging designed to allow travelers to park their car immediately outside their room's door.

But just as all the elements of the American road trip experience were coming together, it would come to a crashing halt with the collapse of the stock market on October 29, 1929. The Great Depression had begun.

Despite the bleak times, construction of new highways continued through the 1930s. In fact, the famed Route 66—the historic "mother road" that began in Chicago, snaked around the Grand Canyon, and ended in Los Angeles—was largely built and completed during the thirties. Americans would also keep buying cars, only in far fewer numbers, throughout the Depression. Midway through the malaise, there was still one car for every one and a half adults in the United States. But it wouldn't be until after World War II that Americans got back to taking road trips. When they did get behind the wheel again, they'd never look back.

It took a worldwide depression to hit the brakes on road trips and a world war to get them going again. The reason is simple: money.

People travel when they have it and not so much when they don't. With post–World War II America's economy booming as the world clamored for its products, more citizens were flush with cash than ever before.

For nearly two decades after the war, America's economy grew at a stunning rate of 3.5 percent per year. With it, so did the incomes of American workers. By 1960, the typical American made nearly one and a half times what he or she had in 1946. In real income, a factory worker in 1960 made as much as a plant manager just a decade before. What's more, between 1930 and 1960, the number of Americans considered middle class doubled. Americans weren't just doing better; they were doing significantly better.

Much of the extra income Americans brought home was discretionary, meaning they could spend it on whatever they wanted. As it turned out, Americans wanted cars. By 1960, an astounding 77 percent of American families owned at least one car, a figure that rose throughout the decade.

Beyond having more money in their pockets, Americans had more time on their hands. The growing influence of labor unions made the forty-hour workweek common even before it was formally sanctioned by the Fair Labor Standards Act of 1938. As early as 1948, a Department of Labor report declared, "Paid vacation clauses are now a standard feature of union agreements in most industries." By 1957, 91 percent of blue-collar workers received up to three weeks of paid vacation.

One more factor was fueling the postwar travel boom: Americans had been bitten by the travel bug. By one estimate, the U.S. armed forces collectively discharged 7 million soldiers in the two years following World War II. Many returned from conflict not just as veteran soldiers but also veteran travelers. When not in combat, they'd walked the romantic boulevards of Paris, admired the majestic cathedrals of Italy, and savored the crimson sunsets of the South Pacific. They'd seen much of the world, only to return home after the war with the realization that they hadn't seen much of their own country. Suddenly blessed with the means to do so, they were determined to take full advantage.

And they wouldn't be traveling alone. Aside from delaying the plans of couples already headed down the aisle, the war made those of family-rearing age realize life was precious and fleeting. The time to settle down and begin a family was now. So the Greatest Generation set to work creating an even greater generation, at least in number. In the years leading up to the war, American women gave birth to around 2.5 million babies a year. In 1946, the first full year following the conflict, that number rose 40 percent. And couples were just getting started. Births continued to climb each year until 1957, when 4.3 million babies made their debut, a figure that wouldn't be exceeded for fifty years.

Postwar Americans had fat wallets, new cars, paid time off from work, the curiosity to see new places, and lots of kids with whom to share the experience. One thing they didn't have was cheap air travel. That's not to say America didn't have planes. In fact, as a result of the technological improvements in airplanes spurred by the war, the aviation industry was thriving. All of the Big Four domestic airlines—American, United, Eastern, and TWA—were busy shuttling passengers around the country. The largest international airline, Pan American World Airways, began offering transatlantic passenger service as early as 1939, just twelve years after Charles Lindbergh made his historic solo crossing of the Atlantic. But flying still had its drawbacks. As travel editor Scott McCartney recounts in an article titled "The Golden Age of Flight" in the *Wall Street Journal*, "The piston-driven planes of those days, like the Lockheed Constellation and Douglas DC-7, were noisy and ferociously bumpy. They couldn't fly over storms and turbulence the way jet-powered planes can. Engine failures were more frequent. So were crashes. And the cost of a ticket was affordable for only an elite few." McCartney points to the price of a round-trip coach ticket between New York and Los Angeles in 1958: $208, around $1,761 in today's dollars. At such prices, most families were left grounded.

Of course, if families really wanted to see America, there was no better view than at ground level anyway. What's more, automobile travel was cheap and flexible. The whole family could pile in and travel together for the cost of a few tanks of gas—gas that in 1947 averaged around 23 cents per gallon, about a third the cost of a gallon of milk. Cars allowed families to leave when they wanted and travel as they pleased. If Mom lingered too long getting ready, the family wouldn't miss the flight. If one of the kids had to pee, Dad simply pulled over. Best of all, cars afforded everyone the security of something familiar in unfamiliar places. In a way, you could drive anywhere without leaving behind the comforts of home. Carmakers even sold several models as extensions of the family home. In one ad typical of the day, Ford billed its popular 1949 family sedan as "a living room on wheels" with seats that were "sofa wide." Could a built-in icebox and fireplace really be far behind?

In the end, it wouldn't be a question of how families traveled, but how often and how far. The roads were open, and the cars were packed. American families were ready to hit the highways in unprecedented numbers. Halfway through the century, the Golden Age of Family Road Trips was about to get under way.

. . .

With Americans taking to the road in record numbers, Eisenhower's 1954 announcement of his "Grand Plan" of interstates couldn't have been timed any better. Newspapers and magazines were filled with articles touting the project. In a *Better Homes and Gardens* article from January 1956, writer Edward D. Fales Jr. enthusiastically tells readers, "You'll be on one-way ribbons of highway so wide and safe your whole family will feel free from strain and worry." It was as if the new interstates would be giant conveyor belts, effortlessly whisking cars from one side of the country to the other. All automobile occupants would have to do is relax and enjoy a carefree game of Parcheesi before arriving safely at their destination. The article's author went on to declare, without any apparent support, that while traveling on these magical new superhighways, "your family is at least four times safer than on ordinary roads." Apparently the new highways would be lined with inflatable bumpers like a bowling alley.

Americans didn't need convincing. When the first sections of the interstates opened, cars veered onto the on-ramps in staggering numbers. Many were bound for distant vacation destinations.

Where were they all going? Not just to sunny beaches, fancy resorts, or far-off theme parks. Many were on their way to places where families could savor America's natural beauty and connect with its historic past. Throughout the 1950s and continuing into the mid-1970s, attendance at America's national parks and landmarks soared. In 1955, when the country's population hovered around 165 million, America's national parks collectively drew 62 million visitors. In just five years, the number would swell to 80 million. By 1972, that figure would more than double to an astounding 165 million visitors. Families also flocked to the nation's historic Civil War battlefields. Between 1954 and 1964, annual attendance at Pennsylvania's Gettysburg Battlefield tripled to more than 2.2

million visitors—about thirteen times the number of soldiers who fought on both sides of the war's bloodiest battle. The nation's capital also became a popular destination, with families traveling—mostly by car—to Washington, DC, from all over the country. In 1964, 700,000 more visitors climbed the stairs of the Washington Monument than just a decade earlier, and almost twice as many walked the halls of the White House. Finally provided the means to cross the country's vast landscape, Americans also seemed intent on exploring their nation's rich heritage.

Many tourists also followed the sage advice of famed *New York Tribune* editor Horace Greeley to "Go West!" In the 1950s and 1960s, Americans developed a fascination with the Old West. Tales of cowboys and America's pioneer past dominated popular culture. Throughout the 1960s, moviegoers stampeded to theaters to see Western-themed pictures such as *The Magnificent Seven*, *Once Upon a Time in the West*, and Clint Eastwood's series of "spaghetti Westerns" (so-called because while the films were set in the American West, they were produced and directed by Italians and filmed in the deserts of Italy and Spain). In 1960, eight of the top ten TV shows were Westerns, including such classics as *Gunsmoke*, *Wagon Train*, and *Rawhide*. It's hard to say whether Americans' sudden interest in the Wild West was inspired by a pioneering spirit revived by construction of the new interstates or vice versa. But the result was undeniable: the landmarks of the Old West became prime vacation destinations. Decaying boomtowns like Virginia City, Nevada, and Tombstone, Arizona, boomed once again. Instead of gunslingers and prospectors, towns were now swarmed by camera-toting parents and kids with cap guns, often traveling great distances to walk their storied streets.

Attendance also swelled—nearly to the breaking point—at national parks in the western United States. Yosemite in particular was overrun. Between 1954 and 1966, visitors to the park doubled to more than 2 million. The park's modest facilities and staff were often overwhelmed by hordes of guests expecting modern cafeterias, clean restrooms, and prompt service. In part, the surge in attendance was due to renewed interest in camping, another result of the Old West craze. But unlike the cowboys who inspired them, families of the 1960s didn't just spread out a bedroll and sleep under the stars. They hauled along gleaming Airstream trailers, complete with kitchenettes and comfortable sleeping quarters. Parking lots overflowed, and vehicles spilled out onto surrounding fields. Fearing irreparable damage to the natural environment, authorities tried to lure visitors to attractions outside the park, but with little success.

Entrepreneurs were also quick to recognize the popularity of the cowboy fad, finding ways to bring a taste of the Old West to America's East, North, and South. Western-themed restaurants, hotels, and attractions sprang up alongside highways all over the country. The Bonanza chain of steakhouses made its debut in 1963, founded by Dan Blocker, the actor who played gentle giant Hoss Cartwright on the TV show of the same name. Two years later, the Ponderosa chain staked its own claim in the market. (The two chains would merge in 1997.) Of course, hungry travelers also had their pick of any of a number of independent Wild West–themed diners and eateries bearing names like The Wagon Wheel, The Chuck Wagon, and Buffalo Bill's Restaurant. Afterward, they could retire to Mosey-On Inn or Happy Trails Motor Lodge for a good night's rest, all without ever setting foot west of the Mississippi River. Interestingly, the first of the famous chain of Wigwam Village motels, which afforded travelers the opportunity to sleep in teepee-shaped concrete cabins, was built in 1935, well before the Western craze of the 1950s and 1960s. A handful of Wigwams still remain today, most notably in the American Southwest and in Cave City, Kentucky, near Mammoth Cave.

While many off-the-beaten-track states had to adjust to the postwar tourist rush that new highways made possible, Florida had already been drawing vacationers for years—ever since someone had the good sense to put the state at the end of a major road. That someone was Carl Fisher, the same promotional whiz who organized construction of the Lincoln Highway. In 1913, at around the same time construction began on the highway that would link America from East to West, Fisher also started work on another ribbon of asphalt to connect the country from North to South.

Leveraging his auto industry connections and promotional talents yet again, Fisher rallied support for a paved road stretching from his hometown of Indianapolis all the way to Miami (extensions would later be added to funnel in travelers from Chicago and Michigan). It would come to be known as the Dixie Highway. Construction of the route moved considerably faster than for the Lincoln Highway, mainly because it folded in so many existing roads. Not even a year after breaking ground, Fisher himself would lead the inaugural auto caravan from his home city to Florida. He must have decided the warm Florida climate suited him. After his arrival, he didn't just set up a blanket and beach chair. He went to work building an entire beach community, starting with the beach itself. Fisher dredged Biscayne Bay for landfill to pile atop an existing barrier reef. On the new strip of land, he built a series of upscale resorts in hopes of attracting wealthy northerners. Borrowing the name of the nearest city he knew would be familiar to prospective buyers up north, Fisher called his new community "Miami Beach."

As a developer, Fisher profited handsomely from the Florida real estate boom of the early 1920s that his Dixie Highway helped initiate. Soon he'd amassed a fortune worth an estimated $100 million. But his luck wouldn't last. By 1925, Florida's hot real estate market began to cool. The following year, South Florida was devastated by a hurricane, severely damaging five of Fisher's hotels. What money Fisher didn't lose in the hurricane was swept away in the stock market collapse of 1929. By the mid-1930s, the once-wealthy entrepreneur was destitute. He would live out his remaining years in a humble cottage in Miami Beach, the community he'd built literally from nothing, supporting himself doing odd jobs for old friends. Among his final accomplishments was helping to construct the famed Caribbean Club on Key Largo, a project he hoped would serve as a retreat for people who, like himself, had fallen on hard times. Despite his rise from grade school dropout to enterprising bike store owner to highway champion and wealthy entrepreneur, respected by presidents and common folk alike, Fisher ultimately deemed himself a failure. He died a broke—and broken—man in 1939.

But his vision of Florida as a haven for sun-starved Yankee tourists would materialize beyond his wildest dreams. Throughout the 1920s and 1930s, droves of tourists trekked down Fisher's Dixie Highway to the Sunshine State. It wasn't just the elites that Fisher had hoped to attract. Scores of working-class motorists also made the journey in their sputtering Tin Lizzies, as Ford's popular Model T came to be known. Others rumbled along in improvised "house cars," the homemade forerunners of today's RVs. After arriving in Florida, they congregated in open spaces and set up enormous impromptu campgrounds. In time, they even formed themselves into a national club, calling themselves the Tin Can Tourists of the World (TCT).

With each passing year, the most popular TCT campgrounds evolved beyond simply providing basic amenities. They also constructed elaborate wooden dance halls, clubhouses, and year-round recreational facilities. Many campers found the surroundings so appealing that they never returned home. A handful of these improvised communities, like Briny Breezes near Palm Springs, incorporated as towns. Others served as the foundations for major cities that sprang up around them, including Sarasota and Gainesville.

Decades before the arrival of a certain white-gloved mouse, Florida was already drawing carloads of tourists to some of the country's first theme parks. In 1936, Cypress Gardens sprouted up near Winter Haven, initially as strictly a botanical garden. Its founders presumably hoped to attract a horde of horticulture-minded travel enthusiasts. Two years later, Marineland made its debut on Florida's Atlantic coast near St. Augustine. Billed as the "world's first oceanarium," the park drew more than thirty thousand tourists on its opening day, shutting down Highway A1A. The main attraction that day? A single semitrained bottlenose dolphin.

A big reason Florida flourished as a destination following World War II was that so many American GIs had been stationed there during the war. As many as 2 million soldiers were either trained or based at 172 military facilities located across the state. Following America's entry into the war, it didn't take long for U.S. military leaders to realize the state's mild climate and vast expanses of vacant land were perfect for housing and training huge numbers of soldiers, especially pilots and air crews. Almost overnight, Florida became home to some of the largest military bases in the world, including Eglin Army Air Field near Pensacola and the Jacksonville Naval Air Station. At one point during the war, Camp Blanding, a major training center in the state's northern interior, was the fourth most populated city in Florida.

Just as Uncle Sam introduced GIs to Florida during the war, many of these same men wanted to return afterward to show their families the sunny beaches they recalled so fondly. Tourism exploded across the state. Between 1950 and 1960, the number of tourists visiting Florida each year doubled to 10 million. By 1965, that figure escalated to 16 million. And just like the tin can tourists who came before them, many would decide to make Florida their home. During the 1950s, Florida's population increased 79 percent, by far the greatest state increase.

Tourism would continue to boom in Florida throughout the 1960s because of the objects sent booming out of it: America's first manned rockets. After the Soviet Union successfully launched its Sputnik satellite in 1957, America instantly found itself in a space race in which it was running a distant second. In response, President Eisenhower established the National Aeronautics and Space Administration (NASA) to kick-start America's space program. President Kennedy significantly upped the ante in 1962 when he declared that America would be the first country to put a man on the moon. Because of its ideal weather conditions, proximity to the equator, and the fact it had already long served as a missile test site, Florida's Cape Canaveral,* on the state's Atlantic coast, was selected as NASA's primary rocket launch site.

---

*Cape Canaveral was renamed Cape Kennedy in 1963 by executive order of President Lyndon Johnson. He did so in response to a request by Jacqueline Kennedy, who felt the name change would be a fitting memorial to her husband, the president who had made America's space program a top priority. However, local Floridians never warmed to the change. In 1973, the Florida legislature restored the original four-hundred-year-old name. As an alternative way to honor the fallen president, the NASA complex at Cape Canaveral was named the Kennedy Space Center. Today, the two names are used almost interchangeably.

Throughout the 1960s, spectators traveled by the thousands to Cape Canaveral to witness each launch of NASA's Project Mercury, Gemini, and Apollo rocket programs. In the early days, even low-profile launches regularly drew crowds in the hundreds of thousands. Between launches, families could freely range about the Cape Canaveral complex on self-guided car tours. Though the gates were opened only on Sundays during a three-hour time slot, more than 250,000 cars rolled through the site in 1964. (In light of today's tight security restrictions, consider this: all of those vehicles were allowed to pass within yards of millions of gallons of rocket fuel inside the perimeter of a high-security government facility during the Cold War.) When a formal visitors' center, Spaceport USA, was opened in 1967, the attraction drew 500,000 visitors. Two years later, it attracted more than 1 million. Attendance continued to swell every year, even after the Apollo rocket program ended. Without intending to, the US government had created the fifth most popular tourist attraction in a state brimming with them.

Cape Canaveral's popularity as a destination went stratospheric on July 16, 1969, when more than 1 million stargazers gathered on the Florida coast to watch Apollo 11 blast off on the first lunar-landing mission (more than 60 million viewers worldwide also tuned in to watch it on TV). Four days later, when Commander Neil Armstrong took his one small step to the lunar surface, America officially won the space race. Of course, Florida businesses had been winning all along. For nearly a decade, they'd reaped millions of dollars from throngs of hungry, tired, souvenir-seeking tourists streaming to the Space Coast to witness history.

In 1970, 23 million visitors, more than the entire population of California at the time, made their way to Florida, mostly by highway. It was still a year before Walt Disney World opened its gates to hordes of Mouseketeers. For many families living in the eastern half of America, a road trip to the Sunshine State was becoming an annual tradition. It was indeed becoming a small world after all.

While American families were just beginning to discover the appeal of Florida and the Old West, they'd been flocking to other diverting destinations since the days when there were barely roads to reach them. I'm speaking, of course, of America's many great amusement parks.

New York's Coney Island began to draw visitors to its beaches as soon as a private company built a bridge to connect the small island with the mainland in 1829. As thousands of urbanites repeatedly fled the stress and smog of nearby Brooklyn to enjoy the rejuvenating charms of the resort area, a railway line and steamship service were added, cutting the half-day's journey to a mere two hours.

Sensing an opportunity to make a buck, or thousands of bucks, a veteran showman, Paul Boyton, established an "aquatic circus" in 1895 to entertain visitors to the area. Boyton's show, featuring forty trained sea lions, was an instant hit. Hoping to increase his take, Boyton quickly added a log flume ride and then a roller-coaster featuring—amazingly, for a pre-1900 ride—an inverted loop. Enclosing his attractions with a fence and charging a fixed admission fee, Boyton called his property Sea Lion Park. It was the first permanent amusement park in North America.

Unfortunately for Boyton, he created a monster he couldn't control. The public's craving for new rides and attractions ramped up so quickly that he couldn't keep up with demand. Investors with much deeper pockets poured into the area, setting up their own amusement parks and forcing Boyton to sell his park before being driven out of business altogether. Sea Lion Park became Luna Park, joining competing major amusement parks Steeplechase Park and Dreamland, along with an assortment of independent attractions, to form the largest amusement area in the United States. Between the early 1900s and World War II, Coney Island drew several million visitors each year.

Interestingly, instead of bringing more guests to the area, the rise of the automobile actually helped drive families away. As the amusement parks of Coney Island grew more crowded following the war, street gangs began to exert an intimidating presence, especially in the midways, and the parks developed seedy reputations. Afforded the liberty of their own transportation, families living in the upper Northeast increasingly opted to travel to the more appealing state parks of Long Island, especially Jones Beach Island, or take even longer road trips to more wholesome, albeit more distant, amusement parks. These included Rye Playland on Long Island Sound; Seabreeze in Rochester, New York; Riverside Park (now Six Flags New England) in Agawam, Massachusetts; and Lake Compounce in Bristol, Connecticut.

The automobile helped amusement parks in other, less densely populated areas of the country thrive as well. Founded in 1906 by chocolate scion Milton S. Hershey, Hershey Park remained a popular attraction, drawing visitors from all over the Midwest to the tiny town of Hershey, fifteen miles outside Harrisburg, Pennsylvania. Aside from the chance to tour the nearby Hershey Chocolate Factory, Hershey Park (renamed Hersheypark after transitioning to a theme park in 1971) invited guests to swim in several enormous pools and enjoy a merry-go-round, railroad, bumper cars, funhouse rides, and a roller-coaster. On the shores of Lake Erie in Sandusky, Ohio, Cedar Pointe Park gradually transformed from a bathing resort into a full-fledged amusement park, boasting multiple roller-coasters. Though it fell into disrepair during World War II, the park was revived and restored to its status as a major tourist attraction during the 1960s and 1970s.

Meanwhile, across the country in Buena Park, California, a berry farmer was busy with his own budding attraction. In the 1920s, Walter Knott opened a simple roadside stand where he sold cartons of his berries, along with jars of preserves and homemade berry pies. Recognizing his customers were hungry for more, Knott encouraged his wife, Cordelia, to begin frying up chickens to serve as well. Mrs. Knott's delicious dinners proved even more popular. As word spread and more guests found their way to the farm, the Knotts built a proper restaurant, shops, and—to entertain the kids—a replica Old West Ghost Town. It turned out to be more like a boomtown. After adding a steakhouse, saloon, stagecoach ride, and working railroad, the Ghost Town attracted its own following, and soon Walter was installing a carousel, a mine ride, and a fence to surround it all so he could begin charging admission. By the 1970s, Knotts Berry Farm was a genuine amusement park with sophisticated roller-coasters and thrill rides rivaling those found anywhere.

It's unsurprising that Walter Knott felt the need to keep expanding and adding bigger and better attractions. As of the mid-1950s, he faced stiff competition from another park that had opened just minutes down the road. Not only did the competitor have big ideas and substantial financial backing, the new rival was closely acquainted with one of the most recognized and beloved figures in the world. His name, of course, was Walt Disney.

Referred to in early plans as "Mickey Mouse Park," Disneyland was unveiled during a special-event broadcast live on ABC Television on July 17, 1955, hosted by Art Linkletter, Bob Cummings, and a fading movie star named Ronald Reagan. The enormous appeal of Disney and his animated characters, along with such original attractions as Jungle Cruise, Mr. Toad's Wild Ride, the King Arthur Carousel, and Snow White's Scary Adventures, soon had families traveling to Anaheim, California, from all over the country—even beyond. During his 1959 trip to America, Soviet premier Nikita Khrushchev had but two requests: to meet Hollywood legend John Wayne and to visit Disneyland. With Cold War tensions at a peak and security concerns high, Khrushchev's latter request was denied.

Walt Disney's grand ambitions were constrained only by the limitations of his original land purchase. Just years after Disneyland's opening, it became clear to Disney that his 160-acre property was far too small to accommodate his plans for future expansion. What's more, Disney conducted surveys that showed just 5 percent of Disneyland's guests came from east of the Mississippi River, where 75 percent of the US population lived at the time. As early as 1959, he began searching for a site for an even larger, more elaborate theme park—in fact, a complex of theme parks that would include a forward-thinking planned community that could serve as a test lab for innovative new ideas in urban living.*

After considering several locations, Disney settled on central Florida for many of the same reasons the military had during World War II: vast amounts of cheap land, a mild year-round climate, and a well-developed existing infrastructure of highways

---

*This was the genesis of EPCOT (Experimental Prototype Community of Tomorrow). Disney hoped EPCOT would be a functioning city, where residents employed by the Magic Kingdom would live and interact with experimental products and technologies on a daily basis. Moving walkways would render cars unnecessary and a greenbelt of parks would separate the city's public services from where residents lived. Only later, after Walt Disney's death, did plans for EPCOT evolve into a more traditional theme park.

and airports. To avoid attracting the attention of land speculators who might drive up real estate prices, Disney formed an armada of dummy corporations to stealthily purchase more than thirty thousand acres of land near Orlando, Florida. Finally, in October 1965, Disney's secret was revealed by an investigative reporter for the *Orlando Sentinel*.

Walt Disney World opened on October 1, 1971. Unfortunately, Walt himself wouldn't live to see it. He developed lung cancer and died in 1966 at age sixty-five. His brother, Roy O. Disney, would oversee construction. Three months after the park's opening, Roy would also pass away. But together, the Disney brothers planned and built a complex of almost limitless imagination and appeal for children and parents alike. Today, the Walt Disney World Resort is the most visited vacation resort in the world, drawing a mind-boggling 52 million guests each year—far more than twice the present population of Florida.

The opening of Walt Disney World was just one peak of a wild roller-coaster of construction and expansion of amusement parks around the country during the mid-1960s and 1970s. The Six Flags chain of amusement parks began with a single property in Arlington, Texas, in 1961. The "Six Flags" name refers to the six different nations that governed the Texas region over its long history, each commemorated with its own themed area in the original park: Spain, France, Mexico, the Republic of Texas, the Confederate States of America, and the United States. The company went on to build Six Flags Over Georgia in 1967 and Six Flags Over Mid-America (near St. Louis) in 1971, then acquired a series of independently operated parks including AstroWorld in Houston, Texas; Great Adventure in Jackson, New Jersey; Magic Mountain in Valencia, California; and Marriott's Great America in Gurnee, Illinois.

Near Cincinnati, Ohio, King's Island amusement park opened in 1972 after buying and relocating most of the rides of Coney Island, a popular park that had borrowed the name of New York City's famous attraction and was located on the nearby banks of the Ohio River that had become prone to flooding. Taft Broadcasting, the same company that built King's Island, would also open Carowinds amusement park near Charlotte, North Carolina, in 1973, and Kings Dominion in Doswell, Virginia, in 1975.

Meanwhile, just a couple of hours' drive from Walt Disney World in Tampa, Busch Gardens in the seventies hoped to capitalize on Americans' rising interest in thrill rides by adding a few of its own. Once strictly a bird sanctuary and free-range habitat for African animals owned by the Anheuser-Busch beer company, Busch Gardens added a railroad followed by one roller-coaster after another to broaden its appeal to families with children.

Animals remained the featured attraction at another theme park, opened in San Diego in 1964. SeaWorld was the spawn of four fraternity brothers from UCLA who originally intended to open an underwater restaurant and marine show. However, as construction began, it became evident that the aspiring entrepreneurs' vision far exceeded their budget. Instead, the partners settled on building a marine animal park, originally showcasing dolphins, sea lions, and two saltwater aquariums.

The group's big break came in the form a bad blind date. An adolescent female orca captured in Washington State's Puget Sound turned a cold shoulder to her male orca companion at a private Seattle aquarium, so the aquarium sold the finicky finned lass to SeaWorld, where she was trained to perform a series of crowd-pleasing tricks. Shamu became a sensation, making SeaWorld a major national attraction—so much so that when she passed away in 1971, a succession of other orcas inherited her name and were charged with carrying on her legacy. Spurred on by their success, SeaWorld moved to open additional locations, curiously first choosing a site near cold-weather Cleveland in 1970, and then more tourist-friendly Orlando in 1973.

While standing out in the baking Florida sun at his company's newest park, founding SeaWorld partner George Millay heard so many visitors mention how much they wished they could join the animals in the water that he began to seriously contemplate ways to make it happen. Taking inspiration from seasonal "splash pads" and other wet attractions around the country, Millay conceived his vision for the Wet 'n Wild waterpark that debuted in 1977. Many would argue it wasn't America's first waterpark. Even nearby Disney beat Millay to the punch, opening its River Country waterpark area the year before. But Wet 'n Wild took the concept to a whole new level, erecting an enormous standalone park at which guests could plunge into a giant wave pool and hurdle down dozens of winding waterslides for a fixed admission fee. Millay himself would come to be known as the Father of Waterparks.

The success of Wet 'n Wild unleashed a wave of copycats across the nation, giving rise to a new industry. Among the most notable early waterparks were Schlitterbahn* in New Braunfels, Texas, and Noah's Ark in Wisconsin Dells, Wisconsin. Like the big amusement parks, the most prominent waterparks became prime destinations for families looking for fun-packed getaways.

By the start of the 1970s, America was a nation on the move, a trend made all the more possible by the continuing construction of Eisenhower's interstate highways. Families everywhere were hitting the road to explore their country. They were trekking to

---

Schlitterbahn is a German word meaning "slippery road." The park developers chose the name as a nod to the area's roots as a settlement for German immigrants in the mid-nineteenth century.

America's national parks, visiting its historic landmarks, rediscovering how the West was won, gathering to witness history being made, and seeking new thrills at a growing bounty of amusement parks and waterparks. My parents had delayed joining these families on the road until their fourth and final child—me—was out of diapers and at least a little less likely to turn a long drive to Florida into a short trip to hell. They had now waited long enough. It was time to get going.

CHAPTER 4

Packed In Like Sardines

Join Us, Won't You?

From where I sit, or rather from where I *sat*—typically the rear window ledge of one of my dad's titanic Land Cruisers or in the rear-facing cargo seat in one of our family station wagons—there was simply no better time to be out on the highways exploring America than during the 1970s. It was the last true decade of the family road trip (for reasons we'll discover later), and everything that played into those expeditions—the highways, the cars, the motels, the devices we used while traveling, even the food we picked up along the way—had had enough time to evolve to make those experiences truly worth remembering. It was just a happy coincidence, of course, that this remarkable era happened to mesh with my family's years traveling the country together.

I could explain why the seventies were the best time to be roving around America, but the only way to appreciate it is to experience it all yourself. Perhaps you already did with your own family while growing up at the time. Maybe you were even the one driving or trying to keep a car full of young kids from starting a mutiny in the backseat. Or maybe it was your misfortune to have been born too late to know what it was like to experience a *real* family road trip. Regardless, I now invite you to come along and join me and my family on one of our trips—or, rather, several. After all, to understand how family road trips came to be and what made them so special, we've got a lot of ground to cover. And what better place to discuss it than out on the road?

First, you'll want to know a bit more about whom you'll be traveling with, so some brief introductions are in order. Joining us in the rear seat compartment are my two brothers. My oldest brother, Mark, was (and amazingly still is) a full eight years my senior, a gap wide enough in kid world to make us more like distant acquaintances. He liked dance clubs, disco music, and *Saturday Night Fever*. I liked baseball, G.I. Joes (the classic foottall ones with fuzzy heads and beards and cool "Adventure Team Vehicles"), and the *Herbie the Love Bug* movies. Probably the most important time we spent together was on our family vacations.

On our other side is my second brother, Bruce, just eleven months younger than Mark (my parents evidently thought they were working under a deadline). Bruce was nearly Mark's complete opposite: a gearhead, rebellious, loved muscle cars and loud rock. But unlike Mark, Bruce relished spending time with me—most often in one-sided wrestling matches in our family room, ending with me facedown in a full nelson and at least two lamps knocked over. Out on the road, Bruce's mechanical skills would save our bacon more than once.

Up front, my sister, Leslie, would settle into the awkward middle space between my parents. In most of our cars, it wasn't even really a seat at all, but a sort of semipadded fault line dividing the huge driver's seat and passenger seat. Still, it was her only refuge from the horrors taking place behind her. Pretty, petite, and blond, Leslie is five years older than I, making me the baby of the family by a suspicious margin (years later, my mom gently conceded I'd been "an extra special blessing"). A straight A student beloved by teachers and active in every school activity from Key Club to the yearbook committee, Leslie was the type of older sister that a slightly mischievous younger brother like me should have grown up hating reflexively. But she was also so inexplicably nice and generous to me that I found it impossible to dislike her.

Finally, you'll need to meet my parents. My mother, Marilyn, was, as most young boys see their moms, perfect: beautiful, kind, playful, and eternally patient. If Dad was the engine of our family, plowing us through any obstacle, Mom was the power steering, always keeping us headed in the right direction. In addition to raising four very different but all strong-willed children, making our meals, and managing our household, she also worked as a physical therapist at a local hospital. She was amazing.

Which brings us to my father, Charles, or "Chuck," as my mom and all of his friends called him. My father was a force of nature. An only child born to humble laborers on Chicago's South Side, my father proved his smarts and work ethic first to his superior officers in the army during World War II—for which he was promoted at just nineteen years old to the rank of master sergeant—and later to his bosses at the local branch of a large national electronics distribution company. He was a natural salesman, and his gift for gab and unwillingness to take no for an answer had served him well. By the 1970s, he was the leading salesman and vice president at his branch, earning enough to move our family to one of the nicer suburbs of Milwaukee and provide us with all the trappings of an upper-middle-class lifestyle. In stature, my father stood exactly six feet tall and was of average build, belying his oversize personality and presence. He had a head of thinning, extremely blond hair, accentuated by gold-rimmed glasses, and a round face that folded into deep crevasses when he grinned, to reveal a wide set of bright white teeth.

My friends all thought he looked like Conrad Bain, the actor who played Mr. Drummond on TV's *Diff'rent Strokes*, starring the precocious Gary Coleman.

My dad was modest and conservative in nearly every way—except when it came to his cars. In this area, his tastes can most generously be described as endearingly eccentric. Owning full-size luxury automobiles endowed with every fancy trim package and optional extra feature was one of the few indulgences he allowed himself. Part of the reason was what he did for a living. The customers he sold his firm's products to included high-level executives at some of Milwaukee's biggest manufacturing companies. To build relationships with them, he knew he had to swim in the same social circles and, at least, appear to live life on their level. So he talked his boss into paying for his admission to a local country club to which many of these men belonged, and he bought a succession of fancy cars to drive there. That he also passionately adored every leather-upholstered, chrome-trimmed, gas-guzzling inch of these luxury cars was just icing on the cake.

The truth is my dad may have loved his cars a little too much. When it came to selecting optional trim packages, styling accessories, and color combinations, he could go a little overboard. In an era when automobile designers already pushed the limits of good taste, my father was all too willing to nudge them just a little further. He loved whitewall tires and sparkling chrome wheels. He insisted on pinstripes, the more lines the better. He adored monument-size hood ornaments and glimmering side trim. He considered features like carriage tops and burled wood dashboards standard equipment. As a result, one of the two cars my family owned at any given time often resembled the perp vehicle being chased down on the latest episode of *Starsky and Hutch*.

Now that you know *who* you'll be traveling with, I should

probably tell you where we traveled and why. After all, you can't really experience a family road trip unless you feel like one of the family.

Throughout the 1970s and into the mid-1980s, my family took two and sometimes three long road trips each year. Nothing kept us off the road. Not the oil embargo of the early 1970s, or the economic recession of the late 1970s, or even the disco music my oldest brother and sister would insist on playing on our car's stereo. We had places to go, things to see, and, almost invariably, a tee time to make at some sunny golf course at the end of the highway. This was because my father was fanatically devoted to the sport.

Dad had an interest in golf the same way teenage boys have an interest in swimsuit models. Outside of his family, golf was his consuming passion. It filled his thoughts and his time as much as any hobby could for a man who wanted to remain happily married and gainfully employed. Typically my dad played three times a week at the local country club—Thursday afternoons, Saturday mornings, and Sunday afternoons. If he could talk a client into a "business meeting," he might even fit a fourth round into the week.

My parents had actually met while on a golf junket. Well, my father was on a golf junket; my mother was simply vacationing at the same resort with a friend. For my dad, meeting a pretty, vivacious, and intelligent brunette just a five-iron from the eighteenth green must have seemed like destiny. They were married six months later. Though my mom had never set foot on a golf course before, my dad had coached her well enough to join him in a couples' league their first summer together. As for us four kids, Dad made sure we took golf lessons—whether we wanted to or not—as soon as each of us was old enough to hold a club. My brothers eventually rebelled as teenagers and found their own interests, but my sister and I stuck with the sport long enough to keep playing through high school. That was good enough for my dad. Between my mom, sister, and me, he had his little foursome and an excuse for turning our family vacations into his version of the PGA Tour.

My dad's addiction to golf didn't just dictate where we traveled but also when. If he didn't get his fix of fairways every few months, he'd begin to exhibit withdrawal symptoms. It made my parents' choice to live in Wisconsin an unfortunate one. For approximately eleven months of the year, or so it seemed, Wisconsin was buried in a thick blanket of snow, which presents a challenge for golfers hoping to locate a small white ball. To eliminate that problem and, as Dad put it, "keep the shakes at bay," he planned our vacations for the winter months, while just about every other family I knew traveled during the summer. So that we wouldn't miss much school, Christmas and Easter breaks were earmarked for our getaways.

Almost invariably we traveled due south. It was the most direct route from where we lived to golf courses that didn't need to be plowed before they could be played. While most families selected vacation destinations based on their historical interest or striking natural beauty, ours were most often selected for their proximity to a well-maintained golf course with reasonably priced greens fees. If there also happened to be a beach within an hour's drive, it was mostly a happy accident.

Of course, my mom still held veto power over the final selection. And she wouldn't hesitate in using it if there was nothing of interest in the choice for her. She may have allowed Dad to turn her into a golfer, but she wasn't about to let him turn her into a golf *widow*. While she genuinely enjoyed playing an occasional round of golf, she wasn't fanatical about it in the way my father was. She realized there existed a world out there beyond the white boundary stakes of a golf course, and she wanted to share that world with her family. So any destination my father ultimately chose would have to offer something beyond a favorably reviewed golf course.

Most often, our destination would be a golf resort somewhere near the Gulf Coast—the same type of resort where my folks originally met and, just as important, the kind offering deep discounts in ads in the back of *Golf Magazine*. To be honest, these resorts were a sensible compromise. The properties my dad chose were essentially glorified country clubs. Typically there'd be a championship-caliber golf course, or two, or even three, to allow Dad to satisfy his lust for the links, in addition to a collection of other activities and facilities for the rest of us: tennis courts, swimming pools, fishing holes, sometimes even horse stables or yacht clubs. To secure my mom's approval, he'd always select resorts near New Orleans or the beaches of the Florida Panhandle, and take a break from golfing for a day or two to join us for a side trip.

It wasn't the worst fate for my siblings and me to serve as my dad's personal golf gallery on family vacations. In fact, we had it pretty good. At least once we arrived at our resort, we were free to wander off and do our own things. Not all of my friends were so lucky. Some of my buddies spent their vacations being dragged to dreary museums, unimpressive landmarks, and second-tier Civil War battlefields, or they'd loiter for days on end at rinky-dink campgrounds where the highlight of the trip might be raccoons coming to raid the family cooler.

One of my friends' dad insisted on stopping to read every historical marker they encountered, adding hours to each journey.

Another buddy told me that on a journey from the family's home in New York across the country to the Grand Canyon, his father insisted on spending the better part of a day at a site called the Grotto of the Redemption in West Bend, Iowa. There the family was treated to a tour guide's detailed dissertation on how a priest created nine tacky scenes from the life of Jesus using an assortment of biodiesel-fueled machines and a vast collection of semiprecious stones. Thrilling.

Another friend told me of the cheers he and his siblings let loose as they finally crossed the state line into sunny Florida. After being cooped up together in a car for two and a half days, they were eager to finally spend a day frolicking on the beach. Instead, upon seeing a billboard, my friend's dad impulsively pulled over in St. Augustine to tour the home of Prince Achille Murat, the son of the brother-in-law of Napoleon. I'll say that again: *the home . . . of the son of the brother-in-law of Napoleon.*

Yet another friend went on a family road trip in which *there was no destination.* He and the other five members of his family embarked on a giant loop of the American West, proceeding from one scenic mountain range, canyon, or landmark to the next, covering 5,500 miles over seventeen days, never remaining in any one place more than a night or two. They saw some amazing scenery but . . . seventeen days. In a car. With family. That would drive anyone to the brink.

At least my family traveled in style, however garish and gaudy that style may have been. Even with six occupants, my dad's cars were relatively roomy. We had plush seating and—thanks to my father's penchant for loading his automobiles with extras— heat, air-conditioning, a hi-fi stereo, and other amenities. Few of my friends could say the same. Many endured endless nausea-inducing hours facing backward, perched on the thinly padded pop-up jump seats in the "way-back" of their family station wagons. One friend, whose father was an avid outdoorsman, has shared horror stories of being forced to ride for hours in the cap-enclosed bed of the family's pickup truck en route to their distant cabin. While her parents traveled in relative comfort in the cab up front, she and her sister were tossed about in a dim, poorly ventilated compartment crammed with constantly shifting suitcases, tackle boxes, fishing poles, and even the family dog. In those days, this arrangement wasn't illegal. And in the Midwest, where dads who hunt and fish abound, it was likely common.

What's more, my family could at least count on having a place to stay once we reached our destination. Other families brought their accommodations along. By the 1970s, towed campers had been around for decades: Airstream had begun producing travel trailers as early as the twenties and introduced its iconic Clipper in 1936. But not all manufacturers were so adept in their engineering. One friend has described how his family's camper had a propane-fueled heater that supplied its heat through a register located in the middle of the floor. The grate covering the register actually glowed red with heat in the darkened trailer. My friend claims he still bears waffle marks on his feet from inadvertently stepping on the grate one night while answering nature's call.

Another person I interviewed for this book related how his father deplored spending money on motel rooms, so he simply pitched a tent at night for the family to sleep in. The tent this dad purchased was a dime-store special that needed to be secured to an overhanging tree limb to remain standing. One night as the family slept inside the canvas compartment, a fierce storm whipped up. Waking to a loud crack from above, the family members scrambled outside just as the limb fell, crushing the flimsy shelter. There was brief panic as the family noticed that my friend's youngest brother was missing. After failing to locate the child's body inside the flattened tent, the boy's father thought to check the family's car parked nearby. There he found the little guy sleeping soundly in the backseat. Having been frightened by the approaching thunder, the kid had wisely decided that the car was a far better option to spend the night.

That night, my friend's family had gotten lucky. And all told, when it came to how and where *my* family traveled, so had we. Though I'm sure everyone who has fond memories of traveling America's highways with their families believes their way was best, I wouldn't trade our experiences for anything. I expect neither would you.

But enough jib-jabbing. It's time to get going.

CHAPTER 5

Smokeys in the Bush

Dodging Cops (and Stops) on the Interstates

My parents were well acquainted with the perils of the Chicago morning rush hour. My dad was born and raised in nearby Cicero. My mom had attended graduate school at Northwestern University. They knew why the Loop had really been given its name. The city's downtown business district, through which I-94 ran, was essentially a black hole. Drive anywhere near it at the wrong time of day, and you could be pulled into a traffic jam from which you might never escape. Unfortunately for us, because we always traveled south, we really had no other choice than to take our chances and head right into its dark eye. Sure, there was a beltway around the city. But experience had taught my father that that route added miles to the journey and was just as likely to become backed up by an accident or stalled vehicle. So, I-94 through the heart of Chicago we went.

While we couldn't take a different route, we could dodge the delays. The key to avoiding morning rush hour traffic was to beat it. This wasn't easy. We lived in Milwaukee, two hours north of Chicago. To get ahead of the city's morning commuters, we had to leave our house at an hour when even the doughnut bakers were still snoozing. But if we could clear Chicago by 6:00 a.m., we'd have clear sailing the rest of the day.

It sounded easy in theory, but the execution was far more difficult. It was one thing to get the car packed for an early-morning departure. It was another to get four kids, including two teenage boys, up and going at 3:30 a.m. Even my parents struggled to rouse themselves. Electric coffeemakers were just finding their way into homes at the time, and one wouldn't find its way into ours until 1980. If my parents were going to get up and get us out the door before dawn's early light, it would have to be without caffeinated assistance.

The morning march to our garage resembled something out of a George Romero zombie flick—six half-dressed figures, eyes drawn, hair matted, mouths drooling, stumbling about in a comatose parade. Fortunately, only one of us had to be fully awake—my dad, who always took the first shift driving. The rest of us needed only to sleepwalk from one bedroom to another one on wheels. We might as well have carried our beds with us. Before slogging off, we grabbed every pillow, blanket, and stuffed toy within reach so we could reassemble our sleeping quarters inside the car.

We instinctively collapsed into our customary seating positions—three in front, three in back. My father, of course, was in the driver's seat and my mom was in the front passenger seat. Leslie took the spot between them, where the large folding armrests made finding a comfortable position nearly impossible. For her it was still preferable to getting mixed up in the chaos of the backseat, which my brothers and I would turn into something resembling an army barracks after taking a direct mortar hit. We'd mound pillows and comforters everywhere and drape the windows with blankets to keep out sunlight. My brothers would bury their heads in pillows against opposite sides of the car, then spread their legs over the seat to claim as much space for themselves as possible. With no room left on the seat, I'd sprawl out across their laps or crawl up on the rear window ledge. I actually preferred the ledge. It offered an agreeably flat, felt-covered platform on which I could comfortably stretch out. And the sloped rear window above afforded me a spectacular view of the starry night sky.

Of course, the whole arrangement was ludicrously dangerous. Neither my brothers nor I wore seatbelts. If my dad had to slam on the brakes, I would have been launched like a sixty-pound log into the backs of the heads of my parents and sister in the front seat. My brothers wouldn't have fared much better. But this was the seventies. As ill advised as our seating arrangement was, it was also quite comfortable and perfectly legal. In fact, I distinctly remember relaxing up on the ledge one afternoon as a patrol car passed by on the highway. I waved at the officer, and he simply tipped his broad-brimmed hat to return my greeting. Suffice it to say, it was a more carefree time.

The drawback to departing so early was that I would often fall back asleep before we passed two intriguing landmarks between Milwaukee and Chicago. However, I knew both well from passing them on return trips during more wakeful hours. The first was the Mars Cheese Castle, an establishment whose unusual name and iconic roadside sign stirred wild, borderline delusional images in my youthful mind. I pictured little green men in shiny silver spacesuits rolling thick wheels of Swiss and Cheddar around a magical kingdom. Or maybe the castle itself had even been carved from a mountain of Muenster or Parmesan. For years, I begged my father to stop so I could see for myself what was surely a stately citadel of dairy delights. Finally, he gave in—to my eternal regret. The "world famous" Mars Cheese Castle turned out to be little more than a cheap cinder block hut. There were no laser-toting aliens inside. Only aisles of refrigerated cases crammed with blocks of cling-wrapped cheese and racks of even cheesier souvenirs. I was crushed. Of course, the rest of my family had known the truth of the Mars Cheese Castle all along. My dad stopped only to finally shut me up about it once and for all.

The grandly named yet profoundly disappointing "castle" fell to a wrecking ball in 2011, when the adjacent interstate was widened to accommodate more lanes. It would rise again nearby and in a form far more befitting its name. The new and improved Mars Cheese Castle boasts mighty turrets and even a stately drawbridge entrance. Still no Martians as far as I know.

The other landmark that drew our attention was a road sign that never failed to start my brothers and me snickering, though for different reasons. There was nothing special about the sign itself, just plain white letters on a brown board, the kind used for designating a state park or historic landmark. It was what the letters spelled out that made the sign extraordinary: "BONG RECREATION AREA." If we were awake when we passed it, one of my brothers would point to the sign and exclaim, "Dad, there's our exit!" and the three of us would begin convulsing with laughter. I didn't really get why I was laughing, mind you. But my brothers found it hilarious, so I figured I would just go along.

Whatever they assumed, the Bong Recreation Area was not the site of some ongoing stoner festival. It was a property managed by the Wisconsin State Park System. The parcel was named for US Army Air Forces pilot Richard Ira "Dick" Bong (more snickers, I know), who hailed from a tiny town in northern Wisconsin. Dubbed the "Ace of Aces," Bong rose to international fame for his remarkable record as a World War II combat pilot.

To this day, Bong remains the highest-scoring pilot in the history of the US armed forces, with more than forty confirmed kills to his credit. The 4,500-acre plot that bears his name was originally slated to be an Air Force base, but the plan was later scrapped when facilities nearby were expanded. Instead, the area was converted into a wildlife preserve, today also used by mountain bikers, horseback riders, and ATV enthusiasts. However, like the man for which it is named, the Bong Recreation Area is noted for one remarkable distinction: the park's signs rank among the most frequently stolen road signs in the country.

While my family didn't have to worry about authorities tracking us down for stolen road signs, we did have to keep a vigilant eye out for law enforcement. That's because my dad was always pushing to make good time, especially when he was trying to get through Chicago before the morning rush. In so doing, he may have occasionally pressed a little too enthusiastically on the accelerator pedal, putting us at odds with the highway patrol. My dad knew that to elude Johnny Law, we'd have to spot him before he spotted us. That meant we were all expected to help Dad stay on the lookout for any lurking patrol cars.

Chicago is the city that first put speed limit enforcement on the radar, quite literally. The police radar speed gun was invented in nearby Decatur, Illinois, in 1954 (though some credit an earlier device developed for the military by two Connecticut engineers). The man behind its development was Bryce K. Brown, a physicist who previously worked on the Manhattan Project. It didn't take long for law enforcement to put his device to use. Within a month of the gun's initial public demonstration, Chicago patrol officer Leonard Baldy became the first lawman to ticket a driver for speeding based on the readout of a radar gun. Later, Baldy would atone for his deed by helping motorists get where they needed to go faster. After retiring from the force, he swapped his radar gun for a microphone and became a traffic reporter for WGN Radio. An affable and funny man, Baldy became one of the city's most popular on-air personalities. As "Flying Officer Leonard Baldy," he served up witty takes on Chicago's constant traffic jams to lighten the mood of frustrated motorists. Unfortunately, Baldy's new career cost him his life: in 1960, the helicopter he was reporting from threw a rotor blade and crashed in a downtown railroad yard. He was just thirty-two years old. In 2006, the city of Chicago honored his memory by renaming a street Leonard Baldy Way.

By the time my family came tearing down the interstates in the seventies, radar guns had been around for two decades. The devices were now being used to enforce a new, and much lower, highway speed limit: 55 miles per hour.

Those of us who were around at the time will surely recall the highway safety campaign telling us that "55 Saves Lives." But the original goal of the reduced speed limit wasn't to save lives. It was to save gas. The lower speed limit was a response to the oil crisis of 1973. Early that year, Egypt and Syria, with the support of other Arab nations, attacked Israel on Yom Kippur, the holiest day of the Jewish calendar. Israel went on full nuclear alert, readying its bombers and missiles for launch. As an Israeli ally, the United States offered additional military support. In retaliation, the Arab members of the Organization of the Petroleum Exporting Countries (OPEC) cut oil exports to the United States, and the prospect of a long-term oil shortage in America appeared to be a real possibility. President Nixon and Congress immediately examined ways to cut America's fuel use.

Presented with research indicating lower highway speeds could significantly reduce gasoline consumption, Congress decided to act. As part of the Emergency Highway Energy Conservation Act, Congress passed the National Maximum Speed Law, setting the new maximum at a dawdling 55 mph. It was intended to be a temporary emergency measure that Congress would lift when the crisis had passed. Of course, it wouldn't turn out that way.

Technically, the federal government had no power to set such a limit. The states owned the highways within their borders and were free to determine speed limits as they saw fit. Most set a maximum limit of 70 mph, though ten western states, where highways were lightly traveled, allowed drivers to go faster. The government could, however, force the states to reduce speed limits another way: it made setting a speed limit of 55 mph a condition for receiving millions of dollars in federal highway funds. Though most states opposed the new limit, none was willing to concede federal funding. So in 1974, motorists across America were forced to back their pedals off the metal.

The 55 mph speed limit quickly proved popular with no one. Before the ink on the new law was even dry, more than a hundred truckers parked their rigs on I-80 in Pennsylvania to block traffic in protest. The Teamsters petitioned Congress for a separate 60 mph limit for trucks but were flatly denied. Once the law went into effect, motorist compliance was almost nonexistent despite a massive public relations campaign to rally support for the new limit, increased fines, and ticketing binges by law enforcement. In a study of highways in New York, 83 percent of motorists regularly exceeded the 55 mph limit. A follow-up five years later indicated an increase to 95 percent. Out West, where states openly opposed the law, enforcement was lax and penalties negligible. In Arizona, Montana, and Idaho, drivers caught exceeding the

55 mph limit—but not the previous limit those states had set—were handed tickets for a trifling $5 to $15. The official offense? "Energy wasting."

While there was much debate over how much the 55 mph speed limit reduced fuel consumption, there seemed to be no question about its impact on another travel-related statistic: highway fatalities. In 1974, the first year of the new maximum speed limit, highway fatalities dropped 16 percent. As a result, when the United States resolved its differences with OPEC and the oil embargo was lifted, safety advocates argued the 55 mph limit should remain. Supporters made the case that if it was possible to both save lives and conserve fuel by simply passing a piece of legislation, however unpopular, it was Congress's duty to act. In 1975, the temporary 55 mph national speed limit was made permanent.

Or, rather, permanent-ish. As time passed, one study after another pointed to the same conclusion: the 55 mph speed limit, intended to save lives and fuel, in reality accomplished neither. As doubts grew, Congress commissioned the National Academy of Sciences to study the matter. The panel reported that increasing the speed limit from 55 to 65 mph would raise fuel consumption just 0.2 percent.

Equally damning were studies examining why highway fatalities decreased following passage of the 55 mph speed limit. The data indicated a different reason for the drop: fewer people were dying on America's highways because fewer people were traveling them. The spike in gas prices during the oil embargo caused Americans to drastically cut back on driving, especially on weekends and holidays, when most fatalities occur. In some states, highway travel decreased 30 percent. Naturally, there was also a corresponding drop in crash-related deaths. There was simply no evidence to support the idea that "55 Saves Lives."

By the early 1980s, support for the 55 mph speed limit was running on fumes. Oil prices had returned to low levels, safer car design and wider highways had helped reduce crash fatalities, and a growing body of research indicated that the only real effect of the 55 mph speed limit was that it made drivers angry. By 1981, legislatures in thirty-three states debated ways to oppose the speed limit. In 1986, Nevada openly defied it, posting a 70 mph speed limit sign on a stretch of I-80 until the federal government followed through on its threat to withdraw funding. But the tide had shifted. Under mounting pressure, Congress allowed states to raise the speed limit to 65 mph on rural sections of the interstates. In 1995, it struck all federal speed limit laws, once again giving the states full authority to set their own speed limits.

Sure, it was great the government got around to eliminating the national maximum speed limit in the nineties, but it was small consolation for my family. We took our road trips in the seventies and early eighties, when the ludicrously leisurely 55 mph limit was the law of the land. My dad never got over the exasperation of being legally required to plod along at speeds 15 to 20 mph slower than he'd been allowed to drive just a few years earlier. For him, the 55 mph speed limit was like a government-mandated traffic jam.

The law left us two choices. We could slog along at a snail's pace, adding hours to our trip and reducing our precious time in the warm southern sunshine. Or we could join the throngs of drivers willfully flouting the law and get to a golf course lickety-split. For my dad, it was an easy decision.

Exceeding the speed limit, of course, was risky business. And the only thing that would infuriate my father more than wasting our vacation time inching along the interstates would be forking over $100 for a speeding ticket. To minimize our chances of getting caught, Dad employed a variety of strategies. First, he charged all of us kids with lookout duty. He didn't just tell us to keep an eye out for patrol cars, mind you. He assigned each of us a specific sector to monitor. My sister might be told to watch the right side of the highway, while my dad would keep his eyes on the left. One of my brothers would be told to scan for patrol cars attempting to sneak up from behind, and the other would be instructed to keep an eye to the sky for any police planes. One of my dad's favorite tactics was to slip between two cars cruising 15 or 20 mph above the posted limit. His thinking was that any officer with a speed gun up ahead might get a read on the lead car and any squad approaching from behind might be able to pace the rear car, but the guy in the middle would never get nabbed. Finally, Dad always drove in the right lane whenever possible, even if it meant constantly leapfrogging slower cars. His reasoning was that cops were more likely to look for speeders in the fast lane. Law-abiding drivers, as he pretended to be, kept to the right.

To help drivers like my dad outwit the highway patrol, the seventies offered several helpful devices. The first was cruise control. Trademarked under the name Speedostat, cruise control was originally created in the 1940s. Speedostat's inventor, Ralph Teetor, would never be able to use his own device—a childhood accident had left him completely blind. Despite his disability, Teetor developed a passion for working with machinery and became a skilled mechanical engineer. He was inspired to begin work on the device after enduring a torturous ride in a car driven by his attorney, who had an annoying habit of speeding up and slowing down in pace with his speaking. By the time the two made it to their destination, Teetor was exasperated, queasy, and determined to make sure no other passenger would again have to suffer as he had. Or perhaps he just wanted to create a way to help drivers maintain a constant speed. Teetor's system used a solenoid to vary the engine's throttle in relation to changes in the rotation rate of the drive shaft.

Eventually Teetor sold his idea to Chrysler, who introduced Speedostat as an inexpensive option for buyers in 1958. But sales were modest until the 1970s and the nation's first real fuel crisis. It was then that automakers realized they could market cruise control as a cheap fuel-conservation device. By reducing fuel-sucking surges of acceleration during highway driving, cruise control cut down on gas use. At a time when motorists were experiencing sticker shock every time they pulled up to the pump, cruise control seemed a wise investment. What's more, as drivers like my dad began using cruise control, they realized the device offered another benefit: it helped avoid speeding tickets. As police became more relaxed about enforcing the 55 mph speed limit, drivers realized they were unlikely to be stopped for traveling less than 10 mph above the limit. Many highway drivers, my father included, simply set their cruise control at 64 mph and crossed their fingers. At least in our experience, the strategy worked.

Not every driver was so lucky. One unfortunate motorist was Dale Smith, who, while driving one day in Dayton, Ohio, got caught in what he felt was an unfair speed trap (really, aren't they all?). A research scientist for the Air Force and an electronics buff, Smith didn't just get mad; he got inventive. Working in his garage, Smith created a small electronic device that detected X-band radio signals—the kind that police radar guns used—at a distance greater than their functional range. He attached a light that flashed and an alarm that sounded every time such signals were detected. Finally, Smith added a coiled cord that could be plugged into a car's cigarette lighter to draw power. He called his invention the Fuzzbuster and founded a company, Electrolert, to manufacture the device in 1973.

Almost immediately, the Fuzzbuster was flying off store shelves at a pace faster than its buyers drove their cars. Soon the small black box was appearing on seemingly every dashboard moving down the highway—except ours.

I never quite understood my dad's reluctance to buy one. The cost wasn't prohibitive, even for a man as frugal as my father. A low-end Fuzzbuster retailed for less than the cost of two speeding tickets. We'd certainly get plenty of use out of the device, between the considerable amount of travel we did as a family and the many miles my father logged for work. But I'm not sure Dad could get past the stigma that came with it. In a way, plopping a Fuzzbuster up on your dash was like extending a big electronic middle finger to the police. It smacked of the post-hippie, antiauthority sentiment raging at the time, and my father wanted no part of it. After all, he was a dyed-in-the-wool Republican. A family man. An upstanding member of society. He didn't want to join the ranks of the long hairs and scofflaws, the wearers of fringed leather jackets. When it came to the ridiculous 55 mph speed limit, he didn't mind breaking the law; he just didn't want others to *know* he was doing it. Other drivers had no such reservations. Fuzzbuster sales soared, spawning a $400 million industry by the mid-1980s. In 2010, Dale Smith's original Fuzzbuster was named one of *Time* magazine's "All-*TIME* 100 Gadgets."

My dad never bought a Fuzzbuster, but he did come into possession of the other wildly popular electronic device being used on

American highways at the time: the CB radio. It's not that he was suddenly inspired to don a cowboy hat, grow a thick mustache, and begin calling out the locations of "Smokeys," as users of the devices called highway patrolmen on the lookout for speeders. He simply inherited the CB as a built-in feature in a used car he purchased.

That car was a wonder to behold—a 1979 Lincoln Mark V Bill Blass Edition, a car so lavishly endowed with preposterous options and audacious styling that it surely holds a place of honor in some far-flung auto museum. Our Mark V embodied all that was so wrong and so right about the ludicrous excess of the 1970s. In its appearance, the vehicle seemed built to the same specifications as a US naval destroyer.* Parked in our driveway, the car made our ranch-style home look like a dollhouse. The Lincoln's exterior was painted a deep midnight blue with sparkling metallic flecks. Along its broad sides ran two stark white pinstripes, matching the color of the roof, which was a marvel all its own. Called a Landau carriage top, the roof was wrapped in heavy vinyl that appeared to be stretched over a metal framework, creating the illusion of a fully functioning fold-down convertible top (it wasn't). Another faux style element was the rounded hump in the middle rear of the trunk lid that appeared to house a spare tire. It actually served no purpose other than to display the designation "CONTINENTAL" in inch-high chrome letters to drivers following behind. The Mark V's other embellishments included "opera windows" in the roof, flip-up headlight covers, turbine-style chrome wheels, a slatted front grille, and a gleaming chrome hood ornament. Fans of the TV show *Dallas* may recall that Jock Ewing drove a similar vehicle.

*The Mark V was the largest of Lincoln's Mark series. Weighing just under 5,000 pounds, the Mark V was powered by a 400-cubic-inch V8 engine that delivered fuel mileage, if memory serves, of around 3 gallons per mile.

Upon opening either of the car's two doors (yes, it was a coupe!), countless other opulent details could be glimpsed: upholstered door panels, a burled wood dashboard and accents, dual padded armrests, and leather hand straps for rear passengers (essential for anyone hoping to extricate themselves from the rear seat compartment over the massive folding front seats). Finally, your eyes would come to rest on a collection of buttons, switches, and displays nestled in the center of the instrument panel. There rested the highest achievement in 1970s automotive entertainment technology: an AM/FM high-fidelity stereo with an eight-track tape deck and built-in forty-channel CB radio.

Like cruise control, the CB wasn't invented in the seventies, but it became wildly popular during the decade. CB, short for citizens band, radio actually dates back to the years following World War II. That was when the Federal Communications Commission (FCC) set aside a swath of radio frequencies that ordinary citizens could use to communicate with each other. Initially, CBs were popular with truckers and businesses with service staff because they offered an easy and inexpensive way to exchange brief messages. As solid-state electronic technology became cheaper and more portable in the late 1960s, consumers began to purchase CBs for personal use.

But it wasn't until passage of the 55 mph speed limit that CBs really took off. Truckers used CBs to keep each other informed about law enforcement and, during the oil crisis, the location of service stations that still had fuel. Before long, truckers got to know the sound of each other's voices, and conversations turned more congenial. Because many of their discussions concerned tactics for skirting the law, CB users adopted aliases to conceal their identities. These colorful nicknames, or handles, included monikers like Texas Pete, Old Spare, and Mama Flapjacks. Soon ordinary motorists realized CBs offered many practical benefits as well, from having an easy way to call for help in an emergency to being able to learn the whereabouts of patrol cars. Beyond that, tuning into CB chatter was just a fun way to pass the miles. In no time, CB ownership skyrocketed. Between 1973 and 1975, the number of CB license applications received by the FCC quadrupled to 1 million.

By then, the CB was more than a communications device. It was a full-fledged phenomenon. Among those it inspired was William Dale Fries Jr., an advertising creative director, who, using an idea he'd originally developed for an ad campaign to sell bread, collaborated with songwriter Chip Davis to write the trucker-themed country song "Convoy." Fries employed the lively lingo of CBers to tell the story of a renegade trucker leading an outlaw convoy across America. Assuming the persona of a trucker named C. W. McCall, Fries rattled off his tall tale over a catchy guitar groove:

> Well, we laid a strip for the Jersey shore
> And prepared to cross the line
> I could see the bridge was lined with bears
> But I didn't have a dog-goned dime.
> I says, "Pig Pen, this here's the Rubber Duck.
> We just ain't gonna pay no toll."
> So we crashed the gate doing ninety-eight.
> I says, "Let them truckers roll, 10-4."

"Convoy" was an instant smash, reaching number 1 on American music charts and selling more than 2 million copies. The song even inspired a movie of the same name, starring Kris Kristofferson and Ali MacGraw. CBs were featured in other movies as well, including three *Smokey and the Bandit* films starring Burt Reynolds, and on TV shows such as *The Dukes of Hazzard* and *Movin' On*.

Ironically, although the unique language spoken by CBers was intended to disguise the meaning of their messages to law enforcement, CB lingo drew from those same sources. CB patter was an odd combination of police "Ten Code" abbreviations, the phonetic alphabet the military used, southern-flavored slang, and a nearly endless list of creative euphemisms. Colorful and witty, many of these terms and phrases quickly found their way into pop culture. Soon housewives and businessmen who'd never been near a semi were confirming plans with a "10-4, good buddy!" and bidding each other adieu with an enthusiastic "Keep on truckin'!"

Because CBers were often attempting to sidestep the law, many of the terms they used most pertained to the authorities. A patrol officer was a "Smokey" or a "Bear." Both were references to the "Smokey the Bear" character used in public service campaigns to educate the public about the dangers of forest fires. Smokey wore a wide-brimmed hat similar to those worn by highway patrol officers. Depending on her attractiveness, a female officer might be a "Honey Bear" or a "Miss Piggy," and sheriffs' deputies were "Cub Scouts." An officer in a construction zone was termed a "Care Bear," and a cop scanning the highway with a radar gun was a "Bear Taking Pictures" or, more colorfully, a "Hemorrhoid with a Polaroid." Officers who detected a speeder would turn on their "disco lights" or "gum ball machine" and chase down a "customer" to deliver a "paper hanger," after which the violating motorist would be required to "feed the Bear" a hefty fine.

Out on the "super slab" (multilane highway), a CBer might be trapped behind a slow-moving "blinkin winkin" (school bus) or "anchor clanker" (boat trailer), trailed by a "bumper sticker" (tailgater) or nearly run off the road by a "flyboy" (a speeding motorist) in a "Fire Chicken" (Pontiac Thunderbird). Always on the lookout for "seat covers" (attractive female passengers), CBers also had to keep an eye on the road ahead for "brake checks" (traffic backups), lest one plow into a "chicken choker" (poultry truck) or "pregnant rollerskate" (VW Beetle), requiring a "meat wagon" (ambulance) to be called. In the event of a "window washer" (heavy downpour) or to avoid the risk of "Ice Capading" (slipping off the road in icy conditions), one might get on the horn to call out "Breaker 1-9" (a notice you were about to transmit a message on channel 19, the channel frequently used by truckers to keep each other updated on "Kojaks with Kodaks") to see if any "good buddy" (generally any other CB user) had his "ears" (CB radio) on and could point you in the direction of a "chew 'n' spew" (truck stop diner). There, one could kick back and enjoy a "suds 'n' mud" (beer and coffee), take a "10-100" (potty break), or, if necessary, a "10-200" (you get the picture). It was all very colorful—and very popular for a time.

By 1979, the number of licensed CB users in the United States totaled 14 million. Many more didn't bother to obtain licenses. Even former first lady Betty Ford, using the handle First Mama, occasionally used a CB. So did Mel Blanc, the voice of Bugs Bunny, Daffy Duck, and countless other Warner Bros. cartoon characters. Blanc was known to frequently engage in conversations with other CB users in the Los Angeles area, especially kids, while in character.

Given their popularity, perhaps it wasn't so ridiculous that my family also owned a CB. But there was still something patently absurd about a luxury automaker like Lincoln installing in its flagship model a device used mostly by slang-spouting redneck truckers just so a nice suburban middle-class family could break the law.

Truth be told, our CB did serve a practical purpose. While my father was hardly the type to get on the horn and call out for a "good buddy," he'd often keep his "ears on" and tuned to channel 19. There's no question these frequent callouts helped us avoid having to "feed the Bear" dozens of times. What's more, in a time long before cell phones, the CB provided some peace of mind for my mom. She knew that we could always use our CB to contact help in case of a breakdown, or in the far more likely event that my dad pushed his luck too far and we ran out of gas. Also, on more than one occasion, a passing CBer let us know that one of our rear tires looked dangerously flat or that our trunk latch wasn't fully closed.

However, one member of our family was determined to use our CB for a more meaningful purpose—to reach out and engage our fellow roadway roamers. That person was, of course, me. I may have been young but I was confident in my mastery of CB lingo from avid viewing of *BJ and the Bear* and *McCloud*, and completely unburdened by the inhibitions that restrain most people from striking up conversations with total strangers. On the rare occasions I was allowed to sit in the front seat, I took full advantage of my access to the CB handset. Adopting the handle "Blue Thunder," a nod to our titanic Lincoln, I launched into monologues of breathtaking incomprehensibility.

"Uh, Breaker, Breaker, 10-20. Blue Thunder here, gobbling up the zipper dashes like PacMan rollin' for a power pill. Lookin' for some good buddies out there to croak back a 10-4 on, uh, any hungry Smokey the Bears looking to chase down a Fire Chicken on roller skates. Roger Dodger, out and over!"

Anyone tuning in must have thought I was in dire need of psychiatric treatment. Most often, my nonsensical callouts were met with silence. But occasionally, someone who figured out I was just a dumb kid would take pity on me and respond. We'd then engage in some awkward conversation about where we were headed, what mile marker we were currently passing, and such. I'd try to force in some out-of-context references to "Cornfield Cadillacs" and "County Mounties." Finally, Papa Bear would snatch the handset away and suggest we just listen to some music instead.

But my efforts weren't in vain. Thanks to my rambling and the mindless musings of millions of other "ratchetjaws" (novice CB users) flooding the airwaves, most real truckers either cut way back on using their CBs or turned them off altogether. I may not be able to take credit for the demise of disco or those outrageously heeled shoes called clogs, but I can honestly say I played a role in bringing the CB craze to a merciful end.

Despite the tools at our disposal to help us avoid tickets, there were still places where speeding just wasn't worth the risk. As we repeatedly traveled the same highways over the years, we got to know these areas well. These high-risk zones were made apparent by the sheer number of aggravated drivers we'd see pulled over at the side of the road. The Illinois-Wisconsin border was always a speed trap, as was the short stretch between Chicago and Gary, Indiana. Southern Indiana and Illinois were relatively safe, as was most of Kentucky. It was best to back off the accelerator in Arkansas. Tennessee offered relatively clear sailing, but it was wise to tap the brakes in parts of Alabama. Finally there was one place we knew, without question, where it was never a good idea to push our luck, where both sides of the highway always seemed to be lined with flashing lights, like the gutters of a house decorated for Christmas. That place was Georgia.

There is perhaps no other state in America better positioned to balance its budget by handing out speeding tickets to out-of-state motorists than Georgia. After all, Georgia's southern border stretches across nearly three-quarters of the state of Florida, home to many of the most popular tourist destinations in America. Next to California, no other state attracts more tourists—most traveling by car—than Florida. And except for a few motorists entering Florida along its panhandle from Alabama, all traffic heading south into the state—on the way to Disney World, Miami, Fort Lauderdale, the Space Coast, and other top destinations—has no choice but to cross hundreds of miles of Georgia highway. Since the advent of the automobile, no one has been more aware of this fact than the Georgia Highway Patrol.

Hard data are difficult to gather for the 1960s and 1970s due to the difficulties of collecting records from multiple jurisdictions. However, according to the National Motorists Association, only one U.S. state handed out more traffic tickets in 2010 than Georgia. That state? Florida. What's more, the AAA has for decades advised motorists to beware of "overly vigilant" law enforcement on highway 301, a particularly perilous passage between the two states.

It's along this highway that one can find the tiny hamlet that helped cement Georgia's reputation for being particularly—even unlawfully—hard on out-of-state motorists: Ludowici. At one point, this small town drew national attention for setting the most crooked speed trap in America. It was a place so notorious for shaking down Yankee motorists that even Georgia's own governor, Lester Maddox, once described Ludowici as "lousy, rotten, corrupt, nasty and no good"—and he never even got pulled over there.

In the days before the interstates, Ludowici sat squarely on the trigger of the Georgia speed trap. Situated at the junction of three federal highways (301, 25, and 84), Ludowici was the main gateway into Florida throughout the 1950s and 1960s. Only a thousand residents lived in Ludowici, but more than a million motorists passed through the town every year. Seeing all those happy tourists stop to fill their gas tanks and pay with crisp $20 bills, unscrupulous town leaders and business owners schemed more ways to profit from their prime location.

At first, the shakedown was limited to aggressively enforcing traffic laws. At the edge of Ludowici, where the posted speed limit dropped dramatically without warning, the town's patrol officers waited to pounce on any driver who didn't react in time. They didn't even use speed guns to nab alleged violators. The speed of an offending motorist was simply "estimated" by the officer, using his "best professional judgment." But things quickly took a shady turn. The town's single stoplight was rigged with a switch located behind a nearby billboard. As an unsuspecting motorist entered the intersection, the switch would be flipped, changing the light instantly from green to red, at which point the driver would be chased down by a patrol car waiting in an adjacent alley. Local residents knew to take a side street bypassing the intersection, ensuring the ploy caught only drivers from out of town.

Essentially Ludowici became a sort of tourist turnstile at the entrance to Florida—only one at which tickets were handed out instead of collected. According to a story by Morris Shelton appearing in the *St. Petersburg News*, a newspaper from a nearby town in Florida, on July 5, 1970, Ludowici police issued tickets totaling $43,000 over a single four-month period. One woman received a ticket on entering the town and another on leaving it. Authorities at multiple levels were in on the action. For each ticket they issued, patrol officers were paid $2.50. Long County, where Ludowici is located, cleared $15 per summons. Offending motorists were expected to pay cash on the spot or be forced to appear before the local magistrate at his convenience, which could be days later. In total, Ludowici was said to have relieved motorists of more than $100,000 in fines annually throughout the 1960s.

The town's corruption didn't end with the police. Dodgy local business owners also appeared to be in on the money grab. When drivers stopped at a local service station and requested to have their oil level checked, attendants allegedly disabled the cars by tinkering with their generators or pouring water into their crankcases. When their vehicles wouldn't start, motorists would be directed to a nearby garage for repairs—for an outrageous sum. The name of the repair shop's owner? Billy Swindel.

Unsurprisingly, scores of irate motorists who'd been bilked in Ludowici lodged complaints with state authorities. Fearing the town's unseemly practices were tarnishing the reputation of the entire state—which, of course, they were—three different Georgia governors attempted to force Ludowici to clean up its act, without success. At one point, Governor Lester Maddox even threatened to move the state capital to Ludowici, giving him jurisdictional authority over local officials. Maddox settled for posting state-funded billboards leading into town from every direction offering drivers the following warning:

BEWARE! You are in Long County and approaching Ludowici, Georgia. Don't get fleeced in a clip joint. Don't get caught in a speed trap.

By the time the billboards appeared in 1970, however, Ludowici's days of squeezing motorists were already numbered. East of town, the new I-95 superhighway was already under construction.

When it opened two years later, the interstate offered travelers from the Northeast a faster, more direct route to the Sunshine State. Shortly after, I-75 opened to the west, doing the same for motorists traveling from the Midwest.

But Ludowici's crooked schemes had garnered national notoriety. The town even earned its own spread in *Time* magazine, in an issue dated April 27, 1970. Ludowici's infamy bolstered Georgia's reputation as a place where out-of-state motorists had to be wary. By the time my family came trundling down I-75 in the late 1970s, it appeared that nothing much had changed. Even my dad conceded that Georgia was one place it made no sense to push the limit.

From the day the first speed limit was posted, motorists and patrol officers have sought to outwit each other in a fiercely contested game of cat and mouse. But it was a game my dad had mastered. Not once in more than a decade of our family's travels—covering tens of thousands of miles of open highway—was my father ever stopped for speeding. What's more, if he were still around, I know he'd take great pride in pointing out we always "made good time."

While Dad had to keep a sharp eye out for the fuzz in the front seat, my brothers and I were always looking for ways to stay busy in the backseat. After all, we had plenty of free time on our hands. And even more ways to fill it.

CHAPTER 6

Time to Pass

Diversions, Directions, and Discoveries

When you're just six years old, a twenty-hour road trip represents a significant portion of your lifetime. Trapped in the backseat of a car, squeezed between two hulking teenage brothers, and piled under an assortment of blankets, pillows, jackets, and grocery bags filled with snacks, comic books, and magazines, it's a span of time that seems closer to an eternity. And as any parent knows, if time begins to feel long to a young kid, that kid will make time feel longer for everyone around them.

Like all kids, I needed to be provided with an endless stream of diversions or I'd begin inventing my own, usually involving singing, humming, or some other noisy annoyance. This would begin a predictable series of events, the first of which would be my receiving a swift noogie from one of my brothers. I would respond by bawling hysterically, prompting my dad to snarl "Don't make me pull over!" and angrily throw his right arm over the front seat to grab the neck of my assailant while struggling to maintain control of the steering wheel with his left hand. He'd veer onto the shoulder, causing my mom to begin screaming at my dad to mind his driving before he got us all killed, at which point my sister would curl into a fetal position in preparation for impact. Just in the nick of time, Dad would swerve back onto the road and we'd continue on our way. Having barely escaped death, we'd all sit in stunned silence for the next twenty minutes as though none of it ever happened. On most trips, this would play out a dozen times a day.

To prevent this potentially lethal chain of events from unfolding, my mom often took charge of our family entertainment. This was an especially important job as we traveled south of Chicago, when the need for vigilant cop spotting diminished and the boredom of driving through endless miles of cornfields would set in. She'd begin by initiating the traditional games of I Spy, the license plate game, or the alphabet game, a contest in which we'd try to be the first to spot words on passing billboards or highway signs starting with each successive letter of the alphabet. Given her prime viewing spot in the middle of the front seat, my sister would generally dominate these competitions, while my brothers would just sink their heads into magazines to avoid participating altogether. Eventually the rest of us would lose interest as well, at which point my mother would produce the game bag.

The game bag was a paper grocery bag filled with every novelty, travel puzzle, and cheap toy my mother could buy at the local dime store. For starters, there were those handheld games in which the object was to navigate a tiny ball bearing through a maze or into the eyeholes of a cartoon face. Then I'd move on to the Magic Slate Drawing Pad, a rectangle of cardboard with a drawing area covered in a sheet of gray film. Wherever I pressed the film with a thin red stylus, a black line appeared. The sheet of film could then be lifted to erase the image, presenting a blank page for another drawing. Next, there was Wooly Willy, a personal favorite. Wooly Willy was the cartoon face of a nerdy-looking white guy on cardboard covered with a canopy of clear plastic holding black metal shavings. You used a magnetic pen to pick up the shavings and drop them over Willy's face to create amusing beards, mustaches, and—my preferred embellishment—an enormous afro. Willy didn't seem to mind. Mom would also include several Invisible Ink books produced by a company called Yes & Know. These books included an invisible ink pen that allowed you to reveal answers to trivia questions, hunt down hidden submarines on printed grids, and play hangman, among other games.

But for my money—more accurately, Mom's money—no item in the game bag delivered more entertainment than Mad Libs, a series of activity books created by the commendably juvenile minds behind *Mad* magazine. Each page of Mad Libs featured a short story with key words left blank. You filled in these blanks with random suggestions from others. If a noun was required, the "author" (usually me) asked for a random noun; if a type of animal was needed, I'd ask for animal suggestions, and so on. Finally, the story was read aloud with all the out-of-context suggestions included and hilarity ensued. A completed Mad Lib might read something like this (the words we added are in bold):

On July 20, 1969, America became the first country to land a **pineapple** on the moon. Millions of **armadillos** all over the world watched on television as the lunar landing module touched down gently on the moon's **stinky** surface, in an area known as the Sea of **Polyester**. The mission's landing crew included Commander Neil Armstrong and Edwin "**Ol' Blood 'n' Guts**" Aldrin, while a third astronaut, **Gomer Pyle**, piloted the **unicycle** alone in lunar orbit above. As the first human being to set foot on the **diaper**, Neil Armstrong courageously declared, "This is one small step for a **Dodo bird**, one giant leap for **underwear**." The duo then spent nearly a full day on the **nacho-flavored** lunar landscape, collecting **boogers** and conducting **duck-duck-goose**. After blasting off from the **waterbed**, the pair rejoined their colleague, **Gomer Pyle**, for the return flight back to **Toys 'R' Us**. The **Green Bay Packers** had begun the Space Race with their successful launch of the satellite **Mayor McCheese**. But **dentists** had won the race, when the crew of **Tidy Bowl** 11 safely splashed down in the ocean and emerged smiling and **juggling chainsaws** from the capsule as millions of people **farted**.

It was extremely silly and very fun. What made it all the more entertaining was that everyone in the family enjoyed taking their turn to contribute—even my brothers who avoided participating in every other family activity. Sometimes when I broke out the books after dark and we were a little giddy from a long day of travel, reading the best Mad Libs aloud would have us nearly convulsing with laughter. It wasn't the sort of travel activity that broadened one's horizons, but it did—for a short while—bring us all a little closer.

The fun of Mad Libs sessions could last only so long, however. Sooner or later, I'd overplay my hand and suggest *poop* as a noun or *fart* as a verb once too often, causing my mom to give me the evil eye. Usually we'd just run out of funny-sounding adjectives and lose interest. Then my mom would hand me the one item in the game bag sure to end my pleas for another round of Mad Libs: the Mattel Electronics handheld football game.

Resembling a large LED calculator, the game didn't look very interesting. Except for a small helmeted player molded into the plastic at the bottom, the device didn't appear to have anything to do with football—or, for that matter, fun. The screen where the action happened was tiny, about the size of a stick of gum.

The game play appeared equally uninspired—a few tiny red LED diodes blinking on a small black grid. The player assumed the role of running back, represented by a bright red dash, and—much to the little dash's chagrin, I'm certain—was one of just two offensive players on the field. Confronting the player was an army of defenders, represented by equally sized but dimmer red dashes. That's right: the only way to determine the good guys from the bad guys was a slight disparity in how brightly the dashes glowed. As the defensive dashes advanced toward the running back, they constantly changed positions, usually at completely predictable intervals. To elude the menacing minus signs, the player pushed arrow buttons to move his running back up, down, and forward toward the end zone while attempting to avoid being "tackled." The player's computerized companion attempted to throw "blocks" by positioning itself in front of approaching defenders. Of course, the graphics couldn't actually depict anything as exciting as a tackle or even show two dashes colliding. Instead, a tackle was indicated by having the two involved dashes simply blink beside each other as a tinny little speaker spat out a few sad-sounding tones.

The player could choose to play against another person or against the computer, selecting one of two skill levels. For an experienced player, it was almost mindlessly easy to beat the computer even on the higher skill setting. In a competition between two veteran players, the loser would nearly always be the player who failed to score a touchdown on just one of his possessions before time expired.

At the time of its debut, few thought Mattel's football game would be a success. The game's visuals were so primitive it made early arcade games like *Pong* and *Breakout* seem like virtual reality simulations. In 1977, when the game was originally released, only

Sears carried it. Sears quickly determined the game would flop and production was halted. But Sears couldn't predict how inexplicably thrilling the game would be to kids like me, who were just beginning to experience our first eight-megabyte rushes of adrenaline in the arcades. Soon *Mattel Electronic Football* games were flying off shelves and production quickly resumed. By early 1978, Mattel was selling half a million units a week.

Based on the game's monstrous success, Mattel and other game companies scrambled to create similar games, including other sports games and classics like *Simon* and *Merlin*. The portable game device market was born. Eventually spawning the hugely successful Nintendo Game Boy and other sophisticated handheld game systems, Mattel's primitive yet powerfully addictive electronic football game was named, like the Fuzzbuster, one of *Time* magazine's All-*TIME* 100 Gadgets.

The items included in the game bag had to meet certain requirements. They couldn't be too big or too noisy, or include too many pieces that could be lost (or angrily hurled at a sibling) or—with the exception of my Mad Libs booklets—require the participation of more than one player: me. That meant we never brought board games on our road trips like other families did. It wasn't that I wouldn't have wanted to play them. I relished playing games like Candyland, Battleship, Sorry! and Monopoly back home. But for me to play them out on the road, my parents would also had to have brought my friends. As teenage boys, my brothers (and backseat traveling companions) were far more interested in hot rod magazines, catching some zs, or doing just about anything besides keeping their kid brother entertained. This precluded me from partaking in one of the more popular pastimes of the prime road trip era: travel chess.

Actually, playing chess while en route to a distant destination vastly predated road travel—or even cars. Well-heeled passengers traveling on ships or riding in carriages and stagecoaches had long passed the endless hours of their journeys playing chess using sets with peg-in pieces that fit securely in holes drilled into game boards. But the practice of playing chess while traveling wouldn't truly explode until after World War II.

To support the American war effort, the Drueke Company of Grand Rapids, Michigan, once the country's oldest manufacturer of traditional board games, designed and produced pocket versions of popular games including chess. The sets were then shipped by the boxcar-load to GIs fighting around the world. Compact, self-contained, and eminently portable, these pocket-size sets were highly prized by soldiers and went far in popularizing chess among an entirely different class of players. Following the war, Drueke introduced a new version of their portable chess set with flat, disc-shaped magnetic pieces, making the game easy to play anywhere—even the backseat of a moving car. Sales of magnetic travel chess sets exploded as soldiers who'd grown to love the game overseas took their families out on America's highways, and the games continued to sell well into the 1970s. Of course, it only made sense: after all, chess is a game of war.

While I was dodging diodes in the backseat, my parents and sister were all business up front. In addition to taking charge of our family entertainment, Mom dispensed snacks and beverages, doling out more or less depending on when our next food stop was scheduled. When Dad wasn't swinging an arm over the front seat to keep the peace, he was vigilantly scanning the road for Smokeys. That left Leslie to fill the role of chief navigation officer. In an era before GPS and smartphones, it was a critical job. With far fewer exits back then and much smaller built-up areas around cities, a wrong turn or missed exit often meant traveling 10 miles or farther down the interstate to find a turnaround. Or worse. Every kid under the age of twelve in those days had heard the terrifying stories of families who got off at an incorrect exit, ran into a band of homicidal fiends, and were never heard from again.*

Fortunately for us, highway navigation had come a long way since the days of the Blue Books and their directions to "turn right when you come to the large oak stump." Map publisher Rand McNally had begun producing road maps in 1904 and published its first road atlas in 1924, under the more colorful title *Rand McNally Auto Chum* (*chum* meaning friend or pal, rather than the word's more modern use, a slurry of fish guts dumped over the side of a boat to attract sharks for Discovery Channel TV specials).

Realizing better maps encouraged motorists to travel more and, consequently, to consume more fuel, Gulf Oil Company contracted Rand McNally to print road maps for free distribution at its service stations beginning in 1920. The idea proved so popular that every major oil company soon followed suit. Service stations continued to provide free maps, which also helpfully highlighted the chain's locations and maintenance services for decades. One 1950s-era Gulf Oil map pledged that "weekly and daily cleaning and maintenance schedules are followed, and hourly inspections made to further assure you and other members of your family of finding restrooms in the cleanest possible con-

---

*These stories appeared to be based entirely in legend. At least, until 1995, when a Los Angeles family returning from a cookout made a wrong turn into an alley claimed by a local gang calling themselves the Avenues. The gang members riddled the car with bullets, killing a three-year-old girl and injuring her stepfather and brother.

dition at all times." Judging from our experience, that commitment had waned considerably by the 1970s. What hadn't faded, however, was the popularity of free maps. In 1972, service stations handed out more than 250 million free road maps, far more than one for every American at the time. Never one to pass on free anything, my father made sure to grab a couple or six maps on every visit. But for longer trips, he provided my sister with a vastly superior navigation tool, the TripTik, a personalized travel guide lovingly handcrafted at the local branch of the AAA.

In its day, the AAA TripTik was the pinnacle of sleek, user-friendly highway navigation. The TripTik was and still is—Trip-Tiks are still offered at a limited number of AAA branches—a long, slender flipbook of paper maps, each detailing a short stretch of highway along the route to a selected destination. On each page, the route was visually lifted off the surrounding landscape and highlighted in bright orange marker by an AAA travel specialist. Rest stops were called out and exits listed by number, and symbols indicated AAA-approved service stations, restaurants, and other services. The idea was that drivers could travel from the top of a page to its bottom, then flip to the next, seeing in advance what they could expect along the way. Each TripTik had to be compiled and collated by hand, from the point of origin to the destination and every section of highway in between. This time-consuming process was conducted in a face-to-face meeting between the AAA specialist and member at a local branch, during which the specialist might also note areas of road construction, can't-miss attractions, and other items of interest. For my father, TripTiks alone were worth the cost of his annual AAA membership dues. The discounts he received by flashing his AAA membership card at hotels and restaurants were just icing on the cake.

In the 1970s, TripTiks seemed modern and efficient, but

the idea had been around for decades. In 1911, an adventurous motorist visited an AAA branch for assistance planning a drive from New York to Jacksonville, Florida. Realizing he couldn't offer the man a single map that detailed the complete route, a helpful AAA employee pieced one together using portions of several maps and some tape. The concept proved so useful that AAA adopted the idea for use nationwide.

TripTiks were terrific in concept, but not without drawbacks in actual use, as we discovered. Unlike modern GPS devices, Trip-Tiks were created from pages of highway sections printed far in advance of when they were used, meaning they couldn't be quickly updated for road closures caused by construction or other issues. This was a particular problem for us, as many of the roads we traveled into the Deep South were prone to flooding. When authorities were forced to close highways, we had to improvise our own detours on the spot. For this purpose, TripTiks were unhelpful, to say the least. All the features that made the TripTik so easy to use—the way the route was visually isolated from the surrounding environment, the long, skinny design that made the booklet easy to hold—also made it useless if circumstances required us to stray from the designated route. The TripTik showed exits, but not where they led. The lines representing these roads just faded off into a white void, apparently indicating the world came to an abrupt end just a few miles in either direction. By the look of it, circling around a closed highway put us at considerable risk of driving off the edge of the Earth.

Making matters worse, my father refused to "waste" money on a road atlas. After all, he reasoned, gas stations gave away road maps for free and he kept a glove box full of them. This was true. My father did have dozens of free maps of the Milwaukee and Chicago metropolitan areas in his glove compartment.

It's just that these maps provided little help navigating the roads of rural Tennessee or Mississippi, where we ran into problems. And although every TripTik booklet included a national map in back, each state was about the size of a quarter—hardly the scale needed to chart an alternate route on state and county roads. As a result, we often found ourselves hopelessly lost.

Sometimes we'd lose our way in relatively populated areas, where our biggest challenge would be deciphering verbal directions offered by locals speaking in thick southern accents. On one occasion, after getting directions from a helpful pedestrian in Atlanta, we spent hours searching for "Pass Road," the thoroughfare the woman told us would lead us back to the highway. After driving up and down the main drag looking for our turn, it finally occurred to my father that maybe—just maybe—the PARIS Road we had passed thirty-four times might be the turn our helper intended us to take. More often, though, we found ourselves lost in unsettling hinterlands, where death could wait around any turn. One evening, when we got turned around in a remote area of Louisiana, our car was literally chased out of a dark swamp by what I believe to this day was a band of werewolves. My parents claimed it was just a pack of wild dogs, but that was only because they didn't watch *Scooby-Doo* as I did and were unaware of what really lurks in the depths of bayou country at night.

Even when we managed to remain on the highway, we found trouble on occasion. Sometimes it was our own fault. And by "our," I mean it was my dad's fault. Such was the case with the series of heated skirmishes between Mom and Dad in what came to be known as the "Battle of E."

The "E" in question referred to the letter on our fuel gauge, the one indicating the gas tank was near empty. At least it indicated such to most people. To my father, the "E" stood for something more like "Eh?"—a sort of halfhearted heads-up that somewhere along the next hundred miles, if it was convenient, it might be good to look for an exit with a service station.

Based on previous experience and an understanding of automotive engineering standards known only to him, my father claimed that every automaker made sure at least forty miles worth of gas remained in the tank after the needle dropped to "E" and the low-fuel light blinked on. He insisted that engineers intentionally calibrated fuel gauges to be "on the safe side." To be fair, my father had gathered considerable support for his case, having personally tested his theory many times over the years, much to our collective dismay. And though we'd never run out of gas, I was positive that on more than one occasion, we'd rolled up to a fuel pump on nothing but the last lingering fumes remaining in the carburetor.

As a rule, the needle of our fuel gauge would always drop to "E" when we were as far as possible from, well, anywhere. In the 1970s, this was a much easier place to be. There was far less development, particularly along the new interstates. Urban sprawl was still in its infancy, making the distance between cities seem far greater. What's more, there were fewer exits with services along the interstates.* In fact, when the routes of the interstates were being determined, one of the main objectives was to bypass towns where services such as gas stations and restaurants were already

---

*Interestingly, there were actually more gas stations in the United States in the 1970s than today—substantially more. For a variety of reasons, including gas shortages, shrinking profit margins, and the consolidation of major oil companies, the number of gas stations in America has decreased virtually every year since 1973.

located. This was to hold down costs, as real estate in developed areas was more expensive.

Making matters worse, our family trips nearly always led us into the Deep South. We traveled through large swaths of Tennessee, Arkansas, Mississippi, and Louisiana, some of the least-developed and most sparsely populated areas east of the Mississippi. As a result, my father's stubbornness in pushing the limits of our fuel tank often left us facing the possibility of spending much of our vacation stranded on the shoulder of a lonely highway rather than relaxing on a sunny beach.

My parents' difference of opinion over the best time to refuel made for some uneasy moments. Upon seeing the fuel needle drop below a quarter tank, my mom would begin dropping not-so-subtle hints.

"We should probably think about getting gas soon," she'd casually mention to my dad. "There's an exit coming up. I think I saw a sign a ways back."

"We've got plenty of fuel yet," Dad would respond. "No sense stopping sooner than we have to. We'll lose twenty minutes just getting off and on the highway."

It's here that I should point out my father's motivation for stretching every tank. He was obsessed with what he called "making time." Essentially, "making time" meant nothing more than progressing toward the day's destination as quickly as we could. It was a sort of competition between my father and the laws of physics. He wanted to get wherever we were headed in a time faster than should be possible.

"Hey, we're making great time, everybody!" Dad would announce at random intervals. "We're averaging 57.3 miles per hour—with stops! At this rate, we'll make Murfreesboro by six!"

Of course, it made no difference if we made Murfreesboro by

six o'clock, seven o'clock, or ten o'clock. For my father, that wasn't the point. He just wanted to prove it could be done.

In his ongoing quest to make time, my father was relentless. Speed limits were pushed, meals skipped, and requests for potty stops mercilessly ignored. To this day, I'm convinced my bladder is stretched to four times the size of the average human's because of the countless hours I spent holding my pee as a child in the cause of making time.

As the miles passed and the needle dropped lower, my mom's comments would grow more pointed. "We're on 'E' now, Chuck. We should get off at the next exit."

At this point, Dad would employ his favorite delaying gambit: *The Small Town Up Ahead with Added Bonus.* "You know, hon, we should be able to make Bumbleburg, no problem," he'd begin. "It's just a few miles farther, and I think they have a McDonald's there too. We could get gas, coffee, and burgers for the kids—all in one stop!" And with that, we'd pass by the next exit with its easy off-ramp leading directly into a brightly lit Sinclair gas station just off the interstate.

Without fail, just past the exit we'd see a road sign listing the distances to upcoming destinations. Sure, there might be exits for a town or two in the next ten miles. But they would have names like Diresville or Desperation Point. What's more, a quick check of the TripTik would show that although they had exits, the actual towns lay literally off the map and had no symbols for services of any kind. Then, at the very bottom of the sign, we'd see the town Dad had mentioned as our destination and its distance: thirty-nine miles. It was at this point, as we continued along a highway suddenly devoid of other traffic, that our car would grow very quiet. We would each retreat into our private worlds, hoping against hope that Dad's theory held water—not to mention forty miles worth of fuel.

As the reality of our situation settled in, Mom would read Dad the riot act. She might even work in a few tears as she'd let loose on how he never listened to her about filling up when it was convenient, how he always had to push it. Ever the cool customer, Dad would confidently reply there was nothing to worry about; we'd make it to Bumbleburg with fuel to spare. But afterward he'd become as silent as the rest of us, knowing deep down it was going to be close. And though we'd all been down this road many times before—literally and figuratively—he knew that this just might be the day his luck, and our tank, would run out.

As the minutes passed along with the miles, we'd all edge up on our seats and crane our necks to get a better look at the fuel gauge. Just as the fuel needle would drop below the white line pointing to "E," we'd see the next road sign: BUMBLEBURG, 17 MILES. We'd swallow hard, and our eyes would dart from side to side like the crowd following the action at a tennis match—from the fuel gauge to the road, to the fuel gauge, to the road—searching desperately for an illuminated sign, a billboard, any trace whatsoever of civilization ahead. More than once I'd also looked over at Dad to see the calm expression on his face betrayed by tiny beads of perspiration.

Whether by divine intervention or sheer luck, we always made it to Bumbleburg or Snipesville or whatever other town would be our salvation. Like the lookout up in a ship's crow's nest searching for land, one of us would finally thrust a finger forward and cry out that a gas station sign was jutting up from the horizon. Then we'd sweat out a few last anxious moments as our car coasted on its last drops of fuel into the station and up to the pump. Without a word, we'd simultaneously pop open our car doors, as much to release the pent-up tension as to file outside to use the restroom and offer up a silent prayer of thanks. After a short break, we'd return to our seats and head back out on the highway, only to repeat the whole episode all over again, exactly one tankful of gas later.

And so the "Battle of E" would play out time and again, trip after trip, tankful of fuel after tankful of fuel, that is, until one rainy evening on an interstate outside Little Rock, Arkansas, in 1978. That's when the great debate over "How Far Below E Is Empty" came to its inevitable, sputtering conclusion. Just as we neared the exit that would convey us to the gas station that would be our salvation, the engine of our Ford Country Squire station wagon wheezed a gasp and quit. As my father struggled to guide our suddenly silent car, now without the benefit of power steering, over to the shoulder, no one spoke a word. What was there to say? My father couldn't offer up a word in his defense without it sounding as hollow and empty as the gas tank that had betrayed him. My mother couldn't take any satisfaction in being right because she'd soon be looking after four kids in a stalled station wagon on a dark and rainy highway. And perhaps all of us knew this would be the end of a family tradition. There'd be no more squabbling about when we'd stop to refuel, no more anxious moments of suspense to punctuate the hours of monotony out on the open road. Clearly, the future would be less exciting.

So we just sat quietly, staring into the drizzly darkness of the Arkansas night. Not far off in the distance ahead, we could make out the hazy white glow of fluorescent lights hanging above the gas station that was our destination. My father zipped up the collar of his jacket, pulled a hat down over his brow, and pulled the car door handle. Then he set out into the night, no doubt muttering unspeakable curses under his breath about a nameless negligent Ford engineer who'd calibrated a fuel gauge to leave just thirty-nine miles worth of fuel below the line pointing to "E."

• • •

On our family road trips, nearly running out of gas wasn't a rare event. It was as common as having to roll down the windows because someone released a silent but deadly fart—a frequent occurrence in a car packed with six people whose every meal consisted of greasy fast-food hamburgers, fries, and Coke. Sure, my dad's ongoing crusade to make time accounted for many near misses. But there were other reasons. It didn't help that we drove gas-guzzling land yachts that averaged ten miles per gallon even before being loaded with six people and a mountain of luggage. At the rate our cars burned gas, we went through a half tank before we made it from the pump to the on-ramp. But another factor was the swift demise of a once popular chain named Stuckey's.

One of the greatest success stories of the American highway boom, Stuckey's began as a single wooden stand located along US Route 23 near Eastman, Georgia, in the early 1930s. It was there that Williamson S. "Bill" Stuckey, a pecan farmer sitting on a bumper crop, decided to hawk some nuts to the scores of motorists zipping along the highway en route to Florida. The stand was an instant hit.

Sensing an opportunity, Stuckey sent his wife, Ethel, into the kitchen. Soon motorists were toting off bags of Ethel's original pecan log rolls, pecan divinity, and other tasty homemade pecan treats as fast as she could pull the trays from her oven. As word spread and customers returned year after year, Stuckey built a permanent structure boasting a sit-down restaurant, souvenir shop, gas pumps, and, most notable, a teal shingled roof that would become Stuckey's trademark.

Like the stand it replaced, the new Stuckey's was a resounding success. Bill Stuckey began opening new stores as fast as he could secure financing. Corporate lore holds that he determined locations based on a simple but reliable tool: his bladder. Starting from nearby Atlanta, Stuckey set out on the highway and drove until he could no longer hold back the urge to relieve himself. Reasoning that other travelers would have to do the same, Stuckey marked the spot (presumably on a map and not by—ahem—other means), then drove until he felt the urge again. He noted the new spot on his map, and so on. The system likely not only determined the placement of Stuckey's stores but also inspired its commitment to clean restrooms.

After franchising the concept, Stuckey's stores fanned out across America's Southeast. By the mid-1960s, the chain's signature teal-roofed buildings were nearly as iconic as the golden arches of McDonald's. Even more ubiquitous than Stuckey's stores were the chain's distinctive yellow-and-red billboards. Not wanting to leave a customer's decision to stop at one of his stores strictly to the call of nature, Bill Stuckey erected an astounding six thousand billboards on highways across the South—as many as fifty for a single location. Years later, it would be these billboards that would often result in my family's nearly getting stuck instead of at the site of an operating Stuckey's.

With sales still on the upswing, Bill Stuckey decided to sell the prospering chain in 1964. But the new management failed to keep Stuckey's in tune with the times. By the early 1970s, traveling families were bypassing Stuckey's and its sit-down diner fare for the faster meals available at McDonald's, Burger King, and Hardee's. Gas-pumping convenience stores like 7-Eleven and convenience-pumping gas stations like Amoco Gas & Food Marts introduced more competition. After peaking at 360 locations in the early 1970s, Stuckey's stores closed in scores. By 1984, fewer than 75 remained. In many locations, franchise owners simply locked the doors and walked away. In others, franchisees stopped serving food and pumping gas, focusing instead on selling the pecan treats and kitschy novelties that had originally built the brand.

But while Stuckey's stores disappeared or changed, their billboards didn't. Thanks to Bill Stuckey's overly diligent efforts decades before, dozens of boards remained by the roadside, promising motorists delicious food, cheap fuel, and clean restrooms just ahead. Preoccupied with boarding up windows and tearing out gas pumps, owners of many failed or foundering Stuckey's franchises never thought to take down their billboards. It was an oversight that proved particularly vexing for travelers who rolled into the parking lot of a Stuckey's store with full bladders and empty gas tanks, only to find a chained front door and cobweb-covered gas pumps. All too often in the late 1970s, those travelers were us.

On more than a few occasions when we were running on empty, we'd spot a Stuckey's billboard. "Look," my dad would announce, pointing to the garish red-and-yellow sign. "See? We've got nothing to worry about. There's a Stuckey's eight miles ahead, and they've got gas!"

We'd all let out a sigh of relief, confident we'd once again taunted the fuel gods and lived to tell the tale. Or so we thought. After traveling the eight miles, another Stuckey's billboard would appear, and Dad would exit. Meanwhile, my brothers and I would prepare to jump out of the backseat to use the facilities or just browse the novelty aisle for a genuine imitation animal skin Indian drum, while Dad filled up. Perhaps we'd even try to talk Mom into purchasing a box of pecan caramels to gobble on the road.

But as we'd pull into the parking lot, our hearts would sink.

We'd see that the store's interior was dark, or spot a torn screen hanging forlornly from the front door, a sure tip-off that something was amiss. Other times, the store would be open, but the gas pumps were wrapped tightly in plastic. We'd watch through the front windows as my dad would go inside to ask about gas, only to see the manager shrug his shoulders and point a finger down the highway.

Exasperated, my dad would climb back behind the wheel. The rest of us would slump back into our seats. Without a word, Dad would turn the key and steer our car back onto the on-ramp. With our fuel needle sinking ever lower below "E," we traveled on.

Somehow we always managed to make it, though, and Stuckey's would too. Stuckey's salvation would be Bill Stuckey Jr., who repurchased the failing chain in 1985 in hopes of restoring its former glory. Under Bill Jr.'s direction, Stuckey's updated its approach and has modestly rebounded, with more than one hundred franchises in seventeen states. For the record, though, you may want to note that while you can look forward to stopping at Stuckey's for tasty pecan candies, nuts, and souvenirs, the chain no longer sells gas.

Motorists didn't always have to wait until the next exit to find some essential services. Thankfully, the planners of the interstates built some handy stops right into their highways. I'm speaking, of course, of the nation's collection of rest areas. While rest areas didn't sell gas, they did and still do offer travelers convenient places to pull off the road and enjoy a picnic lunch, use the restrooms, consult a map, and, in many locations, even get a quick education in the history and culture of the local surroundings.

My family stopped at rest areas only in the most dire of circumstances—when we were dragging a sparking muffler down the highway or my dad had miscalculated the effect an extra cup of coffee at breakfast would have on his bladder. But for many families, stops at rest areas were a mainstay of the family road trip experience. And for that, they owe a debt of thanks to a considerate young man employed by a midwestern highway department, at least, according to an article printed in *American Road Builder* magazine in 1957.

As the story goes, sometime in the late 1920s, Allan Williams was driving along a rural highway when he came on an amusing scene. A traveling family had parked its car in a shady spot near a small pond and was attempting to enjoy a peaceful picnic lunch. Only no one appeared relaxed.

The harried mother hovered over a tree stump she was using as a makeshift table, trying to fit one more serving dish on top without knocking several others off. With no place to sit and eat, a child sat cross-legged on the grass, eating her sandwich while keeping a watchful eye on an approaching squirrel. A few yards away, a boy was awkwardly perched on a large rock, his plate sliding off his lap. Meanwhile, the father stood nearby and danced a kind of jig, balancing several plates and glasses in his arms while attempting to shovel a forkful of food into his mouth.

Williams simply smiled and drove on. But the scene stayed with him. After all, he wondered, shouldn't travelers have convenient places to pull off the road and take a break? Somewhere to get out, stretch their legs, and grab a bite to eat after driving long miles of bumpy roads?

Fortunately, Williams held a position in which he could act on his idea. As a young engineer and manager for the road commission in Ionia County, Michigan, it was Williams's job to make the roads in his jurisdiction safe and pleasant for motorists.

Months later, an opportunity presented itself. Williams found himself holed up in a county garage with an idle snow-plowing crew, awaiting the arrival of an expected snowstorm. Rather than fritter away the time playing gin rummy, Williams set his men to work on a project. Using odd lengths of two-by-four scrap lumber piled in a corner, Williams directed his crew to knock together a few simple picnic tables. Finding some leftover paint, the men brushed a thick coat of pine green on each.

When spring came, Williams and his crew loaded the tables on a truck and drove them to a scenic spot he picked out along Route 16, three miles south of the village of Saranac. The tables were neatly arranged on a patch of grass in the shade of some sturdy oaks, within clear sight of passing motorists.

Not long after, a trickle of letters began arriving on the desk of B. C. Tiney, chief maintenance engineer of the Michigan State Highway Department. Each dispatch had been sent by a delighted traveler, lauding the department for its thoughtfulness in providing such an inviting picnic spot. Confused, Tiney looked into the matter. Learning what Williams had done, Tiney decided he liked the idea—not to mention the attention it brought his department. He authorized the establishment of more roadside picnic sites along Michigan highways.

Word traveled fast, as you might expect of an idea spread mainly by tourists, and soon states across the nation got to work creating their own roadside stops. In the blink of an eye, rest areas became as common along America's highways as patrol cars and roadkill.

Technically, these first rest areas weren't known as such. They were called "roadside parks" or "waysides." The transition to a new term didn't occur until planning began for construction of America's interstate highway system in the late 1950s. Even then, such off-road refuges were officially designated *safety* rest areas.

As the term implies, safety rest areas (SRAs) were included along the interstates as much to offer motorists a safe place to pull off the road in the event of emergencies or mechanical issues as they were to offer road-weary travelers a place to enjoy picnic lunches and use the toilet. In outlying areas, developers of the interstates knew it would be years before motorists could depend on finding nearby restaurants and service stations. SRAs were intended to help fill that void.

In 1958, planners of the interstate highway system issued a policy document spelling out a standardized basic layout for safety rest areas. In general, each SRA was to consist of a main building providing toilet facilities and a drinking fountain, a separate picnic shelter, a kiosk to provide basic travel information, and a large parking lot. Freeway-type entrance and exit ramps were to be built to provide safe and easy access, without requiring motorists to actually leave the restricted space of the interstate. Finally, the SRAs were to be staffed or visited regularly by state employees to ensure proper maintenance of the facilities and to render any necessary assistance to motorists.

But while federal policy dictated how SRAs should be constructed and function, it offered no guidelines on how the buildings should look. This meant the aesthetic design of the facilities was left largely up to state officials and the architects they hired. As federal funding for SRAs was continually slashed and the burden of paying for their construction shifted to the states, local decision makers gained even more creative latitude. The results were often charming, sometimes quirky, and, in some instances, nothing less than dazzling.

To understand why local officials became interested in making rest areas more than functional public facilities, it's important to remember that prior to the interstates, road travel was a much more leisurely proposition. Motorists navigated the country on two-lane highways, and stops and slowdowns at crossroads and intersections were common. In towns, traffic could back up for any number of reasons, from a slow-moving wagon making deliveries, to a community festival in the central square. Travelers might decide to stop off and buy fresh produce at a roadside stand or enjoy a meal at a local café or diner. It made for slow going. But it also offered tourists the chance to look around and absorb the local flavor, with each region and community leaving its own indelible impression.

The construction of the interstates changed all that. By design, the new superhighways minimized motorists' contact with the world beyond the asphalt. To keep traffic moving at top speed, intersections were eliminated and access limited. Faster travel speeds also demanded that drivers keep their eyes on the road ahead rather than the scenery off to each side. Even when travelers could cast a glance off the interstate, they were able to see far less. What's more, to promote rainwater runoff and prevent flooding, the new interstates were elevated well above the surrounding landscape. It meant that motorists on the interstates now traveled *over* the country rather than *through* it. In a very real sense, travelers were able to cross vast swaths of America without ever seeing or experiencing anything.

This notion wasn't lost on state officials in the early 1960s. But they realized that there was one place where they could still make a favorable impression on the growing number of travelers passing inside their borders: the rest areas they built and controlled. As a result, the stop-offs that had previously been treated as mere public facilities were promoted to a far more important role in public relations. They became state ambassadors.

The elevated status of rest areas was often reflected in their aesthetic design. Rest area architects increasingly viewed the projects as important venues for showcasing a region's rich culture, history, and vision for the future. The designs they created often distilled building styles common in the area, using noteworthy local building materials—signature types of stone in the Midwest and Northeast, heavy timber in the Northwest, adobe in the Southwest, and so on. Artistic tile mosaics on interior walls became a popular way of sharing the traditions, activities, and themes unique to each area. Outside, commemorative plaques and kiosks often told the stories of significant historical events that had taken place nearby.

Planners didn't always look to the past for inspiration. Sometimes they chose to cultivate more progressive perceptions of their state by borrowing from popular modern architectural trends. In the mid-1960s, these included low horizontal structures with flat or butterfly roofs, decorative screen block entrances, and open interior spaces with severe geometric lines. During the 1970s, modernist trends veered toward rectangular buildings with tall, vertically sloped, low-hanging shingled roofs.

Rest areas also became important places for large-scale pieces of public art. In some cases, the buildings themselves became works of art. Some of the most noteworthy examples are scattered across America's Southwest, where rest area designers transformed simple picnic shelters into giant teepees, oil derricks, stylized longhorn cattle, rockets, and other symbols of local industries and heritage.

In performing their function as state ambassadors, rest areas assumed another role as well as the years passed: that of cultural custodians, capturing and safeguarding the past, present, and even future aspirations of a region and its people at a particular moment in time. In so doing, many of the classic rest areas have become all the more fascinating to stop off and see today.

However, you might want to make those visits soon.

Unfortunately, like many other fixtures of the heydays of the highways, the original rest areas are disappearing quickly. As our interstate highways have become more built up and technology has advanced, the need for rest areas today just isn't what it used to be. With another McDonald's or Wendy's waiting just a few miles down the road, few travelers pack picnic lunches anymore. Smartphones have dispensed with the need to stop to ask for directions. Safer and more reliable vehicles mean breakdowns are far less common. And if anyone has to use the restroom, well, if they can hold it until the next exit, there will be a Starbucks where they can also grab coffee.

Of course, rest areas will always have some place along our highways, especially along remote stretches. At state borders, large and modern "welcome centers" will also likely forever await visitors to dispense information on local attractions and offer helpful guidance. But as state budgets grow ever tighter and aging rest area facilities become more costly to maintain, it's not hard to guess what will become of the classic SRAs from America's golden years of road travel. And as we move on down the road, it's only natural to feel a little wistful for the things we leave behind.

As for now, let's keep moving.

State authorities weren't the only ones trying to promote their interests to passing tourists. Plenty of local officials and private businesses tried to capture travelers' attention—and lighten their wallets—as well. One could write an entire book about America's most notable and curious roadside attractions. In fact, many people have. But in the interest of "making time," we'll just pull over to cover a few of the best attractions.

One of the earliest and most beloved is the famous Mystery Spot located near Santa Cruz, California. According to legend, in 1939 a handyman named George Prather went out for a walk in some woods near Highway 17 one afternoon when he began to feel slightly dizzy. Checking his compass, Prather watched dumbfounded as the arrow inexplicably spun about. He soon discovered other anomalies in the area. Prather was fascinated—and thought others would be as well. He purchased a three-acre parcel of the land, then built a shack on the side of what came to be known as a "gravity hill." For a small fee, Prather led visitors out to the shack, where balls appeared to roll uphill and guests could lean far out over their feet without falling over, seemingly defying the laws of physics. After being featured in a 1948 issue of *Life* magazine and later on the television show *You Asked for It*, the Mystery Spot began to draw hordes of fascinated tourists from around the world. Years later, the mind-boggling phenomena were attributed to Prather's own cockeyed perspective—he'd simply built a tilted house. The structure's imperceptible slant and lack of a visible horizon throw off visitors' ability to correctly perceive what is truly level. Yet the Mystery Spot's intriguing illusions continue to amaze visitors, and it remains open to this day.

Well south of the Mystery Spot, travelers since 1969 have been tempted to discover The Thing near Texas Canyon, Arizona. The attraction is hard to miss. Motorists are confronted with, by one estimate, as many as 247 billboards touting the mysterious "MacGuffin" along the highways between Phoenix, Tucson, and El Paso. In the interest of keeping the secret, I won't divulge exactly what The Thing is except to say that the exhibit was originally created by a man known for peddling faux shrunken heads, mermaids, and other biological oddities as sideshow attractions.

To see a "real" mermaid in the flesh, motorists needed to head much farther east, to Florida. There, in tiny Weeki Wachee, a former stunt swimmer named Newt Perry established his famous Mermaid Shows in 1947 in hopes of netting travelers heading south to destinations like Fort Lauderdale and Miami. Those who stopped were treated to an underwater ballet performed in a natural spring pool by beautiful women dressed in fetching fish tail costumes. Elvis Presley and Esther Williams are among the many luminaries who attended a performance. You can too. Even today, the shows remain an immensely popular attraction.

It didn't take anything as exotic as sultry, slippery sirens to lure travelers headed west along desolate I-90 to Mount Rushmore. All it took was the promise of free ice water. With few other places for motorists to stop, the offer, now posted on billboards for hundreds of miles in both directions, was sufficient to turn Ted Hustead's humble small-town drugstore into a bustling cowboy-themed megamall. Since Hustead's wife, Dorothy, first conceived the free water promotion in 1941, Wall Drug has evolved into what is likely the nation's most famous roadside attraction, drawing 2 million thirsty visitors to a remote South Dakota town each year.

Perhaps nowhere else in America did businesses work harder—or show more creativity—in enticing motorists to pull over than along the famous Route 66, stretching from Chicago to the West Coast. Traffic along the highway was often seasonal and sporadic. To survive, businesses that lined the route had to try every means possible to get motorists to stop and spend their money. The most obvious of these tactics were the colossal fiberglass "people attractors": giant hotdogs, guns, pies, cow heads, ice cream cones, and other items associated with the goods each proprietor was hawking.

Before long, the buildings themselves took on attention-getting shapes. Restaurants morphed into gigantic shoes, sombreros, and UFOs. Diners were served in retired trolley cars, cabooses, and airplanes. Motels assumed the appearance of log cabins, alpine cottages, and, of course, Indian-style teepees. At the Wigwam Village chain's peak, seven of Frank Redford's unique roadside inns lined Route 66.

Other oddities appeared as well. Along the highway in Catoosa, Oklahoma, motorists were amazed to come across a beached blue whale. More than eighty feet long and sporting a friendly smile, the whale sits in a small watering hole, inviting overheated travelers to take a quick dip. Interestingly, the whale wasn't originally built as a tourist attraction. It was a wedding present constructed by a man named Hugh Davis for his bride, Zelta, and intended for use by their family only.

A little farther along Route 66 in Tulsa, road trippers ran into the Golden Driller, a towering brass-toned oilman wearing a hard hat built in 1952 to tout the area's good fortune as the "oil capital of the world." A newer, even taller, and bare-chested version replaced the original in 1966. At seventy-five feet in height, it's one of the tallest freestanding statues in the United States—so tall he requires an actual retired oil derrick on which to support his gloved right hand.

Of course, it wasn't just the cities and businesses along Route 66 vying for the attention of motorists. Outlandish oversize objects could be found beside highways all over America. The World's Largest Catsup Bottle awaited tourists in Collinsville, Illinois, and the World's Largest Light Bulb became a beacon for visitors to Edison, New Jersey, home of the inventor's Menlo Park Laboratory. Honoring its hometown's rich automotive history, the World's Largest Tire (eighty feet tall) can be seen near the Detroit Metro Airport.

For years, there was a running duel between two parties for the title of World's Largest Ball of Twine. The ball got rolling . . . er, winding . . . when a Minnesota farmer named Francis A. Johnson, the son of Senator Magnus Johnson, began tying the ends of spare bits of sisal and coiling them up in 1950. Inspired by newspaper accounts of Johnson's curious, and ever-expanding, creation, Frank Stoeber of Cawker City, Kansas, set to work on his own ball in 1953. Stoeber wound so diligently that he eventually surpassed the size of Johnson's ball despite his later start. In 1973, Stoeber's ball of twine was the first to be recognized by Guinness as the world's largest, measuring in at more than eleven feet in diameter. However, Stoeber's death the following year gave Johnson the opportunity he needed to once again surpass his rival. After several years of furious winding, Johnson finally succeeded, as confirmed by Guinness in 1979. And Johnson wasn't done. Despite failing health, he continued adding to his enormous orb until finally reaching the end of his string on his death in 1989. Now twelve feet in diameter and weighing 17,400 pounds, Johnson's ball was gifted to the nearby town of Darwin, Minnesota, where it is celebrated exactly as its sole creator left it, housed in a glass-enclosed gazebo in a central park. Unwilling to accept second-class status, however, authorities in Cawker City opted to turn Stoeber's sphere into an ongoing pursuit, setting up the ball in an open-air pavilion where tourists were encouraged to make their own contributions and help reclaim the record. Today the Cawker City version is generally considered the biggest of its kind,* at last check measuring in at more than forty feet in cir-

---

*Incredibly, there are two additional contenders, though their claims to the title are controversial. A ball exhibited in the Ripley's Believe It or Not museum in Branson, Missouri, was certified as the largest by Guinness in 1994. However, rather than traditional brown sisal twine, the Branson ball is composed of lighter

cumference and more than 8 million feet of twine. Johnson's ball remains the largest wound by a single creator.

The competition between the two towns certainly wasn't the only "World's Largest" rivalry. Fittingly, there have been even bigger ones. Six parties around the country have laid claim to possessing the World's Largest Frying Pan. Most are well over twelve feet in diameter and are used to fry eggs or chickens at local fairs. Such skillet braggadocio pales in comparison to the dozens of businesses claiming to be sitting on the World's Largest Chair, each padding its claim to its own advantage. While a lumber store in Binghamton, New York, boasted of building the World's Largest Ladderback Chair, an office supply dealer in Anniston, Alabama, declared that it had created the World's Largest Office Chair—and at least a half-dozen claimants feud over the record for the World's Largest Rocking Chair. You get the idea.

Even harder to keep track of back in the road trip's golden era were all of the World's Largest Animals. Depending on where your journey led you, you might run into the World's Largest buffalo, bull, Holstein cow, turtle, prairie dog, musky, clam, sperm whale, loon, hippo, jackalope, or just about any other animal (real or imaginary). In tiny Enterprise, Alabama, you can still find the World's Largest (and only) Boll Weevil monument, erected by the town after a plague of the insects destroyed surrounding cotton crops, delivering a tough lesson to local farmers on the importance of crop diversification. True story.

---

weight and multicolored plastic twine, which many dismiss as a disqualifier. A fourth ball, created in eccentric isolation since 1979 by a man in Lake Nebagamon, Wisconsin, is made of short strands of multicolored twine and was wound in a way that is many times denser (and heavier) but significantly smaller than the Cawker City ball. It appears that the true claim to the World's Largest Ball of Twine lies in the eye of the ballholder.

. . .

With so many competing attractions lining America's highways, it should be no surprise that billboards touting them all started to become a real issue. By the 1960s, the saturation of billboards in some areas got so bad that it became nearly impossible for traveling motorists to see the land they'd set out to explore.

Among these motorists were Lyndon B. Johnson and his wife, Claudia, known by most as Lady Bird. During the time Lyndon served as a US congressman and senator, the couple often drove from their ranch in Texas to Washington, DC. While on the road, Lady Bird frequently expressed her frustration at the number of billboards, junkyards, and other unsightly scenes spoiling the view from her window. So when Lyndon became America's thirty-sixth president, she pressed him to do something about it.

President Eisenhower had made an earlier attempt to deal with the problem, offering states an extra half percent in federal highway funding if they controlled the spread of billboards along the interstates. But the powerful and well-funded billboard industry was largely successful in blocking the effort. Clearly, the Johnsons would have a fight on their hands.

Locked in a pitched battle with the Outdoor Advertising Association of America, Johnson and his congressional allies struggled to pass the Highway Beautification Act in 1965. They succeeded, but not without making major concessions. Billboards were banned along interstates "except in those areas of commercial and industrial use," a vague phrase the billboard industry would continually exploit. What's more, where companies were required to remove their billboards, they were handsomely compensated. Still, the Highway Beautification Act inspired by Lady Bird Johnson did limit the growth of billboards, required junkyards and other roadside messes to be screened, and provided funds for local highway cleanup efforts.

That's not to say the highways were free from junk, especially by the time my family came rolling along in the 1970s. In an era when many cars weren't yet equipped with air-conditioning, motorists often drove with their windows down, making it all too convenient for occupants to simply throw used wrappers, cans, and cigarette butts into the breeze. Even worse, many people (my parents being exceptions) considered the practice *acceptable*. I can still vividly recall seeing the shoulders of highways cluttered with mounds of paper cups, pull tabs, and other jettisoned trash, even outside urban areas.

Fortunately, those responsible for creating the mess were also among the first to work toward cleaning it up. In the 1950s, the country's leading can and bottle manufacturers joined Coca-Cola, PepsiCo, Philip Morris, Anheuser-Busch, and other consumer products companies to form Keep America Beautiful (KAB), an organization promoting antilitter efforts. The consortium's goals weren't entirely noble. Sure, KAB sought to reduce the amount of trash, but it also wanted to shift blame for the litter problem away from producers of disposable packaging to consumers—so-called litterbugs.

As part of its effort, KAB was responsible for creating one of the most memorable TV commercials of all time. Debuting on Earth Day in 1971, the spot depicted a Native American rowing his canoe through a river of floating garbage. After the Indian reached shore near a busy highway, a passing motorist tossed a bag of trash out of his car's window that landed at the man's feet. As the camera dramatically closed in, a tear rolled down his cheek as an announcer gravely intoned, "People start pollution. People can stop it." The face of the "Crying Indian" became one of the most indelible images of the 1970s. It was also one of the most deceptive. The actor who portrayed the Indian was a full-blooded Italian, born Espera Oscar de Corti. In his twenties, de Corti contrived the false persona of "Iron Eyes Cody" to win Native American roles in Hollywood Westerns.

Being a kid, I wasn't overly concerned about the enormous amount of pollution cluttering the nation's highways. Instead, my mind was on junk of another kind: souvenirs. Knowing I would inevitably have to give some sort of speech about my trip at school, it was crucial that I bring back something remarkable to impress my classmates and help me nail down an easy A from my teacher.

After all, I had a reputation to uphold. From previous presentations, my classmates knew my family traveled a lot, and I'd already hauled in an impressive array of extraordinary pieces from our earlier travels: a plastic bottle of water from the "real" Fountain of Youth in St. Augustine, Florida; a cool wide-brimmed Union Cavalry hat from Gettysburg; even a genuine voodoo doll wrapped in creepy Spanish moss from the French Quarter in New Orleans.

I was also the proud owner of what I assumed was the world's most expansive collection of Mold-A-Rama figurines. Mold-A-Rama machines were freestanding blow-molded plastic vending machines placed in zoos, museums, and other popular attractions beginning in 1962. Their allure was the magic of seeing figurines made right before your eyes. You'd drop a few quarters into the slot, then press your nose up against the clear plastic viewing bubble to watch two hydraulic arms push the halves of a complete mold together. Then the machine would light up and start shaking and whirring as hot liquid plastic was injected into the mold and air was blasted inside to push it into every crevice. After a moment of suspenseful silence, the arms would pull the halves of the mold apart to reveal a shiny single-color figurine that would drop down into a bin where it could be retrieved. When you pulled it out, it would still be warm and fill your nostrils with the intoxicating aroma of molten resin. Individually, the cooled figurines were nothing special. But a collection like mine was. It included an ape, lion, panther, robot, rhino, polar bear, sea horse, dolphin, *T. rex*, stegosaurus, and more. I was a Mold-A-Rama mogul.

I also felt pressure to keep the competition at bay. Other kids in my class traveled as well, and several had begun returning from their trips with impressive specimens of their own. One boy brought in a genuine tin deputy's badge from the real O.K. Corral. Another kid exhibited a fully "inflated" blowfish from Florida coated in a thick layer of lacquer to maintain its shape. Still another girl boosted her popularity by distributing handfuls of saltwater taffy from the boardwalk in Atlantic City.

To stay on top, I would need to choose carefully because I'd get only one shot. One pricy souvenir would likely be all I'd be able to shake down from my mom per trip. To make a solid selection, I needed to meticulously preview the itinerary for our trip and identify the stops or attractions where I'd likely find the best souvenirs. On one trip to Florida, I'd foolishly opted for a cheesy coconut shell bongo set when, if I'd waited a few days longer, I could have brought home an entire box of foil-wrapped packets of freeze-dried ice cream—*the same kind eaten in space by real astronauts!*—from the gift store at NASA's Kennedy Space Center.

On those occasions when distractions like the game bag had lost their power to divert and I wasn't preoccupied with whether we'd reach a gas station, I found other ways to pass the miles. Sometimes I'd climb up on the rear window ledge to take in the scenery or try to coax truckers to sound their airhorns by clenching my fist and gesturing up and down on an invisible pull cord. Often I'd fall asleep on the ledge and wake up to find that hours—even entire *states*—had passed while I snoozed. I might doze off in Indiana and wake up in Tennessee. To a kid my age, it was as amazing as teleportation or time travel.

Almost as fascinating was monitoring the changes that took place as we progressed to warmer climes. During our travels over Easter break, in particular, it was almost magical to observe the transition from the bluster and gray of the Midwest, and its drifts of snow, to the vibrant greenery and budding blossoms that were already heralding the arrival of spring just a few hours south. Aboard our land yacht, we were watching the seasons change right before our eyes, like the time-lapse nature sequences they'd sometimes show on *Sesame Street*. The experience of piling into a car in the morning, shivering and bundled in thick winter jackets, then stepping out into warm sunshine at a gas stop just hours later was almost surreal. We were like bears taking our first steps outside the cave after a long winter's hibernation.

As the weather changed, so did the scenery. Heading south, the rolling hills of Wisconsin gradually leveled off into the wide, flat cornfields of central Illinois. In the lower part of the state, we'd pass through vast tracts of oil pumpjacks stretching as far as the eye could see. With their steel heads bobbing up and down atop long-legged stands, the pumpjacks resembled enormous animals grazing in pastures. I'm told that farmhands who worked the pumpjacks commonly referred to them as "thirsty birds" or "nodding donkeys." To my eyes, they looked more like a herd of dinosaurs feeding on the crops of cabbage and soybeans growing at their feet. Though these *Jurassic Park*–like scenes along the highways were once common, oil pumpjacks are mostly extinct in the Midwest today, the victims of more efficient oil-gathering technologies.

As we crossed the northern borders of Arkansas or Tennessee, we'd all try to be the first to spot one of the sure signs that we'd finally arrived in the American South—a field of cotton, perhaps, or a sharecropper's shack set back far from the road, its corrugated tin roof clinging to a collapsing frame. There wasn't anything particularly noteworthy about spotting a crumbling hovel with a washing machine rusting away on its front porch, I suppose, but I remember that such sights had a visceral impact on us. They marked our passage from a land that felt familiar and comfortable to a place that seemed foreign and strange.

We were leaving behind a world where we—and everyone we knew—lived in roomy and well-built suburban homes in neighborhoods with wide green lawns and friendly neighbors. A place where dads went off to work in concrete and glass office buildings and moms went shopping at palatial malls and sprawling supermarkets, while kids spent sunny Saturday afternoons playing kickball in the backyard or blasting alien invaders on video games in their basements. On seeing that first tiny ramshackle hut, we knew we'd entered a land where at least some people lived in homes with roofs that probably didn't keep the rain out. A place where entire families worked the surrounding fields to scratch out a living, and kids the same ages as us may not have even had the chance to attend school or watch TV because their families lacked the necessary income. What made observing these scenes from our car all the more unreal was knowing that we hadn't crossed a border into some neighboring impoverished Third World country. We'd simply gotten in a car and driven a few hundred miles south in our own country. This was still America. It just wasn't the America we knew.

To kids who grew up living a relatively sheltered life in the suburbs, the experience of seeing the harsh realities of lives so different than ours was striking. On our family road trips, we were traveling to new places indeed.

CHAPTER 7

Eating Up the Miles

Dining While Driving

My father was one of those people born with no "stop" gene. He always had to be on the go, always had to be doing something. Even if he was sitting still, his mind was always racing, thinking about the next item on his to-do list: his next sales call, his next round of golf, his next Rotary meeting, his next whatever.

In short, my dad's disposition made him ill suited for fifteen- to twenty-hour road trips. The advent of the 55 mph national maximum speed limit only exacerbated his restlessness. But what really aggravated him was having to make stops he judged unnecessary—which is to say, any stop at all. If my dad had his way, we wouldn't have ever stopped—not for meals, not to refill our gas tank, not even for potty breaks. And he wasn't alone in this thinking. A friend of mine told me that his father became so fed up making constant potty stops for the eight kids in his family that he rigged up a toilet in the back of their family van. The "facilities" consisted of a funnel with a hose fed into a plastic milk jug. Fortunately, our dads weren't well acquainted.

My dad also couldn't do much about our need to occasionally refuel—at least, beyond stretching every tankful of gas to its gauge-defying limit. But he could control how often we stopped for meals. His main strategy was to forget meals altogether. As lunchtime approached after a long morning's drive, he'd click off the radio and announce, "Why don't we all take a break for a while? Maybe you kids can get a little extra sleep. You'll want to be rested for the beach tomorrow!" We'd settle into our corners to read magazines, click away on our electronic games, or just doze off, only to awaken hours later with rumbling stomachs.

Finally, one of us would say, "Dad, I'm hungry! When are we stopping to eat?"

"Oh, look at that," he'd respond, playing dumb. "Did we miss lunch? Well, no point stopping now. We'd just ruin our appetites for dinner!" Then he'd ease into the passing lane just in case any exits appeared.

As dinnertime neared, our only hope was that Mom would join our protests and make him stop. Unfortunately, she was often exhausted from looking after four kids and would often sleep right through our meal negotiations with Dad. So we'd simply cruise along until we reached our hotel for the night. By that time, most of the restaurants in the vicinity would be closed for the evening and we had no other option but to grab snacks from the vending machines and hit the pool. This, of course, was just fine with Dad. The way he saw it, the sooner we turned in for the night, the sooner we could skip breakfast the next morning and get back on the road.

My family saved a lot of money on meals while traveling.

By the time I was nine, I'd traveled with my father long enough to know if I was going to stave off starvation during long days on the road I had to rely on myself. So I began to pack my own provisions.

A few days before we'd leave, I'd make my way to the village of Elm Grove, our local commercial hub, atop my five-speed Schwinn Orange Krate.* Once in town, I'd head straight to Phillips Pharmacy, one of the last of the classic pharmacies—the kind with a stainless steel lunch counter and waitresses wearing "cat eye" frame eyeglasses and hairnets who would mix cherry Cokes by hand. Phillips Pharmacy boasted the best candy counter in the area, at least within Orange Krate riding distance, and it was there that I stocked up on all the supplies I'd need for a week on the road.

I'd begin by grabbing a few proven staples, selections I could count on to fill me up between meals. These included a one-pound bag of Twizzlers licorice, Three Musketeers bars, Milky Ways, and perhaps a Reggie! bar. This last choice was a gooey lump of caramel, nuts, and chocolate named for New York Yankee and World Series hero Reggie Jackson. As a loyal Milwaukee Brewers fan in an era when the Yankees were a perennial roadblock to my team's path to a league pennant, I detested Jackson as a player, but I couldn't deny his abilities as a confectioner. The Reggie! Bar was unquestionably tasty, even if it was a blatant rip-off of the Baby Ruth.

I also reserved a portion of my budget for bubble gum, mainly because of its favorable flavor-to-mile ratio. This was no small consideration when I was about to embark on a two-thousand-mile road trip. While a typical candy bar provided a few moments of tasty indulgence, a pack of bubble gum offered hours of sat-

---

*The Orange Krate was a bike of almost indescribable beauty. It was one of Schwinn's Sting-Ray bicycles, a line of bikes designed to resemble the top fuel dragsters popular in the 1970s. The Orange Krate came complete with raised handlebars, functional rear shocks, a banana seat with racing stripes, and a sweet five-speed Stik-Shift mounted on the top bar. The proud owners of these magnificent machines were the envy of every other kid in Kid-dom.

isfying chewing. I was also certain that one day, my considerable bubble-blowing skills would earn inclusion in the *Guinness Book of World Records*.

During my younger years, my preferred brand was Rain-Blo, which was really just a pack of oversize gumballs coated in bright colors with fruity flavors to match. Rain-Blo's two primary rivals for my allowance money, Double Bubble and Bazooka, were nearly impossible to chew just out of the wrapper. Both required concentrated effort to gradually grind into a pliable gob. But the problem with all three choices was that none seemed capable of producing a bubble larger than the size of an orange.

That all changed in 1975, when Life Savers introduced Bubble Yum, the first soft bubble gum. Unlike Rain-Blo's hollow gumballs, Bubble Yum came in thick, individually wrapped blocks that felt heavy and substantial. And unlike Double Bubble and Bazooka, Bubble Yum had a pleasant, spongy texture that was pliable and easy to chew right out of the wrapper.*

Most important, a single piece of Bubble Yum, skillfully blown, produced a bubble nearly the size of one's head.† With two pieces, one could blow a bubble the size of a watermelon. With an entire

---

*Bubble Yum's texture was so different from other brands that it sparked a pernicious rumor. According to some, the reason for the gum's pliability was a secret ingredient—spider eggs! The rumor became so potentially damaging to sales that Life Saver was compelled to place a full-page ad in the *New York Times* and other publications to deny its veracity.

†Bubble Yum's key asset—its stickiness—also became its chief liability once the joy of blowing an enormous bubble had burst. It was nearly impossible to remove the tacky aftermath of a large Bubble Yum bubble explosion from one's face and hair. In an attempt to exploit that disadvantage, rival gum manufacturer Wm. Wrigley Jr. Company introduced a similar but less sticky brand of bubble gum, Hubba Bubba, in 1979. American Chicle launched another competitor, Bubblicious, in the late 1970s. But I remained a Bubble Yum loyalist throughout my youth.

pack who knew what was possible. A bubble the size of the *Hindenburg*? I became an instant Bubble Yum convert.

Once I had the basics covered in stocking up on pretrip supplies, I indulged in a few more exotic choices—candies of the most resplendent cheapness and novelty. Razzles were a favorite because their gimmick appealed to my sense of value. I mean, how could one top a confection that was first a candy, then a gum? I also always picked up a box of Lemonheads because their sour finish provided a nice palette cleanser. Ever the little ham, I'd also throw in some wax lips or wax mustaches that I could pull out to get a laugh out of my mom. The downside to buying wax candy was that after playing my little joke, I was left with candy that tasted like, well, wax.

As an alternative paraffin-based pleasure, I might include a bag of wax bottles. These were pinky-size vials of wax shaped like tiny Coke bottles filled with colorful syrupy goo flavored like popular brands of soda. In reality, they all just tasted like Kool-Aid that had been left out in the sun too long. Wax bottles didn't remain in my routine long. During one trip, my brother Bruce shifted himself onto my candy sack while sleeping and smooshed the goo of a half-dozen or so wax candy bottles onto the velour upholstery. After returning home, my dad made me spend hours scrubbing the stain out with soapy water. I never bought wax bottles again.

Nearly everyone smoked in the seventies, and I was no exception, even if my smokes were of the confectionary kind. To my mind, the only proper way to conclude a sugary snack was with, well, more sugar. My indulgence of choice: candy cigarettes, which were white sticks of chalky candy with one end dipped in bright red coloring to simulate a lit ember. (These sugary totems of adulthood are still sold today, mostly online, despite laws banning them in many communities.*)

Candy cigarettes were nearly as addictive as real ones. They had a smooth flavor, like a wintergreen lozenge, and their sweet taste (along with a telltale white powder mark) clung to your lips long after taking a drag. Candy cigarettes offered another pleasure too—watching adults in passing cars do double takes after glimpsing a nine-year-old puffing away on what appeared to be an unfiltered Camel.

Hey, they were long car rides. Sometimes you had to invent your own fun.

Finally, no trip to the candy counter in the late 1970s would have been complete without picking up at least a few foil envelopes of Pop Rocks. Introduced midway through the decade, Pop Rocks were an instant hit because of the way they literally exploded with flavor, popping and sizzling like tiny firecrackers on your tongue. Pop Rocks were just small chips of hard candy that had been carbonated and cooled to trap tiny bubbles of gas. When exposed to liquid—saliva, for instance—the candy dissolved and the bubbles burst apart, causing a startling tingling sensation in your mouth.

The candy's popular pop went from mildly disconcerting to downright alarming because of a nasty rumor, similar to the one attached to Bubble Yum. Talk began to circulate that the child

*Candy cigarettes were sold in packs of ten, in boxes resembling those of their tobacco cousins, in boxes resembling popular cigarette brands but with fictitious names like "Kings," "Target," and "Stallion." In the 1950s, actual cigarette brand names were used—Salem, Pall Mall, Winston, and others. The only discernible difference in the packaging of the two products was the addition of the word *candy* next to *cigarettes* in tiny type beneath the logos. Apparently tobacco companies were willing to overlook a little trademark infringement if candy cigarettes helped them recruit a new generation of customers.

actor who portrayed the character Mikey in a popular TV ad campaign for Life cereal had died after washing down a pack of Pop Rocks with a bottle of Coke. Supposedly the combustible combination caused his stomach to explode. The story was hokum, but the Food and Drug Administration received so many calls from concerned parents that it was forced to set up a special hotline, and General Foods, the maker of Pop Rocks, launched a costly PR campaign to reassure the public about the product's safety. For my buddies and me, the "danger" only made Pop Rocks that much cooler. I made sure to pick up a few packs on every trip to the candy counter.

Once I had made my selections, I would bike home and hide my candy on the highest shelf in my closet. It would take all my willpower to resist dipping into my stash until the moment of our departure.

Not all kids had to resort to such drastic measures to stave off starvation on road trips. Though I have little knowledge of such things from personal experience, I'm told some families once even stopped for minutes—*maybe an hour!*—to enjoy freshly cooked meals—*served on actual plates with silverware!*—while out on the highways. In fact, one man built an empire preparing such meals for hungry travelers. His name was Howard Deering Johnson.

Johnson inherited his entrepreneurial spirit from his father, who owned a Boston cigar store and export business in the early 1920s. Unfortunately for Johnson, he also inherited the equivalent of more than $100,000 in debt when his father died and left him the foundering business. Quickly concluding that the cigar business might not be the best for striking it rich, Johnson decided to try his hand at another, buying a small drugstore and soda fountain in the Wollaston neighborhood of Quincy, Massachusetts, in 1925.

Business was brisk at the soda fountain, but competition was fierce. To help his business stand out, Johnson decided he needed to offer truly outstanding ice cream—like the kind made by a local pushcart vendor, an elderly German immigrant. Learning the man was contemplating retirement, Johnson paid the handsome sum of $300 for the vendor's recipe. The secret, Johnson learned, was doubling the typical amount of butterfat and using only natural ingredients. But for Johnson, even that wasn't enough. He locked himself away in his basement and used a hand-cranked ice cream maker to create and perfect twenty-eight different flavors, a number Johnson believed covered "every flavor in the world." The flavors included coconut, macaroon, fruit salad, and frozen pudding.

Before long, customers were lining up for Johnson's tantalizing array of frozen treats. He quickly opened another stand at a local beach—it served as many as fourteen thousand cones in a single day! Leveraging the popularity of his ice cream, Johnson began serving freshly grilled meals as well and soon opened a full-blown restaurant. Besides hamburgers, "frankforts" (as Howard Johnson called his hot dogs), chicken potpies, and other staples, the menu also included another New England favorite: fried clams. Unlike other restaurants, which served whole clams, Howard Johnson's prepared and fried only the meaty foot of each clam, calling them "clam strips." The item became Howard Johnson's signature dish.

Still, Howard Johnson's might have remained a local favorite were it not for open discussion of adultery and abortion. It was those topics, among others, that spurred Boston's mayor to ban a planned production of Eugene O'Neill's play *Strange Interlude*. The play moved to nearby Quincy, near the Howard Johnson's restaurant. The five-hour performance included a break for dinner, affording thousands of wealthy and influential Bostonians the opportunity to discover the culinary delights awaiting them just down the road. Word of Howard Johnson's spread quickly. However, just as Johnson was hoping to take advantage of his growing fame by opening another location, the stock market crash of 1929 intervened.

Unable to find financing, Johnson hit on the idea of leasing his restaurant's increasingly famous name and recipes to the owner of an existing restaurant. This location, on the tourist mecca of Cape Cod, also proved fabulously successful. Soon other restaurant owners were clamoring to borrow the Howard Johnson's name and purchase his food. Howard Johnson had invented franchising.

It wasn't long before Johnson purchased the exclusive rights to build restaurants in service plazas along the new Pennsylvania Turnpike, Ohio Turnpike, and New Jersey Turnpike. Striving to appeal to traveling families, Johnson designed the exteriors of his restaurants to resemble inviting colonial-style homes. The buildings were sided in white clapboard with dormers and multipaned windows around a central cupola with a clock. Atop the cupola was a weathervane designed by artist John Alcott featuring Simple Simon and the Pieman from the famous nursery rhyme. And to ensure motorists noticed and instantly recognized his restaurants, Howard Johnson had every one of his shingled roofs painted a vibrant shade of orange.

Road trippers saw the restaurants, all right. They also stopped, in droves. By 1940, more than one hundred Howard Johnson's lined the turnpikes along the East Coast all the way to Florida. World War II hit the chain hard, as it did most other businesses. But afterward, Howard Johnson's returned better—and brighter—than ever before with a new design that replaced each building's staid dormers and clapboard siding with stucco walls and huge floor-to-ceiling plate glass windows in the counter areas. The colonial-style cupolas transformed into teal space age pyramids perched on low, wide roofs of sleek orange porcelain. But the Simple Simon weathervanes remained, as did the chain's appeal to travelers. By 1954, Howard Johnson's had rebounded from near extinction, with four hundred restaurants along America's highways.

Still, Johnson wanted more. Having seen independent motel operators build thriving businesses by locating near his popular restaurants, Johnson decided to get into lodging as well. Although the new interstates prohibited service plazas, Johnson aggressively purchased property near the end of exit ramps to build combined restaurant and lodging operations. As travel along the interstates exploded, so did Howard Johnson's. In 1965, Howard Johnson's sales exceeded those of McDonald's, Burger King, and Kentucky Fried Chicken combined. By the late 1970s, Howard Johnson's—now run by Johnson's son, Howard B. Johnson—controlled more than a thousand restaurants (under several names) and five hundred motor lodges, making it the largest hospitality chain in the world.

It didn't last. Facing the same competition and changing tastes that had doomed Stuckey's, Howard Johnson's lost its bright orange luster. Sold to a British company in 1980, Howard Johnson's restaurants were separated from the motor lodges and resold to Marriott, which rebranded most locations under new concepts. While Howard Johnson's motor lodges continue today as Wyndham Worldwide properties, just one Howard Johnson's restaurant remains open: in Lake George, New York.*

But for several generations of families, especially those who

*Aside from its fame as the last remaining Howard Johnson's restaurant, the operation is also significant for giving one of America's most famous chefs her start. Rachel Ray worked there as a teenager.

traveled America's East Coast highways, Howard Johnson's offered a comforting taste of home—along with twenty-eight flavors of ice cream.

If you want to start a food fight, there's no better way than to declare where to find the world's best barbecue or proclaim who invented the first drive-through restaurant. In his book *The American Drive-In: History and Folklore of the Drive-In Restaurant in American Car Culture*, Michael Karl Witzel makes a strong argument that credit for both should go to Texas entrepreneur Jessie G. Kirby and his chain of roadside Pig Stands, the first of which opened along the Dallas–Fort Worth highway in 1921. Declaring "people in their cars are so lazy that they don't want to get out of them to eat," Kirby's brainstorm was to employ a fleet-footed staff of order takers. The carhops (so named because the tip-motivated servers would sprint out to hop up on an approaching automobile's running board) would take food orders right through the customer's car window, then hustle back with the chain's signature barbecue pork "pig sandwiches" and other food items moments later. Billed as "America's Motor Lunch," the new system launched a craze.

Technically, Kirby's idea of using carhops qualified his Pig Stand only as America's first drive-*in* restaurant. The first drive-*through* would come later, and once again Kirby's Pig Stand would be the originator. In 1931, it occurred to the owner of Pig Stand No. 21 in California that managing an unreliable group of young carhops required altogether too much energy. So he simply sawed a window into the wall beside his grill, allowing customers to drive up alongside the building, place their own orders, and collect their food directly from the cooks who prepared it. It was a classic example of eliminating the middleman.

And so ends the debate about who invented the drive-through window, right? Well, don't go pulling off just yet. Other sources claim the idea was conceived by a young ginger-haired entrepreneur named Sheldon "Red" Chaney. Fresh out of business school, Chaney recognized the potential of the burgeoning travel craze in 1947. Scraping together some cash, Red and his bride, Julia, purchased a small gas station along Route 66 in Springfield, Missouri. After spending sixteen hours a day pumping gas and observing customers, Red concluded two things: one, he didn't want to spend the rest of his life pumping gas, and two, people hate getting out of their cars.

The Chaneys decided to get out of the business of fueling cars and into the business of feeding motorists. For menu inspiration, they needed only to catch sight of a nearby pasture of suddenly very nervous cattle. Redecorating their station on a shoestring, Red and Julia painted white clouds on the ceiling with blue skies and green pastures on the walls to resemble a picnic scene. They covered the dining room's tables in red-checkered tablecloths and topped each with a button-spigot Coleman cooler and stack of paper cups so diners could dispense their own water. But the couple's most radical idea was adding a small window in the building's west wall, allowing drivers to pull up and order food right from their cars.

Not everything went as planned. In his haste to convert the gas station into a restaurant, Red neglected to take a few simple measurements before ordering his new roadside sign. The design he selected was in the shape of a tall cross, with the word *Giant* intersecting the word *Hamburger*, which ran vertically down the post, at the letter *a*. It was only when the delivery crew attempted to hoist the sign into place that Red realized his mistake. The towering sign was too tall to fit beneath a run of utility cables draped overhead. His options limited, Red picked up a saw and made a quick edit. And so "Red's Giant Hamburger" became the eminently more memorable "Red's Giant Hamburg."

The name piqued customers' curiosity, but it was the drive-through window that prompted cars to line up around the building. Whenever the line became too long, Red would bolt out the side door, pen and pad in hand, and scurry to each car's window to take orders before drivers pulled away. Meanwhile, Julia remained at the grill, flipping burgers and dispensing bags of food. Eventually Red installed an intercom system so drivers could dictate orders before advancing to the window to collect their food. *Voilà!* Red's Giant Hamburg became the first modern fast-food drive-through restaurant . . .

. . . *if* you ignore the accounts of dozens of other journalists, authors, corporate PR departments, and Wikipedia citations. The catalog of those assigning—or claiming—credit for inventing the drive-through is longer than the list on McDonald's Dollar Menu Board. Depending on whom you choose to believe, Harry and Esther Snyder created the drive-through, complete with a two-way speaker for ordering, when they built the first In-N-Out Burger in 1948. Or Fred Angell should get the credit because he pioneered drive-in service at his Maid-Rite restaurants in 1927 (six years *after* Kirby's Pig Stands). Jack in the Box claims to be the first fast-food chain designed specifically for drive-through service, placing two-way speakers inside its friendly and colorful— or for you coulrophobes, horrifying and menacing—clown heads as early as 1951. Wendy's Hamburgers also claims credit for developing the "first modern-day drive through window" in 1971, though on what basis, it's not clear.

About the only thing most credible sources agree on is that none of these restaurants can take credit for inventing the drive-up window. Instead, the idea seems to have originated with an institution not typically associated with daring innovations: a bank.

In 1928, Rufus Crosby Kemper, the ambitious young president of City Center Bank in Kansas City, Missouri, watched a routine repeat itself day after day. Just as his manager approached the bank's front doors to lock up at the close of business each day, the man would be nearly trampled by a stampede of local business owners and managers streaming in from nearby stores and diners to make their daily deposits. It gave Kemper an idea. As a convenience to his business customers (and to spare himself the headache of constantly replacing flattened bank managers), Kemper installed an after-hours collection window in the side of his bank. The fortified deposit window permitted customers to drop off each day's collections at their leisure on their drive home. Not long afterward, the Grand National Bank across the state in St. Louis one-upped Kemper's idea by adding a teller at their window. This allowed customers to conduct other types of transactions from their cars during normal banking hours. It was just a matter of time before restaurants and other businesses followed suit and added their own drive-through windows.

To cater to a new generation of car-crazy consumers, America quickly became a drive-in nation. In addition to drive-in banks and drive-in restaurants, Americans could catch the latest shows at drive-in movie theaters, pick up food at drive-through grocery markets, and, in many states, swing by for a six-pack at drive-through liquor stores. In 1961, in Garden Grove, California, Pastor Robert Schuller founded the nation's first drive-in church to keep the faithful rolling on the highway to heaven.* It was during

---

*I like to think that a few of Pastor Schuller's faithful flock completed their mortal journey years later in New Roads, Louisiana. It was here, in 1977, that the Point Coupee Funeral Home introduced the nation's first drive-through funeral service.

this same period that In-N-Out Burger, Jack in the Box, and other chains began staking their claims as the originators of the drive-through window.

But it wasn't until the seventies that drive-through restaurants really became a phenomenon. Before then, many folks who didn't live on the West Coast—my family included—had never even seen a drive-through restaurant. While Wendy's Hamburgers' claim that it installed "the first modern-day drive-through window" may be dubious, there's little doubt the chain was responsible for helping grease the wheels, so to speak, for drive-through windows to spread across the country. After opening his first Wendy's restaurant in Columbus, Ohio, founder Dave Thomas insisted on adding a drive-through window at his second location in 1971 and in nearly every location thereafter.* As Wendy's restaurants quickly fanned out across the nation, so did the idea of drive-through windows. Soon, hungry motorists across America were able to purchase their meals on wheels.

It took McDonald's a bit longer to pull ahead to the drive-through window. Though McDonald's restaurants had been around since the 1940s, the chain didn't introduce its first drive-through window until 1975. Even then, it was a window added by a single franchisee to accommodate the unusual needs of his principal customers. The McDonald's store in Sierra Vista, Arizona, was located just down the road from the Fort Huachuca military base, making

---

*Dave Thomas never lost his enthusiasm for drive-throughs either. Long after his face became familiar to millions in countless Wendy's TV spots, Thomas would regularly visit restaurant franchises around the country. On occasion, he'd don the headset of the drive-through worker and surprise customers by personally handing over their orders.

it a popular lunch stop for soldiers. Military rules at the time prohibited enlisted personnel from exiting civilian vehicles dressed in fatigues, even if only to step out and pick up a Big Mac. To accommodate the soldiers, the franchisee, bucking corporate policy, installed a drive-through window. Soon, the only ones dealing with issues of fatigue were the fry cooks scrambling to fill orders for hungry customers. With the drive-through window a proven winner at the Sierra Vista location, other franchisees began lobbying McDonald's headquarters for permission to add their own.

For McDonald's, the revelation couldn't have come at a better time. The company was in the midst of a growth spurt, fed by families like mine in search of cheap, dependable, kid-friendly meals while on the go. In 1970, McDonald's reported $580 million in sales from 1,600 restaurants. By the decade's end, it would collect $6.2 billion from 6,200 stores. More than half of that cash would be handed over through drive-through windows.

My dad didn't care how it had all happened. He was just happy it happened at all. In fact, I can say with relative certainty that had he been asked to rank the greatest advancements of the twentieth century, my father would have placed the drive-through window somewhere near the polio vaccine, well above personal computers, not quite as high as graphite-shafted golf clubs. Finally, he had a means to put an end to his family's incessant—unreasonable, he might argue—demands to eat more than once a day while on the road.

Of course, the explosion of McDonald's restaurants and drive-through windows along the highways only solved the problem of quickly feeding the family. Inevitably, with six people in our car, at least one of us would also have to use the restroom. To complete both tasks with maximum efficiency, my father devised a plan that my family, after regular and rigorous practice, eventually executed to perfection. The goal was simple: keep the car's wheels moving forward at all times. Prior to getting into the drive-through line, my father would take everyone's food orders and pull up along the side entrance to the restaurant. Any prospective pee'ers would be quickly discharged onto the curb. As the youngest, I never really had any choice about getting out of the car. I was simply pushed out as my brothers bolted through the door. In keeping with his goal, my father never stopped to let us out. He'd simply slow down enough to allow us to leap and still have a chance of landing on our feet.

Once inside the restaurant, we'd sprint to the restrooms while Dad eased the car ahead to place our order. At the time, McDonald's goal was to provide each drive-through customer's order within fifty seconds. Factoring in a few additional moments for my father to pause—not stop!—while drivers ahead of him ordered, we had about ninety seconds to pee, wash up, and dash out the door to intercept our passing car.

Usually we ran the drill to perfection. When we were all on our game, we could go from hungry family on the highway to happy family on the on-ramp in seven, maybe even six minutes (Dad actually timed our performance). There were occasional hiccups, often due to circumstances beyond our control. There might be a line at the urinal. One of us might have to go #2. There could be a backup at the pickup window. Any of these delays could add seconds, even minutes, to the process, causing my Dad's blood pressure to redline.

But nothing made the curvy vein in my father's right temple squirm more than when he was told to pull forward and park because there'd be a short wait to prepare the plain Quarter Pounder ordered by my brother Bruce. McDonald's simply wasn't set up to accommodate special orders. The chain's assembly line–style "Speedee Service System," which had revolutionized the fast-food industry since its introduction in 1948, was designed to prepare food exactly one way—the "McDonald's Way." It was quick, efficient and notoriously inflexible. When a customer requested a burger prepared any way other than the McDonald's Way—say, plain, with no ketchup, mustard, onions, or pickles—the system broke down, as did my father whenever we sat waiting for my brother's plain hamburger.

Of course, McDonald's inability to handle special orders like Bruce's plain hamburger was also noticed by the chain's rival Burger King. It became the basis for Burger King's long-running "Have It Your Way" ad campaign, launched in 1973. If you lived through the period, the following jingle will now be lodged in your brain:

> *Hold the pickles*
> *Hold the lettuce*
> *Special orders don't upset us*

No doubt you remember the rest.

To my dad's credit, he didn't blame Bruce for wanting a plain hamburger. Heck, the way he saw it, his kid was ordering a burger that required less labor and fewer ingredients; it should have been ready in half the time for a fraction of the price. Instead, all he got was an agonizing delay in getting back on the highway. It wasn't a good way to "make time."

Still, my dad and therefore my entire family remained steadfastly loyal to McDonald's throughout our travels. On many occasions, even when we were famished while on the road, we'd bypass exits with clearly visible signs for Burger King, Arby's, or other chains in hopes of finding a McDonald's somewhere farther down the highway. This wasn't the sure thing in the seventies that it is today. In 1978, there were fewer than four thousand McDonald's scattered across the United States, compared to more than fourteen thousand in 2016. It was even less likely to encounter a McDonald's along highways out in the boonies, where we always seemed to find ourselves around mealtime.

There were many reasons for my father's unwavering devotion to McDonald's, and it wasn't just drive-through windows. For starters, my dad felt a certain kinship with Ray Kroc, the man who turned McDonald's into an international phenomenon. Though my father was born two decades after Kroc, in 1926, both men grew up in the modest suburbs of Chicago, a city where hometown loyalty runs deep. Like my father, Kroc was a salesman who didn't find real success until later in life, after turning fifty years old. Whereas my dad sold electronic fixtures and lighting systems for a living for the first half of his life, Kroc sold restaurant equipment.

In 1954, Kroc's interest was piqued when a small restaurant located on the edge of the desert in San Bernardino, California, ordered eight of the expensive high-end Multimixer blenders he sold—enough to make forty milkshakes at a time. The restaurant was a simple burger stand owned by two brothers, Dick and Maurice "Mac" McDonald. Curious as to why such a modest operation could possibly need such equipment, Kroc decided to fly out and pay the McDonald brothers a visit. What he saw astounded him: a six-hundred-square-foot restaurant, little more than a walk-up stand, with customers lined up by the dozen to order from a simple menu of hamburgers, fries, sodas, and shakes being efficiently churned out in assembly-line fashion by a handful of hardworking staff. The prices were cheap, and the food was tasty and easy to eat on the go. Recognizing the formula's enormous potential, Kroc convinced the McDonald brothers to sell him the McDonald's name and national franchising rights. He then returned to Illinois to begin building an empire.

Headquartered near Chicago, McDonald's initially launched

franchises across northern Illinois and the Midwest, in locations my dad frequently visited on sales calls. Throughout the 1960s, McDonald's opened restaurants as fast as its cooks could flip burgers. By the seventies, no fast-food chain came close to matching the dominant presence of McDonald's in middle America. It therefore only made sense that we found ourselves going to McDonald's more than to any other chain—there were simply far more McDonald's to be found. Along the highways we traveled into and out of the Midwest, McDonald's was truly the Big Mac.

Aside from all else, my family genuinely enjoyed McDonald's food. It wasn't fancy, but it was satisfying and predictable. A McMuffin in Milwaukee tasted the same as the one in Memphis; a Big Mac in Burlington was as big as the one in Baton Rouge. Such consistency was an enormous draw for families like mine while out exploring America—it was a familiar taste of home in places that seemed a world away. Ray Kroc knew the importance of such uniformity, and his obsessive approach to maintaining it became legendary. It was Kroc himself who dictated the strict specifications for a McDonald's hamburger. The beef patty had to be exactly 3.875 inches in diameter and 1.6 ounces in weight, and contain precisely 19 percent fat. Big Mac buns should have on average 178 sesame seeds. He even decreed how much wax should be used on the wax paper in which McDonald's hamburgers were wrapped. No detail was too small.

Most important, eating at McDonald's fit our modest travel budget. After all, the restaurant was cheap, and, well, so was my dad—at least when it came to "discretionary" expenditures such as food. Yet even as inexpensive as McDonald's was, Dad found ways to trim the tab further. Before being dropped off to make our drive-through potty run, my siblings and I would take turns rattling off our food orders. As we did, Dad would mentally combine and edit our orders for maximum value before pulling up to the speaker. If three of us wanted our own regular-size Coke, he'd instead order one large Coke costing half the price and ask for three complimentary kiddie cups. Indeed, long before McDonald's introduced the super-size concept, my father came up with "shrink-a-size." If Dad believed one of us had placed an order that exceeded our appetite, he'd simply scale it back. Hence, many an optimistically ordered Big Mac became a less-than-enthusiastically received regular hamburger.

We discovered these arbitrary changes too late. This was because Dad would collect our food from the pickup window while we were still rushing to relieve ourselves. As we dove back into our seats, he'd casually say, "Hey, let's not make a mess. Why don't we wait until we're back on the highway and not making so many turns before we hand out the food?" Then he'd place the bags of food on the floor at his feet until he navigated back to the on-ramp. It was only after we were at cruising speed and far past any turnarounds that he'd begin distributing the disappointment.

Making matters worse, before Dad handed back the single order of fries he'd ordered for my brothers and me to split, he first shoveled a half dozen or so of the biggest ones into his mouth. It was a subtraction we came to expect and derisively call the "Dad tax." As we grew older and smarter, we'd attempt various strategies to defeat my father's penny-pinching—for example, ordering two Big Macs each in hopes of getting just the one we wanted. But these tactics rarely worked. When it came to deciding what and how much food we'd get in a trip to the drive-through, my dad was—in the most literal sense of the phrase—always in the driver's seat. It wouldn't be until I had my own driver's license that I received exactly what I ordered at a McDonald's drive-through.

CHAPTER 8

Inn and Out

Motels, Hotels, and Invaders from Space

If the idea of briefly exiting the highway to eat or use the restroom irritated my father, the thought of stopping for hours—*hours, mind you!*—just to spend the night sleeping in a roadside motel seemed borderline insane. As my father saw it, ten hours at a motel was ten hours less at our final destination. *Why, a man could play two rounds of golf in that kind of time!*

Of course, Dad *had* considered driving straight through to our destination. He even attempted it on one of our early trips, a marathon nineteen-hour expedition to the Florida Gulf Coast. The trip seemed to go well as far as we kids were concerned. We traveled all day and through the night, leaving behind the blustery Wisconsin winter to awaken the following morning basking in the golden warmth of a Florida sunrise. Sure, we were tired and restless from spending an entire night crammed into our car, shifting about to find tolerable sleeping positions. But we'd made it to our destination safe and sound, and gained an extra day of beach time in the bargain. So it always seemed strange that we never attempted to drive straight through again.

It was only years later that my mom let us in on what happened as we all slept that dark, early morning. Awakened by a loud rumbling under her seat, she initially thought we'd blown a hole in our exhaust. But she quickly realized our car was veering off the highway onto the gravel shoulder. Glancing over at my dad, she saw his eyes were closed and that his head was bobbing, as though he were taking in a Sunday sermon. His pious posture was appropriate, as we were all just a moment from meeting our Maker. Acting quickly, Mom grabbed the steering wheel with one hand and prodded Dad with the other, alerting him that the cruise control was hurtling us at a speed of 64 mph to certain doom. Fortunately, the car remained on the highway.

The whole incident was over in a heartbeat—or in my mom's case, a few hundred heartbeats—and my siblings and I remained asleep the entire time. But Dad had received his wakeup call. He knew how close he'd come to driving us all to our final destination. The idea of ever again attempting to drive through the night had been put to rest.

That being the case, once or twice each way per road trip, depending on the distance to our destination and my parents' tolerance for spending hours in a five-passenger car packed with six people, my dad reluctantly pulled up to a motel to spend the night.

Nearly always, we'd stick to one of the major lodging chains—for a couple of reasons. First, in the same way that McDonald's offered a uniform eating experience, the big hotel chains offered a uniform lodging experience. With the brand names, we knew what to expect: a clean, comfortable room with a few basic amenities at an affordable rate. Second, in an era long before the Internet and Google, the chains were able to provide printed lists of franchise locations (with phone numbers) along our route. These lists came in especially handy because my dad never wanted to be constrained by room reservations. If the open road beckoned him to drive a bit farther, he wanted to do just that. The more cities and towns he could put in our rearview mirror, the better.

The way it worked was that each day around dinnertime, when we'd pull off the highway to grab a bite or fuel up, Dad would pull out the TripTik and motel guides. Then he'd begin popping dimes into a pay phone to try to secure our evening's accommodations as the rest of us surreptitiously listened.

My father always began these conversations with the same question: "So, how's your availability tonight for a tired family a long way from home?" This wasn't just my dad's way of breaking the ice. It was Negotiating 101: Determining Supply and Demand. If the motel clerk responded that she had plenty of rooms and would have no problem accommodating us, Dad would break out his standard follow-up: "Well, what's your special rate for a nice midwestern family traveling on a tight budget?" This was where the bargaining began. Dad's tactic was to launch into a tortuous tale of woe, hoping to appeal to the employee's charitable nature. His sob story would include references to every minor setback we'd faced on our journey. Frequently there was a dissertation on the burden of high gas prices on middle-class families and musings on the uncertainties faced by lodging operators in a flagging economy. No one could plead poverty like my father. He was usually successful in securing some discount, often because the person on the other end just wanted to get my dad off the phone. As soon as we heard Dad launch into this soliloquy, we'd all breathe a sigh of relief. We knew the motel had a vacancy and we could probably look forward to a swim in the pool before bedtime.

But things didn't always go well. Sometimes my dad's second inquiry concerned other lodging in the area, perhaps an exit or two down the road. Often this query would occur in the worst of circumstances—when it was pouring rain and more prudent travelers had already snatched up the available rooms, or when we were in an area where there weren't other motels for miles around. When we'd hear Dad ask about other options, we'd all take a nervous gulp. We knew our chances of having to drive late into the night or spend the evening at the Bed Bug Inn or some similarly named establishment—the kind where we'd find mousetraps under the beds—had just increased exponentially.

Most often, we ended up at either a Holiday Inn or a Ramada Inn. Though fierce competitors, the two chains had much in common. In fact, the men who were the driving forces behind them had strikingly—almost eerily—similar backgrounds.

Holiday Inn was founded by Charles "Kemmons" Wilson in 1952. Two years later, Marion W. Isbell welcomed guests into the first of his properties that would form the Ramada Inn chain. Born just four years apart, Wilson first in 1901, both men grew up in dire straits after losing parents at a young age. Wilson's father passed away when he was just nine months old, forcing his mother to move to Memphis, Tennessee, where she had family who could assist with caring for Charles (who would eventually go by "Kemmons") while she worked as a dental assistant. Isbell lost both of his parents before he turned five years old. He and his brothers were claimed by relatives and raised, in the first of a string of parallels with Wilson, also in Memphis.

Against all odds, both men rose above their challenging circumstances to build modest fortunes through thrift and hard work. Wilson's entrepreneurial inclinations first surfaced at age six, when he began selling subscriptions to the *Saturday Evening Post* door-to-door. To make more money, he recruited classmates as his sales staff. When Wilson's mother lost her job during the Depression, he dropped out of high school to bag groceries and deliver newspapers so the pair had money to eat. Upon turning seventeen, he took a chance to improve their lot by borrowing $50 from a friend to purchase a machine to make popcorn that he sold in a local movie theater. Within three years, Wilson scraped together $1,300 to build a home—literally, with his own hands. Wilson then mortgaged the property to purchase a Wurlitzer jukebox franchise, parlaying the profits into ownership of several movie theaters. After serving in World War II, Wilson realized that millions of his fellow GIs would be looking to start families and purchase houses. Drawing on what he'd learned building his own home, Wilson started a construction business, eventually partnering with the most successful homebuilder in the South. By 1950, Wilson was a millionaire.

Like Wilson, Marion Isbell also began working at an exceptionally young age. Isbell was just eight years old when he entered the fields outside Memphis to pick cotton every day after school. For his efforts, he earned around five cents per day, more or less depending on the weight of the cotton he collected. In another parallel with his eventual rival, Isbell was forced to drop out of school to help support his family. He withdrew from his studies at age twelve to take a job running errands for a local chemical company. By the time he turned sixteen, he was ready to see what the world beyond Memphis had to offer. Along with his brother James, Isbell packed up his meager belongings and moved to Chicago. There, the two boys found employment washing dishes, cooking meals, and jerking at soda counters. As they socked away their meager earnings, they also learned every facet of running a restaurant. In 1934, the Isbell brothers opened their own luncheonette. Within a decade, they owned an entire chain.

Decades of hard work had taken Wilson and Isbell a long way. But both would find the inspiration for their most successful endeavors by taking a little time off. The idea would occur to Marion Isbell first, though it would be two decades before he could act on it.

In 1929, Isbell and his wife, Ingrid, decided to join the legions of motorists setting out to discover America. Touring the country with their three children, the Isbells were fascinated by the scenery and landmarks they saw each day. But the accommodations that awaited them each evening—dingy, often outright dirty motor courts lacking the most basic amenities—left them appalled. Worse, the rundown properties attracted seedy characters engaging in sordid activities. Clearly, these weren't places for respectable young families. Isbell envisioned opening a chain of lodging properties that combined the amenities of pricey downtown hotels with the convenient locations and reasonable rates of roadside motels. But Isbell was just twenty-five years old and already struggling to support a young family. His idea would have to wait.

Inspiration would similarly strike Kemmons Wilson while on vacation with his family. But Wilson didn't embark on his fateful trip until 1951, when he was already a wealthy and successful businessman. It was then that Wilson and his wife, Dorothy, decided to take their five kids to visit the nation's capital. It says much about Wilson that although he could easily afford to do so, he didn't purchase plane tickets for his family. Instead, he piled his seven-member clan into the family Oldsmobile—a vehicle without air-conditioning—and set out from Memphis in the sweltering August heat. It says more about Wilson that along the journey, he refused to pay the expensive rates charged by city hotels, opting instead to stay in mom-and-pop boardinghouses and tourist courts. I have little doubt that Wilson and my father would have gotten along well.

The accommodations Wilson found in 1951 differed little from those Isbell and his family encountered in 1929. Amenities and cleanliness varied wildly from one operation to the next. Worse, Wilson discovered, proprietors nickel-and-dimed him for every little extra, from ice cubes and baby cribs to, in one case, clean sheets. But what really got his goat was that he was charged an additional fee for each child in his family. At one motor court charging $6 a night, he was slapped with an additional $2 fee for each of his five kids, more than doubling his bill. Fuming, he declared to Dorothy that he was going to start his own hotel chain—one traveling families could depend on for clean, affordable accommodations with no surprises or additional charges. Dorothy laughed and asked how many hotels he planned to open. Wilson considered the question a moment and declared that four hundred would be a good start.

Though Wilson's anger passed, the idea didn't. The more he thought about it, the more he became convinced that with so many middle-class families taking to the road, there really was a market for an affordably priced motel chain. He decided that the motels should make standard a variety of family-focused amenities: rooms with television sets (devices just being introduced at the time), air-conditioning (a nod to Wilson's experience traveling in his stifling Oldsmobile), ice machines in every hallway, dog kennels, complimentary baby cribs, in-room phones, swimming pools, free parking, and even a list of nearby babysitters. Oh, and one more item—a Bible in every room. Perhaps he figured parents would be looking for divine guidance after a long day on the road with the kids.

In 1952, Wilson's vision became a reality. The first of his motels opened on Summer Avenue in Memphis, just off a two-lane highway. The property was bathed in bright, cheery green and yellow,

DON'T MAKE ME PULL OVER!

colors selected by Wilson's mother. However, Wilson designed the property's roadside sign himself. Recalling his days working in movie houses, Wilson conceived a sign that resembled a theater marquee. The monstrous structure blazed with the light of fifteen hundred feet of neon tubing and five hundred incandescent bulbs. From the base arose a large yellow arrow that curved around the sign's top, pointing the way to the check-in desk. Tucked beneath the motel's name was a glowing marquee on which employees could arrange black letters to welcome happy honeymooners and local civic groups. And atop it all shimmered a blinking neon star to serve as a beacon for weary travelers. In time, the garish goliath would come to be called the "Great Sign."* It would become one of the true icons of American travel.

The name on the sign? That would be lifted from a 1942 movie musical starring Bing Crosby. Wilson's architect, Eddie Bluestein, had seen the film the evening before completing his final sketch of the motel and scrawled the title above his drawing as a good-natured joke. On seeing it, Wilson thought the title perfectly captured his vision of a wholesome home away from home for vacationing families. The name, of course, was "Holiday Inn."

Holiday Inn's combination of clean accommodations, family-friendly amenities, and low rates—$6 a night with no hidden extras—was an instant success. What's more, Wilson's timing couldn't have been better. America's interstate highway system was just years from approval.

---

*After Wilson retired in 1979, the Great Sign soon followed. In 1982, the Holiday Inn board of directors voted to phase out the expensive sign and replace it with a cheaper, more contemporary-looking design. Furious, Wilson called the decision "the worst mistake they ever made." To punctuate his statement, he even specified that the design of his beloved sign be engraved on his tombstone, an order dutifully carried out upon his passing in 2003.

When the interstate project was given the green light, Wilson followed an expansion strategy similar to Bill Stuckey's. He constructed new Holiday Inns along each highway at a distance of a full day's drive from one location to the next. As a convenience for travelers and a way to lock in business, Wilson instructed his managers to ask guests if they could assist in making reservations for the following evening as well. Of course, all the managers had to do was place a call to the next Holiday Inn located along their guest's planned route. Because every Holiday Inn was nearly identical in construction, rates, and amenities, travelers had no reason to decline the helpful offer or consider alternatives. Wilson's strategy worked like a charm. In 1959, Holiday Inn had one hundred locations. By 1975, there were an astounding seventeen hundred. Wilson himself would appear on the cover of *Time* magazine in 1972 hailed as "The Man with 300,000 Beds."

Marion Isbell and his Ramada Inns would never rise to the dizzying heights of Kemmons Wilson and Holiday Inn. But Isbell did found the company that would, at least for the period of my family's peak travel years in the 1970s, become the second-largest hotel chain in America. Isbell and Ramada would also win the loyalty of a very select but important clientele: my parents.

The idea of a nationwide chain of family-friendly motor hotels dawned on Isbell before Wilson had the idea. But he didn't have Wilson's means or vision to build such an operation from scratch. What Isbell did have were affluent business connections from his years in Chicago. And in the early 1950s, after selling his interest in the chain of restaurants he co-owned with his brother, Isbell found himself with money and time on his hands. As America headed toward building an interstate highway system, Isbell recalled the idea that occurred to him on his trip decades earlier and realized the time had come to act. So in 1954, two years after Wilson opened the original Holiday Inn, in Memphis, Isbell and a group of investors began buying and building motels, primarily in Arizona along Route 66.

By 1960, Isbell's group owned dozens of properties, which he unified into a chain. The name *Ramada* was chosen to honor the company's southwestern roots. During harvesttime in the region, laborers in the fields would assemble temporary shelters from *ramas*—Spanish for "branches"—to provide shade for their afternoon siestas. They called the structures "ramadas." Isbell thought the name was perfect for his collection of comfy roadside inns.

Given the chain's name, one would also expect a southwestern theme for each inn's decor—colorful stucco perhaps and a terracotta roof. But that wasn't the case. Instead, the Ramada Inns were initially built to resemble grand estates straight out of colonial Williamsburg. Each building was a sprawling two-story pile of red brick, with long rows of windows flanked by white wooden shutters. In the center, an imposing porte cochere jutted out over the main entrance, supported by stately pillars. And on the sign out front, waiting to welcome guests was "Uncle Ben"—an affable-looking, balding chap in a colonial-style knee-length jacket and buckled shoes, holding a top hat in one hand and an implausibly elongated trumpet in the other, from which dangled the regal red Ramada Inn banner. Isbell chose the colonial theme as a dignified alternative to the colorful lowbrow tackiness of Holiday Inn or Howard Johnson's. But really it was just cheese of a different flavor.

My parents loved Ramada Inns. To them, Ramada was the classiest of the major chains. My folks were particularly smitten with Ramada's lobbies, which the company obviously emphasized. Most Ramada Inn lobbies were two stories tall, providing space for an almost comically oversize crystal chandelier. Guests were encouraged to admire its twinkling splendor from all angles by climbing a grand staircase up to a banistered overlook. The windows were covered from floor to ceiling in tassel-trimmed draperies that appeared to be plundered from Scarlett O'Hara's Tara. An equally baroque fabric was selected to upholster the Victorian-style high-back chairs and dust-ruffled couches placed here and there throughout the room. The furniture was assembled in tiny islands on a sea of carpeting dyed a retina-burning shade of royal red, the chain's signature color. Ramada intended its lobby to exude elegance. It looked more like the dining room at Elvis Presley's Graceland. Still, my parents adored it.

So while most of America was checking into a Holiday Inn, my family spent the early 1970s bedding down with Uncle Ben (in a manner of speaking). In keeping with Ramada's colonial theme, we were patriotically loyal to the chain. As we did for McDonald's, we'd often go the extra mile, or twenty, driving into the night just to reach one of those foofy foyers. In reality, once you got past the lobby, very little distinguished the two chains. Both charged about the same rate for a same-size room and offered about the same amenities. Aside from the sign out front and the lobby decor, Holiday Inns and Ramada Inns were virtually indistinguishable—that is, until a point in the middle of the decade—no one can seem to recall precisely the date or location—when Holiday Inn began introducing the Holidome.

By the 1970s, the concept of a domed motel offering guests a climate-controlled common area in which to gather and relax had probably become inevitable. It was, after all, an era when America became enthralled with the notion of bringing the great outdoors indoors. Suddenly sports and leisure activities traditionally enjoyed outside were no longer left to the capricious whims of nature—not when they could be brought inside, protected from the elements, synthetically re-created, and artificially regulated for maximum comfort.

The dome craze can be traced back to 1965, when the City of Houston unveiled the Astrodome, hailed at the time as the "Eighth Wonder of the World." But the seventies was the true Decade of the Dome, with domes bubbling up just about everywhere. Following Houston's lead, one city after another cut the ribbon on its own gleaming domed megastadium. Detroit unveiled the Silverdome in 1975, followed by Seattle's Kingdome, and New Orleans's Superdome in 1976. Minneapolis broke ground on its Metrodome in 1979, though it wasn't opened to host events until three years later. More domed venues sprang up to host collegiate sports events at the University of Northern Iowa (UNI-Dome), Idaho State University (Holt Arena), Syracuse University (Carrier Dome), the University of South Dakota (DakotaDome), and Northern Arizona University (Walkup Skydome), to list just a few. On a smaller scale, municipalities and private clubs in northern climates erected giant inflatable domes to house driving ranges, playing fields, and setup areas for wintertime diversions. Even Disney caught dome fever. In 1975, Walt Disney World opened the world's first indoor roller coaster inside a domed structure it dubbed Space Mountain. In the seventies, domes, well, dominated.

Holiday Inn's Holidome concept did more than play into some trendy dome craze, however. It solved a number of worrisome problems for the chain. The first of these was the decline that naturally comes with aging. By the mid-1970s, many Holiday Inns were twenty years old and showing every wrinkle. Even Kemmons Wilson's original Holiday Inn in Memphis had fallen into disrepair and closed in 1973.* Sure, franchisees could have spruced up their properties with a fresh coat of paint and new curtains. Many did. But by erecting a large Plexiglas dome over and around the central courtyard, their motel became something else entirely. Suddenly, a fading Holiday Inn was transformed into a sleek and futuristic climate-controlled oasis straight out of *Logan's Run* or *Battlestar Gallactica* (a pair of seventies pop culture sensations that showcased the virtues of skintight bodysuits).

Another issue the Holidome solved related to a flaw in the original Holiday Inn layout. When first launched, every Holiday Inn offered rooms with doors opening to the outside. But by the seventies, this arrangement, once considered an asset, had become a liability. Whereas traveling families once appreciated the convenience of being able to drive right up to their room's door, now many found that the setup presented a number of drawbacks. Noise and exhaust from the parking lot drifted through the door and into the room. Also, because guests weren't required to pass the front desk, the layout attracted customers seeking private spaces in which to conduct illicit activities and improper, ahem, affairs. It was a situation entirely at odds with Holiday Inn's family-friendly image. By enclosing the properties, franchisees were able to switch their rooms' doors to the opposite side so they opened into a hallway or the domed courtyard. Guests needed to walk past the front desk or through a handful of other entrances to get to their rooms, deterring those who didn't want to be seen coming and going.

The Holidome also helped Holiday Inn franchisees distinguish their properties from nearby competitors, especially in

---

*Despite its historic significance, Wilson's original Holiday Inn, the one that launched the world's leading hotel chain, sat vacant and deteriorating for years. The building finally fell to a wrecking ball in the early 1990s.

colder regions of the country. From his own travels, Kemmons Wilson learned how important swimming pools were to the family lodging experience and how they played a pivotal role in where families chose to stay. It's the reason that Wilson insisted, from the beginning, on making a swimming pool a standard feature of every Holiday Inn. His instincts were dead-on. Lodging research conducted during the 1960s showed that adding a pool increased business as much as 60 percent. That meant a pool paid for its construction in just a few years. But for many Holiday Inn franchisees, the competitive advantage of having a pool disappeared when they were forced to close the facilities during the winter. In much of the country, that was half the year. By adding a Holidome, franchisees were able to promote their pools year-round. And having an edge was turning out to be critical.

While my family was an exception, Americans as a whole pulled way back on discretionary travel during the seventies. By the time Jimmy Carter assumed the presidency in 1977, the country's economy showed signs of recovery. But the optimism wouldn't last. Midway through Carter's term, the combination of high unemployment and high inflation prompted the creation of a whole new economic indicator: "the misery index." At the same time Americans were losing their jobs, inflation was robbing them of their savings. Much as folks needed to get away from their troubles, many couldn't afford to.

But while many Americans decided an extended stay at some distant high-priced resort no longer fit their budgets, they found a shorter stay at a closer, more modest attraction still did. Holidomes fit the bill perfectly. With a large pool and recreational activities for the kids, an inviting lounge area for adults, and a tropical courtyard with warm temperatures for all, Holidomes offered families a reasonable facsimile of a Florida vacation at a fraction of the cost. While many unimproved Holiday Inns struggled to survive the seventies, those with Holidomes largely thrived.

The Holidome captured the spirit of the seventies like nothing else. Everything about it was artificial, tacky, excessive, cheap, haphazardly laid out, and questionably constructed. And, really, that was its charm. The exotic trees and tropical plants were all fake. The oversize tiki figures and towering volcano water slide were fiberglass. The sky over your head was Plexiglas and the grass beneath your feet plastic. The water was highly chlorinated, the temperature overregulated, and the edifice as a whole tastelessly decorated. It was, in short, a majestic synthetic marvel. And it was wonderful.

The only thing inside a Holidome that was genuine was the fun. And thanks to its transparent Plexiglas ceiling, a Holidome offered just about every amusement under the sun. The main attraction, of course, was the enormous swimming pool, often shaped to resemble a tropical lagoon. Sometimes there would be narrow channels to swim through, with walking bridges to swim under or even a waterfall at one end. I used to swim the length of the pool pretending I was navigating a crocodile-infested river like the fantastically bronzed Ron Ely in the 1960s TV revamp of *Tarzan*, which, thanks to reruns, remained in heavy rotation throughout the seventies.*

But a Holidome offered far more than a pool. Though the offerings varied by location, the typical setup might also include

---

*In my opinion, Ron Ely remains the best Tarzan to ever play the role. He didn't just don the loincloth; he inhabited the character, performing many of his own stunts to add realism. Ely said that he suffered two dozen major injuries while filming the series, including two broken shoulders and even several lion bites. He also sported, without question, the most impressive tan in television history prior to the debut of *Baywatch*.

table tennis, air hockey tables, a shuffleboard deck, a miniature golf course, and clusters of stand-up or tabletop coin-operated video games. For adults, there was nearly always a lounge within eyeshot of the pool's shallow end. This arrangement allowed parents to down their gin and tonics and rum daiquiris while occasionally casting glances at little Jimmy or Jenny to make sure they were still bobbing above the surface.

One aspect that never varied from one Holidome to the next was the damp, heavy air inside. The thermostat was always set to sauna-like levels, and the air was so thick with moisture you were never quite certain when you had actually entered or exited the pool. But it was a small price to pay for being treated to a taste of Florida in June when you were actually somewhere in Illinois in December.

While Kemmons Wilson envisioned his original Holiday Inns as a home away from home, Holidomes offered a kind of vacation within a vacation for guests en route somewhere else. If our route led us in the vicinity of one of those tantalizing terrariums, we rarely passed it by. It really was a holiday in a Holidome.

As my parents handled check-in at either the Holiday Inn or Ramada front desk, my siblings and I typically would do a checkout—a quick survey of what our motel had to offer. Because we were expected to help unload the car and haul our own bags up to the room, we had to act swiftly. So like any good reconnaissance team, we'd split up.

If we hadn't eaten prior to arriving at the motel—and we often hadn't—Leslie would determine if there was an on-site restaurant and head off to scan the menu so she could report back to Mom. Mark would locate the pool and dip a hand in to check the water temperature. Bruce, who was inspired to start working on his physique after seeing *Pumping Iron*—the 1977 bodybuilding documentary that made Arnold Schwarzenegger an international sensation—went off in search of the fitness area. And I would embark on the most important quest of all, at least as far as I was concerned: I sought out the motel's video game arcade to check out which electronic marvels would soon be vying for my quarters.

It would be almost impossible to overstate the importance of video games to an elementary school kid in the seventies. Before my friends and I began noticing the merits of the opposite sex, video games occupied our every waking thought. Video games and my generation were coming of age at the same time, and like best friends growing up next door to each other, we made an inseparable pair. It was a relationship few outside our peer group understood. Parents didn't get it. Even my brothers—just seven and eight years older than I—didn't get it. And really that's what made the connection we shared with video games all the more special.

Video games weren't invented in the seventies. Their roots wound back to logic puzzles and data manipulations employed in computer research of the 1940s and 1950s. Those games were created more to test the capabilities of computers than the people who played them. What's more, the only computers on which they could be played were fantastically large and expensive. The first computer designed for commercial sale, UNIVAC I* (short

---

*In 1952, the UNIVAC I gained national fame by successfully predicting the outcome of the US presidential election on live television. While most human pollsters forecast a win for Illinois governor Adlai Stevenson, UNIVAC I projected an easy victory for popular World War II hero Dwight D. Eisenhower. Believing there must have been some sort of error in UNIVAC's calculations, CBS-TV News boss Sig Mickelson insisted that UNIVAC's prediction of 100-to-1 odds in favor of an Eisenhower victory be amended to 8-to-7. When Eisenhower won by a yawning margin within 1 percent of UNIVAC's original projection, the network was forced to admit its change.

for UNIVersal Automatic Computer), produced by the Remington Rand typewriter company in 1951, required a space the size of a twenty-five-meter swimming pool. The computer's control panel alone was the size of a church organ.

It wasn't until the 1970s and the invention of solid-state integrated circuits that computers became inexpensive or small enough to make video games plausible for a mass audience. The men with the vision and know-how to lead the way were two electrical engineers, Nolan Bushnell and Ted Dabney. Bushnell supplied the vision, Dabney the know-how.

Blond-haired, keen-eyed, and quick-witted, Nolan Bushnell grew up in a Mormon household in Ogden, Utah. At the same time he was studying engineering at the University of Utah, he worked at the nearby Lagoon Amusement Park, where he was assigned to the Midway arcade. Besides maintaining the arcade's coin-operated pinball machines, he occasionally assumed the role of barker, persuading park guests to try their luck at Skee-Ball, ring-the-bottle, and other carnival-type games. Day after day, Bushnell would watch players hand over dollar after dollar to hone their skills at a particular game, conquer the challenge, and win a prize.

Back at the computer science labs on campus, Bushnell watched fellow students take breaks from their schoolwork to compete against each other in a game on the lab's mainframe computer. Developed by students at MIT years earlier, the game was called *Spacewar!* Two players, each controlling their own spaceship, were pitted against each other in a laser duel. The object was simple, the graphics were primitive—little more than white lines and dots on a black screen—and, as Bushnell learned firsthand, the game was incredibly addictive.

When Bushnell graduated, he took his experiences with him to a job in Silicon Valley, where he met Ted Dabney, an older, more experienced engineer. Bushnell shared with Dabney his idea for turning the *Spacewar!* concept into a commercial endeavor. Excited by the idea, Dabney collaborated with Bushnell to create a near-clone of *Spacewar!* called *Computer Space.* The game flopped.

Undaunted, Dabney and Bushnell quit their jobs and formed their own company, setting up shop in the quaintly named town of Sunnyvale. For inspiration as to what to name their start-up, Bushnell looked to his favorite board game, a traditional Chinese game similar to chess. Among its many unique Mandarin terms was a word that loosely translated as "checkmate." That word was *Atari.*

After forming Atari, Bushnell and Dabney hired another talented engineer, Allan Alcorn, as a junior associate. As a sort of training exercise, Bushnell tasked Alcorn with designing a game similar to one recently debuted by another game designer. It was an electronic version of tennis included with the Magnavox Odyssey, the first video game console for home use. Alcorn aced the exercise. Like Magnavox Odyssey's *Tennis*, Alcorn's game was a simple two-dimensional re-creation of a racket sport. Two players competed against each other, using blocky pixelated paddles to bat a white dot representing a ball back and forth from opposite sides of a court. To ratchet up the difficulty and ensure each volley would eventually end, Alcorn added several twists. He invisibly divided the paddle into eight segments, each returning the "ball" at a different angle. He made the ball speed up with each successive return. And he added sound effects, including a crowd that booed and cheered along with the players' performances. Bushnell and Dabney were blown away. But wary of their previous failure, they wanted to see how the game would be received in a real-world setting. The game also needed a name. In keeping with their new company's philosophy of keeping things simple, the three men settled on a descriptive four-letter appellation written in all caps: *PONG*.

To test-market the game, Bushnell and Nolan set it up at a local tavern. Days later, Bushnell received a call from the bar's owner—the machine wasn't working. Crestfallen, Bushnell and Alcorn showed up the next morning and found a small group of patrons outside the establishment waiting for the door to be unlocked. As the bar's owner led Bushnell and Alcorn inside, they inquired if customers were really that desperate for a drink so early in the day. Much to their surprise, the man informed them that those waiting were regular patrons who knew repairmen were coming that morning to fix the game and they wanted to stake their place in line. Bushnell and Alcorn looked at each other in disbelief. Unlocking the game's front panel, Alcorn instantly determined the problem. Though the coin box was filled, players had continued thrusting quarters into the slot, causing a short-circuit. *PONG* was a sensation.

Atari released *PONG* in 1972. From the outset, the company struggled to keep up with demand. Despite initial assembly challenges, Atari sold two thousand five hundred games its first year. In 1974, the company sold eight thousand units and was shipping them overseas. Beyond bars, *PONG* machines began appearing in restaurants, bowling alleys, convenience stores, and other outlets. The reason was simple: owners of the machines made money at an astonishing rate, one quarter at a time. Bushnell estimated that each *PONG* game earned an average of $40 per day, four times the daily revenue of pinball and other coin-operated machines. Atari hadn't just introduced the first widely popular coin-operated video game. It had launched a new industry.

Meanwhile, a Japanese engineer employed by Taito was already at work creating the game that would take the craze to a whole new level. His name was Tomohiro Nishikado. He would take his inspiration from H. G. Wells's sci-fi masterpiece *The War of the Worlds*. The idea of battling aliens from outer space solved two problems for Nishikado. First, it allowed him to create a shooting game without making humans the targets, avoiding a sensitive issue in postwar Japan. Second, a space environment provided a logical reason for the game's austere appearance. The technology of the time did not yet permit the use of color in video game design. But for an outer space backdrop, color wasn't needed.* To create a space setting, Nishikado needed only sprinkle tiny white stars on a field of black.

The game's concept was simple. The player's role was to defend his home planet against armies of invading aliens using a mobile laser cannon. The attacking aliens were aligned in columns and stacked in layers. After clearing an entire screen of marauders, the player would advance to a more challenging stage. Nishikado believed this progression would inspire the player to feel a sense of accomplishment. Both the player and his targets had the ability to move back and forth, firing deadly projectiles at each other. What's more, Nishikado designed his aliens to descend toward the player with increasing speed, creating a sense of heightening tension. If the player allowed a single alien to touch down on his planet, he lost.

The name that Nishikado first bestowed on his creation was *Space Monsters*. Later, Taito changed it to *Space Invaders*.

In 1978, *Space Invaders* was initially released only in Japan. It took a while for gamers to discover it, but when they did, its pop-

---

*To incorporate at least some element of color in the design, the North American version of the game included strips of orange and green cellophane physically adhered to the game screen. That way, any white-pixel objects on the screen beneath the cellophane appeared to have a tint.

ularity spread like a virus. Taito sold one hundred thousand *Space Invaders* games in Japan alone the first year. Arcades opened that offered nothing but *Space Invaders*.

A short time later, *Space Invaders* reached American shores, where resistance proved futile. Taito sold sixty thousand machines its first year in the United States—more than seven times the number of *PONG* units Atari had sold in its first three years. The only reason the *Space Invaders* number wasn't higher was that the company held back an additional two hundred thousand machines it had produced to quench demand in its home country. By 1982, *Space Invaders* machines gobbled a collective $2 billion. For comparison, *Star Wars*, then the highest-grossing movie in history, had earned a mere $486 million. *Space Invaders* back then could lay claim to being more than just the best-selling video game ever; it was the highest-grossing entertainment vehicle ever.

Space Invaders began the revolution that elevated video games from curious novelty to mainstream phenomenon. Along the way, it led arcade video games out of the darkened bars, bowling alleys, and pinball halls to which they were previously confined, and ushered them into the most public of places: supermarkets, shopping malls, restaurants, roller rinks, convenience stores, gas stations, and, most relevant to our story, hotels and motels.

My family may have been on its way to Florida or the Gulf Coast. But whenever we stopped along the way, my primary destination, like that of most other kids my age in the late seventies and early eighties, was the hotel game room.

On my mission to locate and scope out the motel game room, every second was critical. Like my siblings, I was expected to report back to the lobby in timely fashion. This was because, after my dad had been handed our room keys, we'd proceed together back out to the car to collect our luggage and haul it to our room. Dad sure as hell wasn't going to get stuck doing the task himself, and he'd be damned if he was going to tip a bellhop, if one was even available, to do it for us.

The consequences for a tardy return to the lobby could be serious. Depending on my mom's mood, she could deduct a dollar from my precious video game stipend or withhold it altogether. But after hours on the road, I couldn't contain my excitement at seeing what pixelated pleasures awaited my later return. Perhaps there'd even be games I'd never seen before—because of frequent production shortages and uneven distribution, game titles that were popular in some areas of the country were often unavailable in others. It's why hotel and motel game rooms played a vital role in spreading demand for new games. Kids would see and play them in distant places, then return home and ask about them at their local arcades.

The task of finding a motel's game room wasn't always easy. Motels weren't originally built with video games in mind, and often owners didn't really know what to do with them. Video games were noisy, and so were the kids they attracted, which meant that games couldn't be placed in the lobby or near guest rooms, unless the manager didn't mind dealing with constant complaints. Sometimes owners of Holiday Inns that featured Holidomes would arrange the games in tidy clusters around the pool, but eventually it occurred to them that putting electronic devices in a steamy environment to be played by soaking children might not be a great idea. Usually the solution was to locate game rooms at the distant end of some far-flung, poorly marked corridor. Even if you found an employee who could provide directions, the instructions were often impossible to follow. The weary hotel clerk or maintenance man would rattle off a long series of turns to take, staircases to ascend and descend, and landmarks to look for, until you were about as likely to locate the Holy Grail as the game room.

If I did find the arcade, I'd poke my head in to take a quick inventory. By 1982, any game room worth its electric sockets offered most of the biggies, the games just about every kid knew and loved: *Space Invaders, Pac-Man, Ms. Pac-Man, Donkey Kong,* and *Asteroids.* All of these titles sold more than one hundred thousand units in the United States and represented the true elite class of arcade video games. I could pick these games out quickly because they were always surrounded by clumps of onlookers hoping to get tips and learn patterns from watching high-scoring players. What's more, these games would always have a long row of gleaming quarters sitting on the bottom frame of their title panels. It was a sort of reservation system for waiting players, who put quarters up to mark their spot in line. Of course, the coins weren't marked, and there were always squabbles over whose quarter belonged to whom. In the end, bigger and tougher kids just pushed the rest aside and took their turns as they pleased anyway.

I didn't like to wait to play games. And as a smallish kid who valued his teeth, I tried to avoid confrontations, especially with acne-scarred teenagers wearing Motörhead T-shirts. So I gravitated to the next tier of games, the ones that were still a blast to play but didn't attract crowds: *Centipede, Defender, Galaxian, Missile Command, Tempest, Dig Dug,* and, for my money the best racing game ever, *Pole Position.* If I spotted two or three of these titles, I'd deem it a quality game room and look forward to my later return.

There were also certain rare titles that really got me excited. If I spotted any of these games, I'd pull out all the stops in negotiations with my mother to secure as many quarters as possible. These titles barely registered a blip on the virtual radar of casual gamers, but video game connoisseurs like me savored them. These rare finds included *Gorf* (short for "Galactic Orbiting Robot Force"), *Rip-Off*, *Battlezone*, and my all-time underrated favorite, *BurgerTime*.

BurgerTime was a game with an unusual premise, even in the weird and wacky world of video games. The player assumed the role of a character named Peter Pepper, a fast-food fry cook tasked with assembling four hamburgers simultaneously. The tiny chef had to scurry up and down ladders to reach multiple layers of oversize ingredients: bun, burger patty, lettuce, tomato, and others. By running across each one, he squashed them down to lower levels and ultimately a plate. Apparently Mr. Pepper's food preparation methods weren't scrutinized by any tiny pixelated inspectors from any health department. Adding more absurdity to the proceedings were three foes—a hot dog, a pickle, and a fried egg, each sporting a pair of spry little legs—that chased the tiny chef all over the screen inexplicably trying to prevent him from making the burgers (perhaps they were militant vegans).

With games like these available, it was beyond me why anyone would wait in line just to drift around space shooting at rocks. Not that I had much time to contemplate the matter. After I completed my quick scout of the game room, I had to hustle back to the lobby. There was still work to be done before I'd be permitted time for play. And I had to earn my quarters.

Transporting our belongings from the car to our hotel room was an undertaking in itself. After regrouping in the lobby from our scouting missions, Dad would march us all back out to our car.

There, my mom would wisely exclude herself from the proceedings to clear out the day's trash from the car's interior.

Dad would load us up, one by one, with suitcases, gym bags, pillows, blankets, and other items until our belongings were piled so high on our arms that we couldn't see. When the trunk was empty, we'd begin the perilous trek to our room. Following one after another in a line, we'd stumble ahead, while my father shouted directions to the leader from the rear. If whoever was leading us unexpectedly bashed into a wall or tripped over a bench or encountered some other obstruction—say, another hotel guest—we'd all squash into the back of the person ahead of us like an accordion being squeezed. To any bystander observing us, we looked like an expedition of drunken sherpas. Of course, we could have made it all easier by dividing our load into two trips. But that wasn't my father's way; in his mind, two trips would take twice as long. Even on the short journey from our car to the room, Dad was intent on making good time.

When our human baggage train arrived at our room, Dad would unlock the door, and we'd lug our belongings inside. Because we mostly stayed at one of the major chains, our rooms were typically clean and reasonably spacious—for a typical family of four. My family, of course, had *six* members, not to mention the extra baggage that came along. This made our accommodations considerably more snug. Our rooms usually provided two modestly sized double beds, so the question naturally arose of where two of us would sleep. This was never good news for the two of us with the least tenure in my family: my sister and me.

The answer would come with a knock on the door. Upon its opening, a hotel employee would wheel inside two rickety rollaway beds that my dad ordered at check-in, no doubt negotiated into our room fee at no extra charge. Dad would direct the employee to push the rollaways inside our room and up against the wall of the narrow entry hallway. This placement would leave just enough space for us to pass through, so long as we exhaled all the air from our lungs. The beds would remain there, folded up, until we returned from dinner or a visit to the pool (or game room) and had washed up for bed. By this time, the room began to take on the claustrophobic feel of, say, a collapsed mineshaft. It would only get worse.

Once we settled in, my father would finally allow himself to relax. For him, this meant slipping off his shoes and sipping a cocktail. Of course, he'd never pay the outrageous prices being charged down at the hotel bar. *What?! Three dollars for a manhattan? The actual Manhattan cost less!* So, my dad always brought his own solution. He called it the medicine kit. Sears Department Store called it the Executive Portable Travel Bar.

Outwardly, the travel bar looked no different from a small suitcase with a handle and key lock on one side. But my father treated it with a kind of reverence not afforded any of our other belongings. The first thing that made the case special was that it was with us at all. Keep in mind, we were a family of six traveling in a car—albeit a large luxury model—packed with luggage for a seven- to ten-day trip. To ensure we had enough space for everything, my parents restricted the number of pairs of underwear we could pack. But there was never a question of there being enough room for Dad's cocktail kit.

Inside our room, Dad would clear off a section of table and gently stand the case on end, indicating the magical moment had arrived. I'd always look on with intense interest. Dad would reach into his pocket and produce a thin brass key pinched between his thumb and forefinger. He'd lift it up in front of his eyes, where it beamed in the glow of the room's TV screen. Then he'd insert the key into the lock and twist it. Like an archaeologist opening a miniature sarcophagus for the first time in centuries, he'd carefully part the two halves of the case, exposing its contents. On one side gleamed silver tumblers, ornate tools, and an intricately etched serving tray. On the other side were three full-size liquor bottles tucked side by side into a cushion of lustrous red velveteen, each held in place with its own leather strap. To my youthful eyes, the setup resembled something fashioned for James Bond by Q back at the spy lab—an entire bar, shrunk down and housed in a small box disguised as an ordinary suitcase. *Cool!*

While my father removed the contents, I'd immediately grab the plastic ice bucket and head off in search of the nearest ice machine. My dad had trained me well—I'd do this without even being asked, and it was a job in which I took great pride. It was like getting to play a role in some sacred adult ritual. Plus, it was always fun to explore the hallways of a hotel unsupervised. But there was no time to dally. I knew that once Dad was in cocktail mode, the clock was ticking, so I tried to hustle back with his ice as quickly as possible. As I handed over the bucket, Dad would thank me with a wink and proceed with his alchemy. Using shimmering tongs, he'd plunk a few cubes into two glasses, one bearing his initials etched on the side and another for my mom. Then he'd use the jigger to meticulously measure out the portions for two separate cocktails, a scotch and soda for Mom and a brandy manhattan for himself. Dad could have dispensed the perfect amounts with his eyes closed, of course, but that would have made his ridiculously well-equipped Executive Travel Bar a bit less essential. And what would be the fun in that?

After both cocktails were prepared, Dad would hand Mom hers. Then they'd clink their glasses to toast the close of another long day on the road. It was a moment of great excitement for all of us. After all, once Mom and Dad were diving into their liquid refreshment, we could do the same—the kind waiting for us down at the pool.

After changing into our swimsuits and squeezing through the harrowing Passage of Rollaway Beds, we made our way through the maze of corridors to the hotel pool. If tables were available, we'd claim one located near the shallow area of the pool so Mom could keep an eye on us—more specifically me—while she and Dad sipped their cocktails. Meanwhile, I'd make my way into the pool to test the water temperature for everyone else, usually after an unexpected push by one of my brothers.

While playing in the pool, I'd keep a close eye on the clock so I'd know when it was time to leave for the game room. My parents would always set a time when we were all required to regroup and return to our room. I didn't want to cheat myself out of time for an extra game, but I didn't want to get gypped out of pool time either.

Around 10:00 p.m., we'd reunite as planned and return to our room to get ready for bed. For us kids, this meant putting on pajamas and brushing our teeth. For my parents, it meant converting our modest hotel room into a scene resembling a Red Cross refugee camp.

While my brothers and I were in the bathroom fighting for a spot at the sink, Dad would push the large folded rollaway beds out of the room's hallway and into the main room. He'd flop one open, then the other, each releasing its own plume of dust gathered from sitting in some musty closet probably since my family's last stay. With both beds opened, not an inch of floor space remained, transforming the room into one gigantic mattress. However, the rollaway beds always sat at a higher level than the room's conventional beds. This meant that if anyone got up during the night to use the bathroom, they'd have to navigate a perilous obstacle course. Not only would you have to clamber from one mattress to the next in complete darkness, trying to avoid any stray limbs or foot-swallowing crevices between mattresses, you also had to be careful not to bang into the elevated sharp metal frames of the rollaway beds. If you did, it would take all your willpower to stifle your screams as throbbing pain erupted from your shin, so you didn't wake everyone else. You weren't much safer sleeping. Your chances of being roused from slumber by a bare foot stepping on your face were always dangerously high.

Of course, before the lights ever went out, the whole setup practically begged for a pillow fight, much to my mom's aggravation. They'd usually start playfully enough, with my sister and me tossing stuffed animals at each other over some mild gripe. One of us would miss and hit one of our brothers (okay, sometimes on purpose) and the real brawl would begin. In a blink, a small skirmish would escalate to a spirited clash, then a heated fracas. Before long, my parents would have an all-out donnybrook on their hands.

As grizzled veterans of many previous fights, most notoriously the Battle of the Birmingham Best Western of '74, we all knew the key to victory was being first to grab one of the pillows we had brought from home to use as a weapon. These pillows were stuffed with hefty goose down and packed a mighty wallop when swung full force. Hotel pillows were usually foam and far too light to deliver anything but a trifling swipe. When forced to defend myself with one of those, my only real shot at survival was to hold the pillow with both arms extended straight out and blindly charge my attacker. As the youngest, I never had much of a chance anyway. These fights would inevitably end with one of my brothers on top of me, pinning my arms under his knees while mercilessly jabbing his index fingers into the ticklish spots above my kidneys.

By that time of evening, my parents were usually too exhausted to make any real effort to break up the conflicts beyond offering a perfunctory, "You kids better stop that or someone will get hurt!" It was usually only a matter of time until we proved them right. My sister would knock her head against one of the metal rollaway bed frames. Or my brother would get his eyeglasses bashed into the bridge of his nose. Or, most often, I'd wind up in a crumpled heap after plummeting headfirst into one of the treacherous fissures in our mattress-scape. At that point, Mom would remind us that we needed to get to sleep before we'd all face an even greater threat: my father's legendary snoring.

As the years passed, Mom eventually convinced Dad to begin paying for two adjoining motel rooms. The constant disputes between six family members fighting over the use of one hotel bathroom had taken their toll on her. And as the size of both our car's interior and our hotel rooms began to shrink in direct proportion to the growth of us four kids, even my dad conceded it was worth the extra money to put a wall between himself and the loudest and smelliest of his clan. So my sister stayed with my parents in one room, where they enjoyed a little more peace and room to spread out. And my brothers and I were banished to our own room next door, where we were free to fight and fart as we pleased.

Still, as much as my brothers and I enjoyed our private space and freedom, I couldn't help but miss the experience of my whole family spending evenings together in a single room: the musty smell and constant squeaks of those wobbly rollaway beds; the relentless jokes my brothers and I would make about Dad's skinny chicken legs and the condition of his saggy, moth-eaten briefs that would be revealed as he undressed for bed; the way we'd keep talking to each other in the darkness after the lights were switched off about what we planned to do the following day; waking to the muffled curses of my father as he'd knock about blindly trying to find his way to the bathroom for his 2:00 a.m. tinkle; and, of course, those epic nightly pillow fights.

Sure, it was crazy. But after all, we were six people locked up together in a tiny padded room.

CHAPTER 9

Heavy Metal Highways

Land Yachts, Station Wagons, and "The Thing"

The practice of American companies testing employees for drug use didn't become widespread until the mideighties at the prodding of the Reagan administration. I mention this in passing only as one possible explanation for automobile design in the seventies.

How else to explain the bizarre AMC Pacer, a car whose design appeared to be based on the Scrubbing Bubbles of TV ad fame? Or the Chevy El Camino, a vehicle that looked like a pickup truck had smashed into the back of a sports coupe?

And it wasn't just American car designers who were coming up with questionable vehicle concepts at the time. Somehow German Volkswagen engineers decided that a vehicle combining the off-road performance of a California dune buggy with the style of a Nazi staff car would be a good idea. They called it The Thing. It lasted two years. At the same time, the normally sophisticated French defiled America's shores with their own abomination, a super-minicompact from Renault called Le Car. It was as hard on the eyes as it was easy on the gas budget, which in fairness was its purpose. The Le Car was so ugly its owners checked to make sure no one was looking before slinking into the driver's seat.

Meanwhile, engineers at Datsun and Toyota released one oddity after another. Among these was Japan's version of the El Camino, the Subaru BRAT, a dubious acronym for Bi-Drive Recreational All-Terrain Transporter. The BRAT's most distinguishing feature was a pair of rear-facing jump seats in its uncovered cargo bed, apparently included to dissuade any friends of BRAT owners from asking for rides to the airport.

It was as if automobile designers of the day weren't even really trying. Consider the origins of the AMC Gremlin, one of the most derided cars of the era. Richard A. Teague, head of AMC Design, admitted he sketched his initial idea for the car on an airsickness bag while on a flight. The Gremlin made its debut on April 1, 1970. Yep, April Fool's Day.

The crazy thing isn't that these cars were ever designed. It's that they were actually produced—in large numbers—by major car companies. Somehow, at no point in the approval process for the Pacer did anyone at AMC say, "Ya know, I'm not sure the world is ready for a car that looks like an underwater base for Sea-Monkeys." But the highways of the era were made all the more interesting for it. With so many weird and wonderful vehicles being produced in the seventies, there was never a better time to be traveling.

While the role that recreational pharmaceuticals played in seventies' car design may be debatable, there's no arguing the impact of two key influences. The first was the US government's introduction of harsh vehicle emissions standards in 1972. The other was the country's first major oil crisis.

As air pollution became an increasing concern in the 1950s and 1960s, particularly in urban areas, studies were conducted to identify its cause. Unsurprisingly, research pointed to America's growing number of automobiles. But evidence of air pollution's harmful impact outside traffic-jammed cities did catch people's attention. Suddenly air pollution wasn't just a local issue, it was a national problem—one that required a national agency to address it. In 1970, the Environmental Protection Agency (EPA) was established to alleviate the impact of pollution.

In short order, the EPA imposed emissions standards for all new vehicles sold in the United States. Automobile manufacturers responded by implementing a variety of "reburning" strategies that made engines less powerful. As a result, in the midst of a fuel crisis, America began producing cars that, over a given span, consumed *more* gasoline.

By 1975, the EPA's tightening standards all but mandated that every new vehicle be equipped with a catalytic converter. The devices did reduce the pollutants expelled by automobiles, but they weren't compatible with engines using regular leaded gas. This set off a mad scramble by oil companies to make sufficient unleaded gasoline available in time for the release of 1975 car models. The introduction of catalytic converters as part of a national effort to reduce the amount of lead in our environment is why we exclusively use unleaded fuel in vehicles today.

Higher emissions standards and catalytic converters all but strangled engine performance—and cars designed for speed and power. Because there wasn't much point in producing muscle cars without muscle, car companies simply stopped making them. By 1975, many of the macho cars that had become synonymous with American horsepower—the Plymouth Barracuda, Chevy Chevelle Super Sport, and Dodge Charger R/T, among others—were put out to pasture. Other models atrophied into unrecognizable versions of their former selves. The venerable Ford Mustang, the car that had long set the standard for power and style, was reintroduced in 1974 as the Ford Mustang II. Built on the same subcompact-size platform as the Ford Pinto, the Mustang II's standard engine wheezed out just 88 horsepower.

Luxury cars and family station wagons were hit by the new regulations as well. While some models remained large—my family's 1972 Ford LTD Country Squire station wagon stretched nearly 19 feet!—many were almost hilariously underpowered. The engine laboring to push our portly 4,500-pound station wagon produced just 200 horsepower. Loaded with six passengers and luggage, the car struggled to break the minimum highway speed limit.

The country's first major oil shortage also reshaped how cars were designed. In retaliation for America's support of Israel during the Yom Kippur War, OPEC in 1973 announced it would cut oil production by 25 percent, prompting the Nixon administration to develop a response plan. To ensure the reduced fuel supply would be distributed fairly, the government decreed that each state would be allocated the same proportion of the nation's total fuel use it had consumed the previous year. Knowing that shortages would mean skyrocketing fuel prices, Nixon also imposed limits on how much gas stations could charge. But the government could do only so much. When rationing became necessary, only motorists with even-numbered license plates were allowed to purchase gas one day, while those with odd-numbered plates could drive up to the pump the next day. Fearing stations would run out of gas, nervous drivers filled their tanks at every opportunity, forming long lines at the pumps. While waiting, drivers kept cars idling, fearing another driver might cut in if they didn't pull ahead fast enough, behavior that needlessly burned more gas and compounded the shortages, of course. Eventually some gas stations did run dry. According to AAA, 20 percent of the nation's gas stations had no fuel to sell during the final week of February 1974. For the first time, Americans realized just how dependent they were on foreign nations for their fuel—and they were shocked.

What followed was a rush to trade in gas guzzlers for smaller, more fuel-efficient vehicles. Sales of the AMC Gremlin, Ford Pinto, and Chevy Vega soared. Buyers also flocked to economical models manufactured overseas. Many imports came equipped with air-conditioning, power steering, AM-FM radios, and other features for which domestic manufacturers charged extra. Buyers also noticed the cars seemed to be built better than similar American cars, and several were earning outstanding reputations for reliability. Among these models were the Toyota Corona, the Datsun 510, the Subaru DL, and, later, the Honda Accord. Detroit's long stranglehold on the automobile market was beginning to slip. Perhaps nothing symbolized this transition more than an event in 1972. Early that year, Volkswagen Beetle No. 15,007,034 rolled off the assembly line, surpassing the Ford Model T as the best-selling car in automotive history. The automobile Henry Ford II once dismissed as "a little shit box" went on to sell more than 21 million units and remained a top seller for decades.

America's first fuel crisis lasted less than a year, but Americans' desire for smaller, more economical cars continued. As a result of the dramatic changes, the highways of the seventies were filled with a menagerie of odd and interesting vehicles not seen before or since. There were enormous land yachts and tiny subcompacts. Overpowered muscle cars and underpowered family sedans. Station wagons with fake wood side panels and luxury cars with phony convertible tops. Cars that aspired to be pickups and trucks that yearned to be dune buggies. Tricked-out custom vans with wild murals and stripped-down minibuses that appeared to be built for people in the witness protection program. Two-tone color patterns, thick racing stripes, and metal chip-flecked paint ruled the day. It was a weird and wonderful time to be out on the roads, especially as a kid in the backseat of a car on a long road trip with nothing better to do than take it all in.

It was easy to get a good look at cars because in the seventies, so many could be seen stalled at the side of the highways. It was not a proud period of quality for the auto industry. Although foreign carmakers weren't immune to quality issues, Detroit's Big Three made regular headlines with one massive recall after another.

Part of the problem was that the industry was struggling with the transition to a new generation of assembly-line workers. In 1970, fully one third of the line workers at America's three major automakers were younger than thirty years old. Having come of age during the freethinking sixties, many of these workers deplored the monotony and onerous demands that came with life on the assembly line—conditions their parents had readily accepted. When in 1970 General Motors suspended two United Auto Workers (UAW) union leaders for balking at an order to speed up production, hundreds of workers abruptly walked off the line.

Workers also found other ways to demonstrate their unhappiness. David Frum summarized the situation in his book *How We Got Here: The 70s*:

The discontent on the line expressed itself not in protest but in spontaneous acts of sabotage. One-quarter of Ford's assembly line workers quit in 1970. Unexcused absences from work doubled at Ford and General Motors between 1961 and 1970, spiking upward most sharply in 1969–70. In the spring of 1970, 5 percent of General Motors' workers were missing without excuse on any given day. On Fridays and Mondays, up to 10 percent of the workforce failed to show up.

Even when workers did show up, management may have often wished they hadn't. According to Frum, "Disgruntled workers took to vandalizing cars, especially the expensive models." *Fortune* reported that "screws have been left in brake drums, tool handles welded into fender compartments (to cause mysterious, unfindable and eternal rattles), paint scratched and upholstery cut."

Resentful employees weren't the only ones to blame for Detroit's quality issues in the seventies. Poor engineering, penny-pinching by management, and questionable decisions by top executives also factored in.

By 1977, Detroit was recalling nearly as many cars as it sold. According to some automobile industry historians, cars that rolled off American assembly lines at the time had, on average, *seven* significant defects. It was a bad time for motorists to have to count on their automobiles. Especially those who were planning on traveling a long way from home.

Because American automobile quality was so poor in the seventies, the potential for a breakdown on a road trip was more a probability than a possibility. Like many other motorists, my father belonged to AAA, in large part for the club's roadside assistance program. But in order to call AAA for help, he first had to get to a phone. That wasn't always easy after breaking down on a lonely stretch of interstate between, say, Memphis and Mobile. Not only were there fewer exits with service stations back then, there were fewer motorists traveling the highways who might offer stranded drivers a lift. In the days before cell phones, motorists who ran into mechanical problems on the highways were largely on their own.

For this reason, my father took every precaution before we set out on a lengthy road trip. Days before our departure, he'd take the car into a dealership for a thorough inspection and oil change. Then he'd head over to Kmart to pick up all the appropriate spare fuses, bulbs, and belts for our car. Finally, he'd scramble about our garage, filling a tool bag with assorted wrenches and ratchets and scooping up giant jugs of coolant and cans of gloopy lubricants. After packing the trunk with our luggage, he'd fill every remaining crevice with the items he had collected. He didn't know how to use many of these tools and supplies, mind you. My father wasn't particularly mechanically inclined, at least when it came to automobiles. But he was smart enough to sire a son who was.

By the time he was a teenager, my brother Bruce was already a seasoned "wrench." From the moment he handled his first Matchbox racer, Bruce fell in love with cars. He read magazines like *Road & Track* and *Motor Trend* cover to cover. He took every automotive shop class offered in junior high and high school. He'd have his head under a hood at every opportunity. And so my family's fate out on the highways often hinged on the automotive acumen of a kid who wasn't even old enough to drive.

On a number of occasions when some mechanical malady or distressing din forced us off the road, Bruce could always devise a solution. When a pinhole erupted in the radiator of our '75 Lincoln Town Car halfway to Florida, it was Bruce who knew of an obscure sealant that could save the day. We found the product at a nearby hardware store and continued on our way. When a blazing sun caused our '77 Oldsmobile Regency to overheat on a remote Alabama highway, it was Bruce who suggested that my dad crank the heater to vent the engine. As crazy as it seemed to crawl along a baking highway in a vehicle with a steaming engine and our heater on full blast, we made it to an exit and help. When the exhaust system of our '78 Cadillac Sedan DeVille became unfastened and began spraying sparks across the highway, it was Bruce who used a couple of wire clothes hangers from Mom's suitcase to secure it back into place. On other occasions, he fixed flats, adjusted alternators, and tightened engine belts to keep us rolling along.

However, with the automobile quality of the day being what it was, there were some problems even Bruce couldn't fix. One nearly caused a complete breakdown—my father's.

In 1974, my father tallied his best year selling commercial lighting fixtures and decided to reward himself. For the first time since my parents started a family—maybe the first time ever as far as any of us knew—Dad allowed himself to purchase a new car. In the past, he'd always bought used vehicles to save dollars for his four kids' college tuitions. But that year, a new model caught his eye. Two weeks before we were to leave on a spring road trip, he pulled into our driveway, smiling ear to ear, behind the wheel of a gleaming new mustard gold 1974 Oldsmobile Toronado.

My father couldn't have been more excited. He called the family out of the house and waved over curious neighbors to have a closer look. Once everyone had assembled, he marched the group in a circle around the car like a tour guide, pointing out every last feature and styling detail. The padded "opera roof." The gleaming chrome wheel covers and whitewall tires. The elegant front grille that narrowed to a sharp point. Hustling to the driver's side, he cautioned the group to step back as he swung open the massive door and dove into the front seat to demonstrate every switch and button within the driver's reach. The telescoping steering wheel. The six-way adjustable power seat. Power windows and door locks. And, placed in easy view of the driver, an advanced new feature Oldsmobile called the Message Center. This was a matrix of warning lights that kept the driver apprised of every possible mechanical issue, from the oil running too low to the engine temperature climbing too high. "The car is so smart it can even tell you what's wrong with it!" Dad boasted.

Finally, as the climax to his presentation, he turned the ignition. The car's massive 455-cubic-inch engine rumbled to life as he pumped the accelerator. The deafening roar raised the eyebrows of everyone within earshot, particularly my mother's. Suddenly sensing his demonstration—heck, his whole choice of car—might have been a bit much, Dad recovered by highlighting what he deemed to be the car's "most important" feature: "The thing that really sold me, of course, was the front wheel drive. You can't put a price on safe handling, especially with our snowy winters!"

Of course, kids and parents will disagree on which features should be considered truly important. For me, the coolest aspect of the Toronado was its built-in eight-track tape player.

Today we tend to dismiss the eight-track as a failed novelty of a bygone era, another Betamax. But in its day, the eight-track player wasn't just a tremendous leap forward in entertainment technology; it was dazzlingly popular. The driving force behind the eight-track was Bill Lear of Learjet aircraft fame. Lear became interested in eight-track players because he wanted to incorporate a high-end audio component into his luxury aircraft. However, he quickly realized that the technology could be installed in automobiles as well. After all, the playback units were portable and designed for use in bumpy conditions, and the plastic tapes were durable and easy to change.

Lear's break came when he convinced RCA Victor to release its entire catalog on the eight-track format. Next, he persuaded Ford to make the players available as an option for the company's most popular 1966 models: the Mustang, Thunderbird, and select Lincolns. Sales of the players exceeded all expectations—sixty-five thousand units in the first year. That success prompted the introduction of eight-track players for home use, allowing music lovers to swap tapes between their cars and living rooms. By the early 1970s, nearly all domestic automakers offered eight-track players as options, though they were often units installed by dealers beneath dashboards rather than integrated into the instrument panel.

By 1974, when my father bought his Toronado, the included eight-track was no longer new technology, but it was new to us. It was also a feature still novel enough for the dealer to throw in two promotional eight-track tapes as an enticing bonus. In our case, these complimentary tapes included a compilation of theme songs from hit TV shows and movies and a copy of Barry Manilow's latest release.

My dad couldn't wait for our vacation to arrive so he'd be able to spend hours behind the wheel of his new Toronado. He knew my mom was skeptical about the wisdom of buying a two-door coupe for a family of six. It meant that every time our family traveled together, three kids would have to climb over the folding front seats to pile into the backseat. But my father was sure that once my mom experienced the Toronado's silky-smooth ride, plush interior, and impressive features, she and the whole family would love the car as much as he did.

The first few hundred miles of our trip passed without incident. But as we crossed the Illinois border into Kentucky, the skies turned dark and raindrops plinked in wide splotches across our windshield. Soon we found ourselves driving through a raging squall. Watching other drivers pull over to seek refuge under overpasses, my mom wondered aloud if we shouldn't do the same. But my father brushed off the suggestion, raving about how well the car's innovative front wheel drive was handling the wet pavement. With a confident wink to my mom, he crowed, "You know, conditions like this are exactly why I chose this car!"

The downpour subsided only as we pulled into the parking lot of our motel. Of course, Dad made a point of announcing that the storm had hardly delayed us at all. Thanks to the Toronado's sure handling, we'd "made great time" and had a couple of hours for swimming and relaxing around the pool. After checking in and conducting our customary reconnaissance, we returned to the car and formed a semicircle around the trunk to receive our loads. But as my dad turned the key to release the trunk's lid, a cascade of water gushed out, nearly knocking him off his feet. The waterfall splashed to the pavement, soaking our shoes as we looked on in shock.

The trunk was a bathtub. Sandals and snorkels and other items bobbed about, tumbling over the sides onto the asphalt. Inside the compartment, our luggage was submerged, and every stitch of clothing we'd brought for the trip was soaked. Our mood, like our clothes, was considerably dampened.

Inspecting the trunk, Bruce quickly determined the issue: the foam rubber seal lining the compartment had come loose. No doubt the assembly-line worker responsible for its installation, perhaps less than thrilled with management's latest request to work the weekend, had neglected to apply sufficient adhesive to ensure a waterproof barrier. The shoddy seal had allowed a steady leak until rainwater filled the compartment. We never had a clue anything was wrong. Apparently Oldsmobile's engineers hadn't thought to include a warning light for excess trunk fluid in the Toronado's innovative Message Center.

My father had been looking forward to spending the evening by the pool. Instead, he spent hours bailing to remove the pool that had formed in his new car's trunk. From that point forward, he would never look at the Toronado the same way again. The problem with the trunk—one that would require multiple visits to the dealership to eventually solve—caused him to question the quality of the entire vehicle. Every minor squeak and sputter caused him to wince in fear that it was just the first symptom of some far more serious—and costly—defect. He finally sold the Toronado for much less than he paid just so he could sleep at night. He'd owned the car little more than a year.

My mom never said a word. She didn't have to. Buying the Toronado had been entirely my dad's decision. She knew he'd beat himself up enough about it without her help. Instead, she went right to wringing out our clothes and loading heap after sopping heap into the two dryers in the motel's tiny laundry room. As I was too young to do anything but get in the way, I was sent off to the game room with a pocketful of quarters, much to my unexpected delight. When I returned to our room hours later, it looked more like the aftermath of an F5 tornado than a '74 Toronado. Damp shirts and pants dangled from curtain rods and coat racks. Soggy socks and nylons were draped over chair backs. Suitcases lay open across every surface. With our pajamas left out to air-dry for the evening, my entire family went to bed wearing nothing but our underwear, much to the amusement of my brothers and me and the utter horror of my sister.

In retrospect, though, we'd gotten off lucky—on that occasion and throughout our other years on the road. Our car problems usually resulted in temporary inconveniences or short delays. Not all traveling families were so fortunate. Unlike today, it was common at the time to see motorists stranded by the highway, the hoods of their cars raised like white flags in surrender. Back home, I'd hear stories of classmates whose families were forced to spend their entire vacation in some backwater motel waiting for a new alternator or water pump to arrive just so they could drive home.

If there was one thing about the cars of the seventies you could count on, it's that it was pure folly to count on them at all. It wasn't so much a matter of *if* things would go wrong with your vehicle, but *when*. And if, like my family, your vacation depended on countless hours traveling in a car to some distant destination, you were always running on borrowed time.

Many children of the era grew up with a very different view of America than their parents did. This was because they spent their childhoods looking at the country backward—from the rear-facing cargo seat of their trusty family station wagon.

Considering all the unusual and outlandish vehicles the decade produced—the mighty muscle cars, the shag-a-delic custom vans, the half-car/half-truck hybrids—it may seem odd that it's the thoroughly square and conventional station wagons that are among the most fondly remembered. But for those of us of a certain age and upbringing, the venerable family station wagon will always hold the prime spot in the cluttered garages of our memories.

Nothing epitomized suburban America in the 1970s quite like

the station wagon. It was the car owned by the Brady Bunch.* The vehicle that harried moms relied on to cart the kids around to dance classes and baseball games and haul groceries home from the supermarket. And, of course, it was the trusty station wagon into which countless parents piled their kids and luggage to make the cross-country trek to Yellowstone National Park or the Grand Canyon.

Like most other suburbanites, we owned a station wagon throughout much of the seventies. Only it usually wasn't the car my mom used to run her daily errands. Rather, it was the vehicle my dad used to make sales calls and haul around deliveries for work. Back then, the Ratay family's very un-Brady-like two-vehicle arrangement was for my mom to drive the showpiece car while my dad puttered about in the wagon. But come the weekend, when it was time to head to the country club for an evening dinner dance—or take to the open road for a long family trip—Dad jumped at the chance to get behind the wheel of his cherished luxury land yachts. We did, however, take a station wagon on a couple of road trips, enough to appreciate the experience so many other families enjoyed.

It was almost mandatory for a family to own a Ford Country Squire at some point during the seventies, and we were no exception. Ours was a classic 1972 model complete with the trademark simulated wood-grain side panels, honey-colored bench seats, and patented Three-Way Magic Doorgate. The "magic" was that

---

*The Bradys, like the suburban families they represented, were a two-car family. The father, Mike Brady, drove the showier, sportier vehicle—usually a Chrysler product, always a convertible, and nearly always blue in color. Carol, the mother, was relegated to the station wagon—always the latest model Plymouth Satellite. Considering the prevailing chauvinism of the day, it shouldn't be surprising to learn that one of the few times Carol was shown driving the car, she caused a fender bender in a supermarket parking lot and wound up in traffic court.

the tailgate could be rotated down and used as a bench or a table for picnics, or it could be swung outward for easy loading of groceries and other cargo. In reality, the most useful aspect of the Magic Doorgate was that it allowed for easy cleaning. Inevitably, it would be showered with the vomit of kids who succumbed to motion sickness from being forced to ride in the side-facing jump seats in the rear.

My dad bought the Country Squire for my mom for the same reasons every other suburban housewife drove one. She almost instantly hated the car. Mom was pint-size, and the Country Squire wasn't. It had a cargo area the size of a football field, and she could barely see out the rear window when backing up. Because Mom was constantly backing out of a driveway with small children running around, it was a serious concern. So she swapped cars with my dad, who had no such reservations. He promptly backed out over my new bike, crushing it into a twisted orange pretzel.

We took our Country Squire on only one family road trip—a trek to the Ozarks during Christmas break 1974. It was on this trip that my dad pushed his luck too far with the fuel gauge and we ran out of gas. The following day, we blew a tire. Not long after returning home, Dad sold the Country Squire to erase any memory of the whole ordeal.

So, while many American families traveled the roads of the seventies in a station wagon, mine usually wasn't one of them. Still, it was easy to understand their allure. Most station wagons could seat up to eight people. At the same time, their gleaming chrome roof racks and spacious cargo areas offered plenty of room for suitcases, sports equipment, and other belongings. Heck, with a rooftop carrier to hold the luggage, a station wagon practically became a living room on wheels. Many models offered all the comforts of home: carpeted floors, air-conditioning, AM/FM stereos, and generously cushioned adjustable seats. And while the large size of station wagons made them hard to navigate around the city, they offered drivers a confident feeling of command out on the limitless stretches of straight highway. In their heyday, station wagons were the cruise ships of the open road.

Station wagons had traveled a long way to reach such prominent status. Their origins were far humbler, hinted at in both their name and signature fake wood paneling.

As the term implies, the first station wagons were standard automobiles retrofitted with wagon bodies for use around stations—train stations, to be specific. In the early twentieth century, trains were still the most common mode of long-distance transportation by a wide margin. But some sort of conveyance was needed to shuttle train passengers and their loads of bulky baggage between their homes and railroad depots. For taxi services of the day, automobiles were just the ticket—the new contraptions offered a cheaper, more practical alternative to horse-drawn carriages. The problem was that most automobiles were really designed only for transporting passengers, with most manufacturers including just small holds for cargo. Sensing opportunity, a few enterprising souls began purchasing inexpensive Ford Model Ts, then sawing off their steel bodies just behind the windshields. Handymen then built new bodies for the vehicles using hardwood, with seating for passengers in front and long compartments for cargo in the rear. These custom contraptions became known variously as "woodies," "carry-alls," "suburbans," "depot hacks" ("hacks" was an abbreviation for "hackney carriages"), and, eventually, "station wagons."

Before long, station wagons were popular for all kinds of delivery services. Because creating all-wood bodies was time-consuming and the market for station wagons was limited, major automakers were initially happy to leave their production to small aftermarket customizers. But as time passed, affluent patrons of taxi services took note of the practical design of station wagons and began ordering their own. As consumer interest in station wagons grew, so did Detroit's interest in making them. Ford was the first major automaker to produce a station wagon. By 1929, the company dominated the market. Other big automakers soon followed Ford's lead.

Throughout the 1930s and into the 1940s, station wagons enjoyed a period of remarkable prestige and status. Because their wooden bodies were expensive to fabricate, station wagons were priced much higher than other models, so only the very wealthy could afford them. To compete for these discriminating buyers, station wagon manufacturers crafted increasingly more elaborate wood bodywork for outside the vehicles, while adding luxurious appointments inside. By 1941, Chrysler's Town & Country station wagon was the most expensive vehicle in the company's lineup. In keeping with the vehicles' upscale image, automakers stopped referring to them as station wagons, marketing them instead as "estate cars." But the market for such vehicles was limited. In 1940, only one in every hundred vehicles sold in America was a station wagon.

That all changed after World War II. Having seen the world while serving in the armed forces, legions of freshly discharged GIs returned home anxious to explore their country—and they wanted to bring their families along. Buyers streamed into dealerships looking for cars not only big enough to accommodate several passengers but all their luggage too. The impressive station wagons these prospective customers saw on the showroom floor fit the bill. But the cars' hefty price tags didn't fit their budgets.

Carmakers determined that if they could create a more affordable version of the station wagon, they could open up a whole new market. What's more, production techniques developed during the war had made manufacturing all-steel bodies for station wagons far more practical. By eliminating wood in favor of all-steel bodies, it was possible to produce station wagons that weren't just less expensive but quieter and easier to maintain.

In 1949, Plymouth unveiled the first all-steel station wagon available in the United States, a two-door model called the Suburban.* Other major car companies soon introduced their own all-steel station wagons, all of which quickly outsold their more expensive wood-bodied cousins. By 1955, only Ford and Mercury continued to sell woodies, but these models no longer truly deserved the title. By that time, the once dazzling lacquered all-wood body panels and trim of Ford's Country Squire had already been replaced by the simulated wood-grain decals with which it would forever be associated. In reality, the age of the genuine woodie had already passed into history when the last of Buick's Roadmaster Estate Wagons rolled off the assembly line in 1953.

While station wagons constructed of real wood would pass into history, the look wouldn't. Every few years, as trends dictated, imitation wood-grain panel decals would reappear on new models to recall the glory days of the wood-bodied station wagons. In the seventies, an era that celebrated all things nylon, Dacron, polyes-

---

*No, Chevrolet didn't later steal the name for its own vehicle. At the time, *suburban* was a generic term used to reference any station wagon. In fact, Chevy had marketed its own Suburban in 1935, before Plymouth did.

ter, and plastic, the notion of incorporating artificial wood into automobile design never seemed more appropriate. Even today, automobile designers often integrate simulated wood-grain panels into minivan designs in homage to the classic woodie station wagons.

Inexpensive all-steel station wagons proved remarkably popular with families anxious to join America's postwar travel boom. Sales exploded. In 1950, just 3 percent of cars produced in the United States were station wagons. By the end of the decade, one in every five cars sold was a station wagon. In 1958, Plymouth sold more station wagons than any other body style. With the nation enthralled by the travel possibilities opened by Eisenhower's new interstate highway system, sales of the vehicles soared.

By the early 1970s, though, the wild joy ride was coming to an end, at least for many full-size station wagons. The OPEC oil crisis and tougher emissions requirements conspired to kill many of the bigger station wagons, just as they strangled the life out of gas-guzzling luxury models and nearly all muscle cars. High gas prices and concerns about the availability of gas in some areas discouraged families from traveling. Those who did, mostly stayed closer to home. The heydays of hefty highway cruisers had passed.

Sales of domestic full-size station wagons bottomed out in 1974. Not long after, Chrysler, Dodge, and Plymouth halted production of their models. Ford, Buick, and Oldsmobile soldiered on making station wagons, but they were never the same. Shorter, lighter, and comically underpowered, the later model Country Squire and its downsize companions were really just the last of the dinosaurs lumbering along to their inevitable doom. The asteroid that would kill them off appeared in 1984. Called the minivan, it hit the family car market with cataclysmic impact. The first of this new breed of kid hauler to arrive was the Chrysler Town & Country. Models from competitors would quickly follow.

From the day they appeared on sales lots, minivans proved so popular that dealers couldn't keep them in stock. Comparing them side by side with hulking station wagons, buyers deemed minivans easier to drive, easier to park, better suited for kids, and far more fuel efficient. Perhaps the biggest obstacle station wagons faced, though, was their wholesome Brady Bunch–inspired image. Baby boomers starting families at the time saw station wagons as the vehicles of their parents' generation. As funny as it may seem today, these young parents viewed minivans as a hip alternative to the square "mom-mobiles" of the past. Minivans were *cool*.

In the 1990s, after SUVs rumbled into the market to offer young parents another sporty option, the few full-size wagons that remained died off one by one. The venerable Ford Country Squire departed in 1991, followed by the Oldsmobile Custom Cruiser in 1992. Finally, in 1996, the last of the full-size, rear-wheel-drive wagons—the Buick Roadmaster Estate Wagon and Chevy Caprice Classic Wagon—breathed their last.

While a handful of scrappy distant cousins of the great station wagons of the seventies remain today, these vehicles as a species have all but vanished from our roads. But for those of us who spent countless hours of our childhoods queasily staring the wrong way down the highway, station wagons will be remembered for far more than fake wood paneling. They'll be remembered as the vehicles that led us on many genuinely fun adventures.

CHAPTER 10

Through the Windshield Together

A Crash Course in Seatbelts and Safety

Maybe the reason they built cars so much bigger in the seventies was because those of us who traveled in them had so much more freedom to revel in the extra space. It's not that safety devices like seatbelts and child safety seats weren't around. They were. But without laws mandating their use, their presence amounted to little more than suggestions. It was, after all, a remarkably less restrictive era. This was as true of the art, fashion, and music of the time as it was for laws pertaining to automobile passenger safety. Generally speaking, there weren't any. This, of course, was just fine by most of us—at least, until the moment we found ourselves screeching into the rear end of a line of cars unexpectedly stopped on the highway.

Like most other kids of the time, I took full advantage of the liberties afforded me. On a road trip, I wandered about the rear seat compartment of our car in the same way a cruise passenger might rove around a ship. I might begin my day by taking in some sun up top on the rear window ledge, lying flat on my back and staring up at the sky through the grid of radio antenna lines embedded in the glass. When lunchtime rolled around, I'd join my fellow passengers/brothers in the lavishly appointed dining

209

area that was the backseat. After finishing my meal, I'd grab a pillow and retire belowdecks to the floorboard, where I stretched out for a nap on the warm and comfy shag carpet, positioning my belly just so over the hump of the transmission housing. After waking, I might check in with the captain on the bridge for an update on progress toward our next port of call. Really, all our car lacked was a shuffleboard deck and poolside bar.

At the time, the idea of wearing seatbelts, especially in the backseat, seemed borderline crazy. Why would anyone wear seatbelts in the backseat? If Dad has to stop suddenly, we have seats right in front of us to prevent us from flying forward. Isn't that why carmakers pad the back of front seats anyway? In fact, the first thing my brothers and I did when we climbed into the backseat before a long road trip was tuck the seatbelt buckles and latches into the crevasses where their sharp edges wouldn't pose a threat to our tender rears.

My mother reluctantly turned a blind eye to our buckle burying. As a physical therapist who worked in a hospital, she saw firsthand the victims of car crashes and understood the tragic consequences of passengers being tossed around cars. But she also knew that if she insisted we buckle up, our griping would be intolerable. *"But nobody else's mom makes them buckle up in back!"* we'd have whined. And we would have been right—almost no one *did* wear seatbelts at the time, especially not in the backseat. My mom, however, always made certain to buckle herself in and insisted anyone else sitting in the front seat did as well. After all, there were no cushiony seatbacks to protect those in front in the event of an accident, only a hard dashboard and windshield. My dad grudgingly complied, more out of a sense of duty as our father and protector than concern for his personal safety. He reasoned that if an accident sent our car into a wild spin, wearing a seatbelt would hold him in place in the driver's seat so he could deftly steer us all away from further peril. But we all knew that when he was in his car alone, he rarely buckled up.

It wasn't that Dad disregarded safety entirely when it came to our cars. If you'd asked him, he'd say that safety was a primary reason for buying the cars he did. The way he saw it, size was the best safety feature—bigger cars, he said, were safer cars. In his mind, there was no better way to protect his family on the road than by surrounding us in an impregnable fortress of steel, an apt description of every car he ever bought.

He was right to a certain extent. Crash tests at the time showed—and still do today—that large cars fare significantly better than smaller cars in collisions, particularly when the two smash into each other. In general, the old joke that "the bigger car always wins" holds true.

However, what my dad (and most other car buyers of the time) didn't realize was that while bigger cars fare better, unrestrained passengers inside them often don't. The real threat to those inside isn't the first collision, when car hits car, but the so-called second collision, when occupants hit the steering wheel, dashboard, windows, or even other occupants. It was a concept researchers had understood for decades, but few people outside the crash test labs were in a rush to do much about.

It was no accident—pardon the pun—that automobile travel in the seventies wasn't safe. The truth is, automakers and auto buyers had informally colluded for years to prevent safer vehicles and smarter driving practices. Locked in an ongoing battle to woo buyers, car companies resisted adding safety features to their vehicles if it meant making them more expensive. For their part, many consumers were just as reluctant to buy cars with safety features because they believed their presence meant the cars must be somehow unsafe.

As an example, take the package of safety features known as Lifeguard, which Ford introduced and aggressively marketed in 1956. Lifeguard was the culmination of years of crash research conducted at Cornell University and Ford's own test labs. The idea was championed by Robert McNamara, president of the Ford Division and one of ten intrepid young "whiz kids" Henry Ford II recruited to turn around his foundering car company.

Launched with great fanfare, Ford's ads for Lifeguard detailed the safety package's many innovations: the Lifeguard steering wheel ("Its deep-center structure acts as a cushion in the event of an accident!"); double-grip door locks ("Designed to give extra protection from doors springing open under shock!"); safety belts ("Provide new protection and peace of mind!"); plus other innovations, such as a cushioned instrument panel, padded seatbacks, and swingaway rearview mirrors. These pioneering advancements helped Ford earn *Motor Trend*'s Car of the Year award for 1956. There was just one problem: hardly anyone bought the optional Lifeguard package. After an initial flurry of interest, sales quickly tailed off, as did sales of Fords.

Meanwhile, Chevrolet was breaking all-time sales records by pushing cars with bigger, more powerful V-8 engines. In 1955, the year before Lifeguard's debut, Chevy outsold Ford by 67,000 cars. The year after Ford spent millions promoting Lifeguard, Chevy tripled that number. A seething Henry Ford II muttered, "McNamara is selling safety, but Chevrolet is selling cars!" The spectacular flop of Lifeguard gave birth to an auto industry mantra: "Safety doesn't sell."

The failure confirmed what many auto executives already suspected: people want to believe they're immune to tragedy. They want to believe car accidents are rare events and automobiles are places where they can enjoy themselves in carefree safety. The last thing car executives wanted to do was dispel those notions. So even as automakers occasionally introduced new safety features—crashproof door locks and padded dashboards among others—such improvements were offered as options rather than standard equipment. Automakers also refrained from promoting the devices. When they did, the advertising portrayed them as helpful conveniences. Safety locks weren't designed to keep doors closed and occupants inside the vehicle in a crash; they helped parents prevent curious kids from unlocking doors when cars were in motion. Power brakes weren't intended to help drivers avoid slamming into a stopped garbage truck; they made it easier to come to a smooth halt at a traffic light.

But car companies went a step further. For much of the first seven decades of the industry's existence, automakers actively lobbied against any safety requirements that would add to their production costs or cause buyers to think twice about automobile safety. By the time devices such as automatic seatbelts and airbags became widely available in the sixties and seventies, American carmakers simply fought them out of habit as much as anything else.

Depending on how you define the term, seatbelts were around long before the automobile. Edward J. Claghorn first patented such a device in 1885, but his safety belt was designed for people who performed tasks at perilous heights, such as firemen, sailors, telegraph linemen, and, intriguingly, according to Claghorn's patent application, "tourists." Wearers strapped the belt around their midsection like a typical waist belt, then used a pair of carabiner-like hooks to secure themselves to a fixed object—a telegraph pole, a ship's mast, or, presumably, for tourists planning on tipping back a few mai tais in the tiki lounge, a high bar railing.

The first true automobile seatbelts appeared around the turn of the century. Most were installed by automobile owners—not to prevent injury in the event of an accident but simply to keep from being flung from their seats when encountering a bump or rounding a corner too quickly. Seatbelts caught on particularly with auto enthusiasts who raced their machines.

Still, few automobile owners went to the trouble or expense of installing them on their own. Some even argued that seatbelts were dangerous. In truth, there was evidence to back up the claim. In some types of collisions, lap belts—the only kind of seatbelts then in use—were found to cause even more serious injuries.

What was really needed was a new type of seatbelt.

Hugh DeHaven was well acquainted with the subject of automobile safety, having survived a deadly crash himself. While training to become a pilot during World War I, another flyer practicing gunnery runs clipped the wing of his aircraft, sending both planes plummeting to the ground. The other pilot died, but DeHaven survived. In fact, the worst injuries DeHaven suffered—ruptures to his pancreas, liver, and gall bladder—were the result of an unfortunately pointed buckle on his safety belt that tore into his abdomen. DeHaven struggled with the mystery of why the fates of two men involved in such similar crashes could have turned out so differently. He would devote a good portion of his life looking for the answer.

Following the war, DeHaven applied his training as a mechanical engineer toward becoming a freelance inventor. Many of his most successful ideas involved improvements in packaging, finding new ways to ship fragile goods with minimal damage. DeHaven's innovations were successful enough that he was able to retire in 1933 at the advanced age of thirty-eight. But fate would have other plans. Two years later, he witnessed a horrific high-speed crash that left a driver horribly injured when his face slammed onto the sharp steel protrusions of his dashboard. Shaken by the experience and recalling his own accident, DeHaven wondered: If fragile goods can be packaged for safer transportation, why can't people?

DeHaven had neither the facilities nor medical background for such research, but he did have a sharp mind and a carton of eggs. Using his kitchen as a lab, DeHaven began dropping eggs from increasing heights onto a scrap of half-inch foam. None of the eggs broke. Eventually DeHaven reached the ceiling—ten feet above the spongy mat. Still, the eggs he dropped remained intact.* For DeHaven, it was promising evidence that even delicate objects could withstand high-velocity impacts, provided there was a modest amount of cushioning.

However, eggs weren't human bodies. To gather more evidence, DeHaven collected newspaper clippings of what he called "miraculous survivals." One account described a sailor who was blown off a cliff by a mighty gust of wind and fell 320 feet onto a sandy beach below. Much to the amazement of several eyewitnesses, the man got up and walked away. And the *New York Times* detailed a

---

* In 1947, DeHaven repeated his egg-dropping experiment for a group gathered outside the Cornell University Medical College. On this occasion, he dropped eggs from a height of one hundred feet onto a rubber mat just three inches thick. From such a height, the eggs attained speeds greater than 50 miles per hour. Many bounced off the mat and sprang as high as thirty feet in the air before being caught by onlookers. Yet not a single egg was scrambled.

young woman's attempt to commit suicide by jumping from her ninth-floor window at Detroit's Palmetto Hotel. Instead of plummeting onto hard pavement, she landed on a freshly tilled flowerbed. When onlookers rushed to the spot, they were astounded to find the woman conscious and talking. DeHaven published his research, concluding that the human body could withstand tremendous impacts as long as the force of the blow was distributed over a large area of the body. In other words, it wasn't the fall (or collision) that killed people, but how and on what they landed. Combined with his ideas on "packaging" occupants in vehicles for safe transportation, DeHaven's findings would guide future crash survival investigations and DeHaven himself would become known as the Father of Crash Survivability.

From his base at Cornell University, DeHaven launched an investigative effort, the Crash Injury Research project (CIR), in 1942. As part of his research, he conducted the first practical crash tests, which initially focused on aircraft safety. After creating the first crash test dummies, he strapped his sensor-equipped mannequins into simulated cockpits and repeatedly sent them hurtling down the rails of a long, descending ramp to a jolting halt. Each time, he measured the forces exerted on the dummies and filmed their movements using special high-speed cameras. Analyzing the data, he reached two conclusions. First, aircraft interiors can be delethalized through better design, particularly by eliminating protrusions and hard surfaces. Second, the severity of injuries significantly increases when occupants aren't wearing safety belts.

Although DeHaven acknowledged that in some types of crashes, seatbelts can exacerbate injuries—such as the injuries he'd himself sustained in his airplane crash years earlier—he concluded the problem wasn't the seatbelts themselves but how they were designed. He began contemplating improvements.

Working with an engineer named Roger W. Griswold, DeHaven made a critical modification to the standard lap belt design. He added an extra strap that crossed the wearer's torso diagonally from shoulder to waist. This strap was designed to restrain the upper body and head in a collision, distributing the force of an abrupt stop over a greater area of the body and minimizing the devastating hinge effect caused by a belt solely worn across the lap. Griswold and DeHaven patented the design, called the CIR-Griswold Restraint, in 1951. It was the world's first three-point safety belt, a device that would ultimately be hailed as one of the most important patents of the twentieth century. Unfortunately DeHaven and Griswold have never received anywhere near the recognition they deserve for the idea.

Posterity would bestow the lion's share of the credit for development of the three-point safety belt to Nils Bohlin, a Swedish mechanical engineer employed first by Saab and later by Volvo.

Bohlin's first modification was to change where—and to what—the belt straps attached. Previous designs attached the top of the shoulder strap to the backs of seats. The problem with this design, as proven in crash tests, was that the seatbacks themselves were often unable to withstand the force of a head-on impact. The seatbacks broke, and the occupants, still strapped to their seats, were hurled forward into the dashboard, to their considerable dismay. Bohlin's design attached the top of the belt to the car frame, providing a solid anchor.

Next, Bohlin repositioned the buckle. Whereas the CIR-Griswold design kept the buckle in the middle of the lap, Bohlin moved it beside the opposite hip. This new position ensured that the lower section of belt was always pulled taut across the wearer's lap, essential for safe use, and also allowed the user to buckle up with a simple motion using one hand.

Bohlin's revolutionary three-point seatbelt design was widely hailed—at least in Europe. After Volvo made the new belt standard for its cars sold in Sweden in 1959, the company eventually took the unusual, and admirably benevolent, step of making Bohlin's patented three-point seatbelt design freely available to all other car manufacturers. By 1965, all cars manufactured in Europe were required to include front seatbelts.

Though Nils Bohlin would never become as internationally recognized as Sweden's other noteworthy contribution to humanity—I'm speaking, of course, of the legendary pop group ABBA—he would be revered in engineering and auto industry circles. Credited as "the man who saved a million lives," Bohlin was inducted into both the Automotive Hall of Fame and National Inventors Hall of Fame, taking his place among Orville and Wilbur Wright and Thomas Edison, among many others.

Bohlin's three-point seatbelt that was enthusiastically hailed in Europe got a cooler reception across the pond. Following the failure of Ford's Lifeguard package, US automakers were understandably reluctant to add any features to cars designed explicitly for occupant safety. And despite the mounting number of roadway fatalities, American car buyers remained apathetic about protecting themselves and their families. If efforts to improve automobile safety were going to gain momentum, they'd need a benevolent sponsor—a party with a vested interest in making the roads safer and with deep pockets to support the cause. That advocate was the automobile insurance industry.

. . .

As a growing number of cars jamming American roads spurred a corresponding rise in collisions and insurance claims, automobile insurance companies concluded it might be cheaper to spend money on finding ways to prevent accidents, or at least minimize the injuries that resulted from collisions. Executives at one of the leading insurance companies, Liberty Mutual, became aware of the work being conducted at Cornell University, home to Hugh DeHaven's CIR project. After meeting with researchers, Liberty Mutual agreed to underwrite their efforts to advance vehicle safety. But company executives had one additional request: they wanted Cornell engineers to showcase new safety innovations in a way that would spark the interest of skeptical car buyers. The result was one of the most simultaneously insane and delightfully daffy vehicles in automobile history.

Dubbed the Survival Car (officially, the Cornell-Liberty Mutual Survival Car), this marvel was first unveiled to the public in 1956. From the outside, the car didn't look much different from a typical sedan. But the audacious interior looked like something straight out of *Forbidden Planet* or one of the many other sci-fi movies of the era. The driver's seat was moved from the left side to the middle of the car to reduce the chance of injury from side impacts. The driver sat in a U-shaped, contoured capsule seat mounted firmly to the floor. To eliminate the risk of the driver's face being smashed into the steering wheel or chest being impaled on a rigid steering column, these components were removed. Instead, the driver steered using two hydraulic levers jutting out from a padded console like the handlebars of a bicycle. An enormous wraparound windshield, which afforded the driver a sweeping panoramic view, was kept spotless by five wipers. One passenger sat in a rear-facing seat behind the driver, while another was positioned to his rear left. Two more could be securely strapped into form-fitting rear seats. A roll bar provided protection overhead while two pairs of folding double doors (like those used in telephone booths) kept occupants safely inside the vehicle in a crash.

The Survival Car was impressively innovative, meticulously engineered, and, of course, wildly impractical. But it drew crowds and sparked publicity at the same auto shows where American automakers spent huge sums introducing their latest models.* By pointing out every stylish but lethal flaw in the design of their newest cars parked just steps away, the makers of the Survival Car drove many auto executives to the brink.

To demonstrate that existing car models could in fact be practically modified to improve safety at minimal cost, Cornell engineers produced a second Survival Car in 1960. To create this version, the team took a base model Chevrolet Bel Air and retrofitted it with many of their most practical and inexpensive safety ideas. Pointy levers and controls were replaced with rubber knobs and recessed buttons, and the dashboard was padded. Seats were outfitted with three-point belts, and mesh "whiplash nets" were added to cradle the heads of front seat occupants in the event of a rear-end collision. Finally, the entire perimeter of the car was wrapped in a ring of thick, protective rubber. Basically, the Cornell team turned the Bel Air into a bumper car.

The Survival Cars didn't stick around long, but the cause they championed did. The intriguing cars proved instrumental in generating public awareness of vehicle safety and helped win valuable allies for the automobile safety movement.

As public opinion swayed in favor of safety improvements,

---

*The Survival Car still appears alongside some of history's most stylish and beloved automobiles at the Henry Ford Auto Museum in Dearborn, Michigan.

lawmakers also backed the effort. In 1961, Wisconsin became the first state to require the installation of seatbelts in the front seats of passenger vehicles. Soon other states followed suit. When the federal government began contemplating stricter measures, automakers raised the white flag and began making voluntary changes. They announced that lap seatbelts (not Nils Bohlin's superior three-point belts) would be installed in the front seats of all cars produced in 1964 and added to rear seats by 1966.

But the Big Three were about to get broadsided from a new direction. In 1965, Ralph Nader's *Unsafe at Any Speed* was published. Remembered today as "the book about the Chevy Corvair," the exposé included just one chapter about the car and its alleged unsafe handling design.* The book's main focus was the auto industry's callous resistance to incorporating sensible safety measures in cars due to cost. Nader further charged that marketing ideas, rather than engineering principles, were given higher priority in how automobiles were designed. As evidence, he pointed to attractive but highly reflective chrome instrument panels that blinded drivers in bright sunlight and "bumpers shaped like sled-runners" that forced pedestrians under a car's front wheels when struck. Nader concluded that only the government had the power to compel automakers to incorporate safer design concepts and install devices already proven to prevent deaths and injuries.

The book's sales took off like a '66 Corvette Stingray. Not surprisingly, Nader's fans didn't include General Motors executives. In fact, the company took extreme steps to silence and intimidate

---

*Ironically, while Nader's concerns about automakers emphasizing style over safety proved valid, his harsh criticism of the Corvair may have been a bit overstated. Assessing claims made in the book, National Highway Traffic Safety Administration (NHTSA) testers showed "the 1960–63 Corvair does not result in abnormal potential for loss of control or rollover, and is at least as good as the performance of some contemporary vehicles."

the author. In a later lawsuit, Nader accused GM executives of tapping his phone, interrogating acquaintances, and hiring call girls to solicit him for sex—and he won his case. GM president James Roche was forced to personally apologize to Nader before Congress for the company's actions.

The firestorm the book created, combined with mounting complaints from the public and insurance industry, led to a series of widely publicized congressional hearings on road and vehicle safety in 1966. The result was that the government did exactly as Nader advocated: it gave itself the ability to establish and enforce national safety standards for highways and automobiles. The Highway Safety Act gave the federal government the power to set strict standards for highway construction, including better lighting, guardrails, and barriers between opposing lanes of traffic. The National Traffic and Motor Vehicle Safety Act created the National Highway Traffic Safety Administration (NHTSA), the agency that would set and enforce vehicle design standards. The NHTSA quickly mandated the installation of seatbelts (including three-point belts in the front two outboard seats), headrests, energy-absorbing steering wheels, shatter-resistant windshields, windshield wipers, standardized bumper heights, recessed control buttons, dual-braking systems, side-view mirrors, and "the padding and softening of interior surfaces and protrusions." For a moment, it appeared that safety advocates had gotten everything they'd sought for decades.

There was just one problem: while the NHTSA could make automakers *install* seatbelts, it couldn't make anyone actually *wear* them. And few did. A report compiled by the Centers for Disease Control and Prevention (CDC) showed that even in the mid-1980s, just 11 percent of automobile occupants were wearing seatbelts. The percentage was no doubt far lower for those of us who'd spent the previous ten years riding around in the backseat. Or in the station wagon's cargo bed. Or up on the rear window ledge.

Old habits were hard to break. By the late 1960s, most adults had spent their whole lives driving without seatbelts and weren't excited to start. Without grown-ups setting the example, few kids were likely to begin buckling up on their own. What's more, old myths persisted. Some people believed wearing seatbelts could inhibit their escape in the event their car became submerged or caught on fire (events they apparently deemed more likely than simply getting T-boned at an intersection). Others maintained it was actually safer to be thrown from a car in a crash, despite experts having proved decades before that the exact opposite was true.

In time, the NHTSA concluded that if people weren't going to buckle up on their own, it had no choice but to force auto-makers to make cars do the job. By 1970, such technology was already in development. Both Volvo and Volkswagen, two foreign automakers, of course, had been working on creating automatic seatbelts for some time. The idea was to mechanize the process of strapping in the driver once he or she had sat down and closed the door or started the engine. Confident any wrinkles could be worked out in time, the NHTSA mandated that all vehicles man-ufactured in 1973 include automatic seatbelts or airbags, another device in development. Though automakers were able to delay the mandate from taking effect, many, including GM, grudgingly began offering automatic seatbelts as options.

Automatic seatbelts were almost universally detested. Not only didn't the systems work well, the equipment could be down-right dangerous. The most common system combined a manually buckled lap belt with a shoulder strap brought into position by an electronic runner traveling along a track built into the door frame. When the door was opened, the runner automatically raced back to its original position beside the dashboard to allow the occupant to exit. However, if the drivers impulsively reached down to, say, pick up a pair of dropped sunglasses before the system initiated, the strap would smack them in the face from the front. If drivers opened the door to check on their parking, the strap could wrap around their neck from behind. And if drivers didn't react fast enough to escape the confused system, the strap could wrap around their neck like a noose. It was, ironically, a safety device that could kill you.

To defend its stance on automatic seatbelts, the Department of Transportation trotted out a study showing how cars equipped with the devices reduced highway fatalities as much as 67 percent. But the argument won over almost no one. People *hated* the newfangled claptrap. They didn't buy cars equipped with automatic belts and evaded using the belts in cars that were. After all, most automatic seatbelt systems still required users to manually buckle their lap belt, and it wasn't difficult to simply duck one's head under the traveling shoulder strap. Also, there was little hope of making automatic seatbelt systems workable for backseat or middle passengers. Worn down by years of consumer opposition and lobbying efforts by the auto industry, the NHTSA finally gave up its effort to make automatic seatbelts mandatory in 1981.

Even with the death of automatic seatbelts, the Battle of the Buckle wasn't over. The cavalry simply had yet to arrive. Once again, the charge would be led by the insurance industry, and in time a state-by-state effort was mounted to pass new laws. Americans may not have liked seatbelt laws, but they did grow to accept them, especially as one generation gave way to the next. One government study showed seatbelt use jumped from just 11 percent in 1981 to 68 percent in 1997. Over that same period, the number of automobile fatalities per million miles traveled was cut in half. While the decrease can't be attributed to seatbelt use alone, there is no question seatbelts played a primary role. Today, the NHTSA estimates seatbelt use runs as high as 85 percent. Our highways are safer too—in fact, they're the safest they've been since 1949. Despite significantly more motorists on our highways, just 32,719 people lost their lives in highway vehicle accidents in 2013. In 1979, the peak of my family's road-tripping days, that figure was 51,093.

For those of us who grew up traveling the highways unencumbered by seatbelts, the passage of mandatory state seatbelt laws was the passing of an era. Sure, we were all suddenly a lot safer on the highways, but that protection came at a price. Gone were the days of lying up on the rear window ledge soaking in the warm sunshine. No longer would we be able to stretch out for a nap on the laps of our older siblings or hoist our elbows up over the front seat to stare out at the road ahead over the shoulders of our parents. And our own children will never know the pleasure of clearing out a space amid the luggage in the back of the station wagon to enjoy a private lunch and wave at passing drivers. Those days are gone for good.

CHAPTER 11

Up, Up, and Away

All Roads Lead to the Airport

America is shrinking. It's a much smaller place today than it was in the 1970s, just as it was a much smaller country in the 1970s than it was in, say, the 1870s. Advancements in transportation will do that. The easier it becomes to travel from one end of the country to the other, the closer it all seems.

Once upon a time, a trip to California might as well have been a voyage to Mars. You loaded up a Conestoga wagon with all your earthly possessions, kissed your loved ones good-bye, and set off into the great unknown. It was a journey fraught with peril to a destination about which you knew little on an adventure from which you were unlikely to ever return—either because it required too much effort and expense or because you'd die along the way. Today the same trip means spending a few hundred bucks for a plane ticket to visit places you've already seen a thousand times in movies and on TV, and you'll be back in time for work on Monday. The greatest challenges you're likely to face are an overzealous Transportation Security Administration agent or being seated next to a colicky baby in coach.

In the seventies, travel was still in many ways closer to the days of Lewis and Clark than the era of frequent flier miles. America was still a country big enough to hold an almost limitless supply of unexpected delights, hidden dangers, and fascinating curiosities. On an extended road trip, you were certain to encounter a few of each. On one stretch of highway, you could discover the world's best roadside barbecue joint (our favorite find was Sammy's Pit Barbecue outside Jackson, Mississippi). On another, you might cross the border between two states by driving straight through a mountain (as you could do via the East River Mountain Tunnel connecting Virginia and West Virginia). And on another patch of highway, you might find yourself stranded at the side of the road with a steaming radiator, miles from anywhere and years before the invention of the cell phone, hoping the driver who stopped to offer you a ride wasn't an escapee from a nearby lunatic asylum. But to have those experiences, you had to travel through the country, not over it.

In those days, we didn't know nearly as much about our destinations, and we knew even less about what to expect once we arrived. At a time before cable TV and long before the Internet, we had only a vague idea of what many distant locations even looked like. It wasn't hard to imagine the beaches of Florida, of course, and like everyone else who watched *The Wonderful World of Disney* every Sunday night, we had a good idea of what we'd find at Disney World. But when my family first arrived in New Orleans's French Quarter in 1976, we might as well have been the Pilgrims landing at Plymouth Rock.

Coming, as we had, from the mundane Midwest, we were truly strangers in a strange land. The colorful stucco and elaborate wrought iron balconies of the buildings were unlike anything we'd seen before. We were awed by the grandeur of St. Louis Cathedral, entranced by the paddle wheel boat churning its way down the nearby Mississippi River, intrigued (and slightly terrified) by the sight of the crumbling aboveground burial vaults of St. Louis Cemetery No. 1. It seemed exotic and foreign. Today, these sights are familiar even to those who've never traveled to New Orleans, simply from spotting them in everything from movies and TV shows to commercials and cable news segments. Back then, you had to spend days driving across the country to see them. And that made the experience all the more worthwhile.

My parents didn't see the fact that America was so big as an obstacle. They viewed it as a challenge. There were a lot of interesting places in the country to visit, and they were determined to take us to see them all—whether we wanted to or not (and just so long as there was quality golfing close by). Setting off in a family cruiser two or three times a year, we managed to tick the boxes on a long checklist of interesting American destinations: Miami, Daytona Beach, the Florida Space Coast, Disney World, Pensacola, Charleston, Savannah, Atlanta, St. Louis, the Ozark Mountains, Memphis, Gettysburg, and more. After falling in love with New Orleans, my parents purchased a small studio condominium at a nearby golf resort in Diamondhead, Mississippi, making that location a regular destination throughout our travel years.

By the time 1980 rolled around, we'd already covered tens of thousands of miles. But things were about to change. As summer 1980 drew to a close, my parents began discussing possible trip destinations for our upcoming Christmas and Easter breaks. My dad had been enjoying a particularly good season of golf that summer, so it came as no surprise when it was decided that we'd be heading down to our tiny studio condo at Diamondhead again for the holidays. Now in his midfifties, Dad knew his best playing days were behind him, and he wanted to ride a hot streak as long as he could. Nor was it a big surprise when, one autumn evening as we were all gathered around the dinner table, my parents announced our destination for spring break: Washington, DC. Mom and Dad had been on a bit of a history kick. On one recent trip, they took us to Charleston, South Carolina, where we visited Fort Sumter and the USS *Yorktown* aircraft carrier turned floating World War II museum. On another trip, we toured the Gettysburg Battlefield. It made sense that we'd finally embark for our nation's capital. But it was what came out of my father's mouth next that caused our jaws to drop: "What would you kids think if we all flew to DC instead of driving?"

Fly? On an airplane? Like, those machines with wings? And pilots who—I had it on good authority from reliable sources (some of my fifth-grade buddies)—invited kids up to the cockpit to fly the plane? And pretty stewardesses who came around and brought as many Cokes as you wanted? And tiny bathrooms in the rear that, after you flushed, dropped your pee from the sky on whoever was below (again, my sources were quite clear on this)?

We were stunned. Speechless. Was this another of Dad's lame jokes? My father certainly wasn't above pulling our legs on occasion, so my siblings and I kept looking at each other, waiting for the inevitable punch line to drop. Instead, Dad launched into an explanation, one he and my mom had obviously discussed.

"Listen, we only have eight days for the trip and there's so much for us to see in DC: the White House, the Capitol building, the Washington Monument, the Smithsonian Museums. We've read that each of those can take a day in itself. If we fly instead of drive, we'll have two extra days to cover as much as we can."

So, we were going to fly . . . to save travel time? Seriously? Had my father suddenly won the lottery without us knowing? But he was too cheap to even buy a ticket! Had aliens abducted our father and replaced him with some pod person? Besides, how would we get around once we got there? Was our car coming on the plane too?

"We'll get a cab from the airport to our hotel," my father continued. "Then we'll just take the subway—they call it the Metro in DC—wherever we need to go. Almost everything is easy walking distance from a Metro stop. We really don't even need a car."

Wait. So in addition to my first flight on an airplane, I was also going to get out of this my first ride in a taxicab? And my first ride on some sort of subway train–type thing? All before I'd even entered the sixth grade? Count me in!

Before Dad could even finish his pitch, my siblings and I were sold. Of course, in reality, the decision had already been made. My dad wasn't seeking our approval; he was just telling us what was going to happen to get us excited about our first family plane trip.

The way he'd explained it, it all made perfect sense—and yet none at all. If flying to our destination was such a smart choice now, why hadn't it been before? It sure would have been nice to have had a couple extra days at Disney World a few years back. Heck, I might have even had time to work up the courage to ride the Space Mountain roller-coaster. It wasn't like we'd needed a car at Disney World either—they had buses and trams and even a monorail to shuttle us wherever we wanted to go.

But the more I thought about it, the more I realized many of my friends also suddenly seemed to be flying with their families to distant destinations. Had something changed about flying I didn't know about? Was there a reason families like mine were suddenly leaving behind their station wagons to go jetting off to their vacation destinations?

As it turned out, there was. I was simply too young to know it.

• • •

It wasn't an empty gas tank or steaming radiator that would bring the era of family road trips sputtering to the shoulder. It was a pen—the one President Jimmy Carter used to sign the Airline Deregulation Act into law in October 1978. With a few sweeps of his hand, Carter almost instantly eliminated the barriers that for decades had prevented most middle-class families like mine from flying and instead had us stuffing ourselves into station wagons (or in the case of my family, loading up our Lincolns) for long road trips.

Deregulation unwound decades of government rules and red tape that had ensnared the airline industry and prevented the free market from working properly. Almost overnight, the cost of flying fell within reach of average American families. According to a report by the Government Accountability Office, the average airfare declined by around 30 percent between 1976 and 1990. Airfares to the most popular destinations dropped even more dramatically, and much sooner.

When flying suddenly became more affordable, more people clamored to get on board. A lot more. In 1979, the first year following deregulation, 317 million passengers boarded US flights, an increase of more than 50 percent from just five years earlier. The bulk of those additional passengers were people who'd never flown before because it had cost too much. Once strictly the domain of the wealthy and well heeled, air travel was suddenly open to just about everyone. In one fell swoop, deregulation had democratized the skies. As *Time* declared on the cover of its August 14, 1978 issue, it was a "New Era in the Air." No wonder so many families, even my own, were suddenly rethinking road travel by the early eighties.

Given the obvious benefits of airline deregulation, why did it take so long? Why were we still heading out on the highways to drive to distant destinations in the seventies at all? To learn the answer, we need to take a short flight back to the beginnings of American aviation and learn why the industry became so regulated in the first place.

As with automobiles, aviation in the United States was pioneered by men whose ambitions often exceeded the limits of good sense. Many of the first pilots had more screws loose than their machines. In hopes of securing lasting fame—or just the satisfaction of outdoing rivals—some sky jockeys would attempt just about any feat, no matter how daunting or how long the odds of success. Pilots continually vied to be the first to fly vast distances across treacherous seas or scorching deserts to exotic destinations. They attempted thrilling stunts such as flying through the opened doors of barns (giving us the term *barnstorming*) to draw crowds and grab headlines. And often they refused to postpone scheduled flights due to threatening weather merely to prove their manliness. Such daring exploits went a long way in capturing the public's fascination with flying and ultimately led to Charles Lindbergh's historic crossing of the Atlantic in 1927. But this reckless ambition also resulted in scores of deadly crashes and did little to instill confidence that aviation was a safe and reliable means of transportation.

By the 1920s, several domestic airlines had been established to carry passengers between select destinations. But if the industry was to grow, aviation leaders realized they needed the government's help to build new infrastructure—airports, landing strips, navigational aids—and to establish safety standards and basic rules of the road—or, in this case, the air.

At the urging of these leaders, Congress established the Aeronautic Branch of the Department of Commerce to ensure civil air safety. The department's purview included testing and licensing pilots, inspecting and certifying aircraft, writing and enforcing safety rules, designating airways, operating and maintaining navigational aids, and investigating aviation accidents. With some basic parameters and policies for the aviation industry set, the job seemed done.

Except, of course, it wasn't. In fact, the government was just getting started. As bureaucracies tend to view such matters, if a few good rules are sufficient, then many more are even better. The aviation industry also became swept up in a wave of sentiment opposing free market competition in the 1930s. The prevailing concern was that unfettered competition could drive down profits to the point that no individual business could survive operating safely and responsibly. As a result, the federal government vastly expanded the regulation of industries it deemed of vital national importance—banking, trucking, railroads, and, eventually, aviation.* Not only was commercial air travel beginning to flourish, but the transportation of soldiers and military supplies by air was increasingly viewed as essential for national defense, so Congress established the Civil Aeronautics Board (CAB) in 1938. From that moment on, individual airlines no longer had the power to set their own fares, routes, and schedules. Instead, these were all determined by a committee of bureaucrats in Washington.

For decades, the airlines essentially operated on, well, autopilot. The CAB assigned each airline a specific service area, dictated the routes it could fly, and determined the fares it could charge

---

*Conspicuous in its absence from this list was the auto industry. As the employer of tens of thousands of American workers and the producer of the country's primary means of transportation, the auto industry would seem to have been one of vital national interest and therefore a target for regulation. That the industry wasn't deemed "vital" by Congress speaks to the power the industry already wielded in defending its interests by the 1930s. Is it really any wonder federal involvement in automobile safety standards remained decades away?

and the amount of profit it could earn. Airlines were even told the models of aircraft they could operate and how they were to configure their seats on each plane. All that remained for the airlines to do was offer passengers a choice of coffee, tea, or milk.

By and large, the big airlines weren't unhappy with the arrangement. After all, they didn't have to worry about things like streamlining their operations to keep airfares competitive—ticket prices were set for them. What's more, the number of flights between cities was limited and competition restricted, all but ensuring that planes were filled with passengers. Profits were virtually guaranteed.

The folks boarding flights, though, were hardly average Americans. Only the very wealthy—or business travelers with expense accounts allowing them to act as such—could afford tickets. To please airline investors and employee unions, the CAB kept airfares high to keep profits high. According to the Air Transport Association, the cost of a round-trip coach ticket between New York and Los Angeles in 1958 was $208, around $1,600 in today's dollars. Such inflated fares typically included gourmet meals with silverware, white-glove service, and loads of legroom, prompting some today to recall the era as a lost golden age of flight. But it was a golden age only for those who had the gold. Small wonder that ordinary Americans of the 1950s and early 1960s, especially families, took to crossing the country by car, while society's upper crust streaked overhead in gleaming silver planes.

It wasn't until the early 1960s that the highly regulated airline system began to encounter turbulence. Ironically, the cause was the arrival of an advancement hailed as the next great leap in commercial aviation: the jet airliner. Jets were faster, safer, and far more efficient than the piston-engine planes they quickly replaced. In fact, jet aircraft may have been too efficient. Because commercial jets were able to carry more passengers farther and faster than ever before, airlines soon found themselves with lots of empty seats. They were also prohibited from dropping their fares to attract new customers who could buy up the extra capacity. At the same time, the number of travelers who could afford to fly remained unchanged. As a result, many planes began flying less than half filled.

With profits in a tailspin by the 1970s, management at the major airlines took what little action it could. Unable to compete on price, airlines found other ways to fight over customers. They secured approval to spread out seating for additional legroom (after all, they had nothing if not extra space). They served up steaks and gourmet fare. They created the first frequent flier programs to inspire loyalty. They hired the most attractive young women they could find as stewardesses and dressed them in miniskirts and go-go boots. In one famous ad campaign, National Airlines featured beguiling female attendants inviting prospective—and presumably male—passengers to "Fly Me." However, it did little to boost sagging revenues.

As it did to American travel in general, OPEC's 1973 oil embargo and the economic turmoil that followed dealt other staggering blows to the airline industry. Unsure of what the future held, many people, even the wealthy, put vacations on hold. Making matters worse, corporations slashed travel budgets, significantly reducing the number of business travelers, the airlines' most important customers.

The airlines were locked on a course for disaster. Because of strict regulation, carriers couldn't reduce fares to fill their empty seats. They couldn't abandon unprofitable routes. They couldn't even open new routes that showed the potential to turn a profit. Though it was possible to file an application to open a new route, the approval process was so slow and complex it was virtually useless to try. In one notorious example, World Airways applied to the CAB for permission to open a new route between New York and Los Angeles in 1967. Finally, years later, the application was returned to the airline with a letter of rejection noting, "This application is 6½ years out of date, it is no longer current or relevant."

Meanwhile, in contrast to the big national carriers, one airline wasn't only surviving but thriving. Its secret? Being small enough to fly through a loophole in all of the regulatory red tape.

In the mid-1960s, as it was becoming clear that regulation was strangling US airlines, it occurred to an attorney named Herb Kelleher that federal controls applied only to airlines that crossed over state lines—not airlines that flew only within them. Without having to submit to the ill-conceived dictates of Washington bureaucracy, Kelleher reasoned, an airline flying within a single state could offer airfares at a fraction of the prices that the national carriers charged. What's more, Kelleher happened to live in a state big enough for such an idea to make sense: Texas. The second-largest state in the nation, behind only Alaska, Texas is distinguished by having numerous bustling cities located hundreds of miles apart, an arrangement ideally suited for an airline formed to operate solely within the borders of a single state. So in 1967 Kelleher and a partner, Rollin King, founded Air Southwest Co., the carrier we know today as Southwest Airlines.

The idea of an intrastate airline wasn't new. Many small airlines around the country flew point-to-point routes within a single state, evading federal regulations. But nearly all were one- or two-plane operations, connecting commuters in major cities to unique destinations, such as islands or specific tourist attractions. Southwest Airlines aimed to operate on a much larger scale, beginning with a small fleet of Boeing 737s flying dozens of daily routes between Dallas, Houston, and San Antonio.

In developing Southwest Airlines and its edgy personality, Herb Kelleher borrowed heavily from the ideas of another intrastate carrier, Pacific Southwest Airlines (PSA), which had operated in California since 1949. Besides offering similarly discounted airfares as PSA, Southwest also copied the airline's hiring strategy. To select Southwest's all-female staff of flight attendants, Kelleher appointed a committee headed by a man who'd handpicked the hostesses for Hugh Hefner's *Playboy* jet. The selected candidates included outgoing and attractive former dancers, majorettes, and cheerleaders whom Southwest dressed in shape-hugging uniforms featuring short skirts. Kelleher even appropriated PSA's risqué tagline for his advertising: "Long Legs and Short Nights." (Today, it's hard to imagine an airline with such a campaign not suffering the wrath of Twitter.)

For its part, PSA openly welcomed the addition of another upstart intrastate airline as a rebel ally in its revolt against federal regulations. The airline invited Kelleher to tour its facilities, assisted in training Southwest's mechanics, and loaned it start-up manuals and other necessities.

The combination of cheap airfares and friendly service was an instant hit with Texans. While the national airlines battled over a shrinking number of wealthy and corporate air passengers, Southwest was attracting vast numbers of new customers from groups that had never flown before: college students seeking cheap travel between school and home, families wanting to take the kids to visit Grandma and Grandpa, and young couples escaping for romantic getaways. Southwest was opening the skies to a whole new class of air travelers. And it was possible only because the airline was able to operate profitably—even grow—by offering airfares that were often half the price of those demanded by national carriers.

Southwest's low fares didn't just attract the attention of travelers. They drew the ire of the major airlines. And who could blame them? While the national carriers were struggling to survive as they coped with the inflexible rules foisted on them by the CAB, Southwest Airlines' success was due almost entirely to the freedom to set its own fares, routes, and schedules.* Unable to compete with Southwest on a level playing field within Texas, three airlines—Braniff, Continental, and Trans-Texas Airways (a regional airline)—sued to stop Southwest from flying. But in 1970, the Texas Supreme Court, and later the US Supreme Court, sided with David against the Goliaths. Southwest Airlines could continue flying free from the constraints of federal regulation within its home state.

National press coverage of the lengthy legal battle only highlighted Southwest's growing success and raised questions about the need for continued federal airline regulations. Across the country, people wondered why, if such benefits were available to the residents of Texas, they shouldn't be available everywhere else.

By the time Jimmy Carter was elected president in 1976, it was clear something had to be done to save the airline industry.

---

*It wasn't a complete free-for-all for Southwest Airlines. The company was still subject to oversight by Texas state agencies and the Federal Aviation Administration, but overall, the regulatory burden was far less restrictive. By comparison, the airline enjoyed the same freedom as, say, the kids in the back row of a crowded school bus with a disinterested driver at the wheel.

Almost immediately, Carter appointed Alfred E. Kahn to head up the CAB. Kahn had no background in aviation and very little in administration. He was an economist and self-described "good liberal Democrat." Yet like many other leading progressives of his day, he believed fervently that government regulation was most often bad for consumers. In his book *The Economics of Regulation*, he asserted that "even very imperfect competition is preferable to regulation." Working with like-minded progressives including Senator Edward Kennedy and consumer advocate Ralph Nader, Kahn spearheaded the effort to deregulate the airline industry. In effect, he made it his mission to kill the agency he headed.

It didn't take long. In little more than a year, the Airline Deregulation Act was passed by Congress and signed into law by President Carter on October 24, 1978. The legislation set forth a plan to remove restrictions on the airlines in phases over a four-year period, with all regulation of domestic fares ending by 1983. In reality, it would all happen much faster.

As each phase lifted a new set of regulations, airfares dropped and more passengers booked flights. Almost instantly, airfares fell within reach of ordinary folks who'd never previously considered air travel because of the cost—a group that included middle-class parents wanting to take the kids somewhere warm for spring break. Deregulation wasn't the only reason for the big drop in airfares. Better planes and new technology also played roles. But it can be argued that deregulation created the competitive environment that prompted airlines to find ways to continue reducing costs.

Substantially cheaper airfares meant significantly more people taking to the skies. In 1977, just prior to deregulation, 240 million passengers bought tickets for flights. Five years after the government began lifting restrictions on airlines, 316 million passengers boarded planes, an increase of 31 percent. Ten years after deregulation began, 89 percent more passengers booked flights on US airlines. Today, more than three times as many people buy airline tickets as in 1977.

Of course, the uptick in air travel wasn't about price alone; it also had to do with route choice. With the government no longer dictating or limiting routes, carriers could offer more service between more places. Prior to deregulation, American Airlines flew to 39 destinations. Today, it flies to more than 350—nearly nine times as many. And that's just one airline.

With the airlines free to offer cheaper and faster access to more places, traveling families like mine were ready to trade long drives for short flights.

In the early eighties, I had no clue about airline deregulation, of course. I was simply beginning to notice that more of my classmates were returning from holiday breaks with sunburns and shark tooth necklaces. They had better stories to tell too. Instead of the usual tired recaps of trips to their aunt and uncle's houses in Indianapolis or Cleveland, my buddies were telling tales of climbing to the top of the Statue of Liberty in New York, getting "attacked" by the giant shark from *Jaws* on a tour of Universal Studios in Hollywood, and brushing their fingers over real bullet holes in the walls of the Alamo in San Antonio, Texas. I'd listen, engrossed, as they recounted how they stood in the very spot where Davy Crockett fell while he and a band of brave souls attempted to hold off hordes of marauding Mexican troops before meeting their grisly end. This was good stuff.

Each of my friends' stories included a detailed description of hurtling down a long runway before lifting off into the sky, being served their choice of tasty meals by a knockout stewardess, and—us being twelve years old and all—paying a visit to a tiny restroom at the rear of the plane with a special toilet that noisily sucked down whatever was deposited in it—well, within reason.

My friends had the goods to back up their stories too. When assigned to make speeches in class, they brought in the coolest souvenirs to pass around: real scorpions frozen in glass from Arizona, boxes of saltwater taffy from the boardwalk in Atlantic City, colorful seashells and dried starfish from beaches all over Florida, and, of course, gleaming silver airline badges shaped like wings. The last of these were personally pinned to their shirts by the cool pilots of the even cooler jets that had flown them to their destinations.

Airplanes, or at least *Airplane!*, dominated our daily discussions. For an extended period after the hit comedy's release in 1980, every conversation between us preteens eventually linked back to the movie. Even if we weren't exactly sure why the Autopilot was suddenly smiling and enjoying a smoke after being inflated by the winsome Julie Hagerty, one of my friends would inevitably declare that he'd picked the wrong week to give up sniffing glue. It became common to strike up a conversation with a buddy by asking if he enjoyed watching gladiator movies or ever spent a night in a Turkish prison. If you grew up during that time, surely you understand. And, yes, I just called you "Shirley." If nothing else, the movie kept airplanes buzzing around our thoughts.

When the day finally came for me to board my first flight and head to Washington, DC, with my family in 1981, I was understandably excited. I could hardly wait to catch my first glimpse of our beaming silver jet through the windows of our gate's waiting area, stride down the narrow jetway and through the jet's vault-like door, and sneak a peek into the cockpit as I filed past the flight crew, confident I'd be invited by the captain to return for a more thorough inspection later. Of course, I was *most* anxious to get up in the air so I could head back to the bathroom to try out the amazing vacuum toilet/bomb bay door for myself. From my friends' descriptions, I fully expected to be able to peer through the hole in the bottom of the toilet and see clear down to the ground to the unfortunate soul who'd soon be drenched with my plummeting pee.

As it turned out, the experience didn't come close to meeting my high expectations. Sure, takeoff was exhilarating—the rumble of the jet engines, the powerful acceleration as we dashed down the runway, the rush of lifting off into the sky as the ground disappeared beneath us. But once we were airborne, things became distinctly more mundane. Rather than a lithe Julie Hagerty in go-go boots, my stewardess resembled a dowdy Ruth Buzzi in a polyester pantsuit. The fancy gourmet dinner I'd been told about turned out to be little more than a dressed-up TV dinner. Even the toilet failed to live up to the hype. Yes, when I pressed the lever to flush, it swallowed up my pee with a forceful sucking sound. But there was no hole in the bottom of the airplane. In fact, it was pretty obvious my pool of urine was simply dropping into a holding tank rather than raining down onto some bewildered farmer's head. It was all very disappointing. Even worse, my invitation to visit the cockpit never arrived. In fact, the captain never once stepped out from behind the closed door at the plane's front. The only time we even heard his voice was when he announced we'd be beginning our descent, and even then it was almost entirely incomprehensible on the staticy overhead speaker. Clearly, he hadn't received word that there was a bright and charming twelve-year-old boy sitting in coach who was contemplating a future career in aviation.

On the plus side, my sister *did* puke on our descent, proving she was just as adept at getting airsick as carsick. It provided me some measure of comfort to know some things would never change, no matter what the future held.

At the very least, I confidently maintained that I'd be handed my own pair of shiny silver wings on my way off the plane, the same kind my friends had passed around during their presentations at school. But as I watched the passengers ahead of me filing out the door, I saw that the only things being distributed by the flight crew were obligatory smiles and "thank yous." Not one to easily accept defeat, I stopped and caught the pilot's attention, making sure to employ the manners and twelve-year-old charm that had always served me so well with adults: "Excuse me, Mr. Captain, sir, do you have any of those wing things I could have as a souvenir? This is my first time on an airplane!" The captain's eyebrows sunk into a furrow. "Hmm, I'm not sure we're handing those out anymore," he replied. "Bill, have you seen a bag of badges?" he asked his copilot. The man shrugged his shoulders and wafted open his palms. "Sorry, I guess we ran out."

So I walked off the plane with nothing. It seemed appropriate, considering the whole experience of flying had left me feeling empty inside. It just hadn't felt much like a family trip. There'd been no 3:00 a.m. wakeup, no sleepy march to the car, no glimpse of the Bong Recreation Area exit sign. No long naps on our car's sun-warmed rear window ledge, no license plate game, no helping Dad spot Smokeys waiting with their radar guns at the side of the road. We hadn't fought over control of the car stereo, my father never levied a "Dad tax" on our French fries, my parents hadn't argued about when it was time to get off the highway and refuel. We never once rolled into the parking lot of a Stuckey's or Ramada, or rushed around to scope out a motel's pool and game room, or started a single pillow fight on the precarious footing of a rollaway bed.

It occurred to me that we'd barely even spoken to each other during the flight. I'd spent most of the time just staring out the window at the clouds, while on either side of me, my mother read her magazine and my sister slept in her seat. My father and brothers, seated in the row behind us, might as well have been on a different airplane. The only time I'd even seen them was on my walk back to the bathroom.

Through the miracle of modern aviation, we'd boarded a plane in Milwaukee and in just two hours—about the time it normally took us just to clear the traffic of Chicago—had arrived in Washington, DC, eight hundred miles away. Somehow it didn't feel right. It felt as though we'd cheated—I wasn't sure who or what exactly. *The travel gods? The great explorers who preceded us? Ferdinand Magellan? Lewis and Clark? Neil Armstrong?*

The plain fact was that other than purchasing our plane tickets, we'd made no real effort to reach our objective, as those men had—or even as we'd always had in the past. There'd been no hardships, no squabbles, no hours of tedium, not even a worry that we'd missed a turn and were suddenly headed for Walla Walla instead of the Washington Monument. Our flight had allowed us to soar over all the things that once made a family vacation . . . a family vacation. We'd taken a trip but we'd made no journey. And somehow it felt as though we hadn't earned the right to enjoy our final destination.

It would be untrue to say our family trip to Washington, DC, wasn't a memorable one. It was. I still recall chasing my siblings up the twisting spiral of stairs inside the Washington Monument, walking the halls of the White House and expecting to bump into President Reagan around every corner, and silently gazing up at the eternally contemplative face of Honest Abe at the Lincoln Memorial. There was also no doubt that the time and energy we'd saved by flying rather than driving allowed us to see and experience much more of the city. It had probably bought us the additional time we needed to visit the Smithsonian National Air and Space Museum—home of Charles Lindbergh's *Spirit of St. Louis* and an Apollo command module identical to the one used in the lunar landing—as well as take a side trip to Thomas Jefferson's Monticello. But for me, without all of us together spending those long hours crammed in our car, bickering over whose foot had invaded whose personal space, and sweating out those long miles trying to make it to the next exit for gas, the trip would always stir mixed emotions.

Perhaps it was because our visit to the nation's capital would also be among the last of our family vacations. As it turned out, the new era of air travel coincided almost perfectly with our final days traveling together as a family. It wouldn't just be jet-powered planes and cheap airfares that would kill our road trips together. It was the simple passage of time: we were all getting older, and life was quickly leading us in separate directions.

By 1980, both of my brothers were at college out of state. My sister would follow in 1982. Until and including our trip to DC, their holiday breaks happened to fall at just the right times to allow them to join the rest of us for our traditional family excursions. But that would soon change as, one by one, each went on to graduate, begin careers, and become increasingly entangled in the responsibilities that are part of growing up. When my brothers and sister could find time for a break, they reserved their precious vacation time to discover their own destinations with friends rather than join my parents and me at some far more mundane vacation spot. Of course, that was a result of airline deregulation as well. Cheaper airfares to distant ports of call opened up a whole new world for the young and adventurous that hadn't existed before 1978.

As for me, I would continue traveling with my parents throughout the decade, even after graduating from high school in 1987. After all, my folks were offering an all-expense-paid trip out of the Midwest winter to someplace warm. And as a poor high school and, eventually, college student, it wasn't as though my other options included a week-long junket in Waikiki. Sometimes my siblings would join us; most often they wouldn't. Sometimes we'd drive; more often we'd fly. Not surprisingly, there quickly developed an inverse relationship between the number of family members choosing to tag along for the trip and the likelihood my dad would spring for plane tickets. And as we boarded each flight, I became ever more aware that our family trips had forever changed. It wasn't just because one or two of my siblings were so often missing. Something else was missing as well—something we left behind in the airport parking garage each time we flew off into the horizon.

CHAPTER 12

Leaving It All Behind

The End of the Road for Road Trips?

One afternoon in late 1978, at almost exactly the same time President Carter was signing the Airline Deregulation Act into law, three musicians gathered in a London apartment for a songwriting session. Building on a catchy riff dreamed up by guitarist Bruce Woolley, musicians Trevor Horn and Geoff Downes spent an hour fleshing out a melody for the verses and adding a bridge, intro, and outro.

Intent on creating a new sound, Horn, acting as producer, spent six months refining the track using the latest audio technology. He added a thumping dance beat, a bouncy bass line, and layer upon layer of shimmering synthesizer lines that Downes composed. The sound Horn concocted created an instantly appealing aural confection that thumbed its nose at the serious and self-indulgent "guitar god" rock dominating the airwaves of the day.

As he was working his wizardry in the studio, Horn mulled lyrics that would match the song's vibrant new sound. Sensing that a new era was about to be born—not just in music but in modern culture—and that his innovative electronic sound could play a role, Horn ran with a novel idea. The lines he penned seemed trite and silly at first. But when they were sung—almost spoken—using an effect that made Horn's voice sound like that of a radio newsman from a bygone era and placed against the backdrop of Horn's infectious synth-pop sound, the words took on new meaning. The lyrics both greeted the new age and eulogized the one that was fading. Horn titled the song "Video Killed the Radio Star."

Calling themselves the Buggles, Horn and Downes released the debut single in 1979, and it soon became a major international hit, topping the charts in sixteen countries. "Video Killed the Radio Star" was among the first in a deluge of tracks produced by a new breed of avant-garde musical artists who became collectively known as the New Wave. The movement included such groundbreaking bands as Duran Duran, the B-52s, Culture Club, and Depeche Mode. Though these acts never quite dominated American music charts, their influence on pop culture far exceeded their modest record sales. It was this music that filmmakers of the early eighties chose as the backdrop for such hit movies as *The Breakfast Club*, *Pretty in Pink*, *Weird Science*, *Top Gun*, and *Say Anything*. In the process, New Wave artists literally wrote the sound track for a generation—*my* generation.

New Wave's influence also ushered in sweeping new trends in art, fashion, and hairstyles. Suddenly in were skinny ties and spandex skirts, neon colors, the androgynous look, sport mullets for guys, big hair for women, Swatch watches, underwear as outerwear, and the exotic painted beauties of Patrick Nagel. Out were platform shoes, flared trousers, long stringy hairstyles for guys, the feathered Farrah look for women, and the psychedelic style of artists like Peter Max.

Also falling out of favor were many of the music acts that had defined the seventies. Led Zeppelin, Pink Floyd, the Eagles, the Allman Brothers Band, the Bee Gees, Peter Frampton, Boston,

Linda Ronstadt, James Taylor, Kansas, and the Doobie Brothers, among others, all struggled to remain relevant in the new decade. New Wave didn't kill them all, of course. Some disbanded due to internal turmoil or the deaths of key members. Some, like Van Halen, Fleetwood Mac, and Tom Petty & the Heartbreakers, found ways to incorporate the synthesizer and aspects of the New Wave sound into their music. Others just faded away because their time had passed. Nonetheless, the rise of New Wave marked a significant changing of the guard.

The times were indeed a-changin' as the seventies gave way to the eighties. The feeling was palpable. It wasn't just the music. It was a cultural mind-set. America had a new president in Ronald Reagan, a new sense of optimism, and, within a very short time, new confidence in its rebounding economy. Americans were ready to dump the anxiety and malaise of the recent past and embrace a prosperous and exciting new future—one that included cheaper air travel made possible by airline deregulation.

It seemed somehow appropriate then that just as my family was about to experience our first taste of that future, "Video Killed the Radio Star" resurfaced. On August 1, 1981, two years after its initial release, the song and its music video launched the debut of MTV. Within months, my family, following in the footsteps of millions of other Americans, would board an airplane to embark on our first family vacation that didn't include a long trip by automobile. Just as MTV and its profound cultural influence would usurp the power of celebrity DJs and FM radio, the allure of inexpensive airfares and quick cross-country flights was about to bring the long reign of station wagons and TripTiks to a close. Just as video killed the radio star, cheap air travel would snuff out the family road trip.

The coup happened quickly. Between 1980 and 2000, the

number of flights booked by Americans more than doubled. As early as 1990, just twelve years after President Carter had signed the Airline Deregulation Act, more adult Americans had flown than owned a car. In the blink of an eye, the world had changed.

As the typical American family's choice of travel mode shifted, so did the vacation experience. Trips that once took days suddenly took hours. Parents no longer had to plan and prepare to keep the kids fed and satisfied on the road. Bags of cold sandwiches, Thermoses of hot coffee, road atlases, tool kits bulging with replacement fuses and belts, planning for gas and potty stops, and the art of trunk packing all became relics of the past. Kids no longer had to steel themselves for endless hours in the backseat. Secret stashes of candy, portable electronic games, stacks of magazines and comics, invisible ink puzzles, magnetic beard games, and other diversions suddenly didn't hold nearly the same importance.

Instead, everyone focused on the destination, wondering what the weather would feel like, planning what they'd do the moment they arrived. The journey became inconsequential, a brief nuisance to be endured until the fun could start. Where once a family trip began when the car pulled out of the driveway, now a vacation didn't really begin until the jet's wheels touched down on some distant runway. In fact, many travelers began thinking so little of the actual journey that they dressed for their destination before ever leaving home. In the middle of December in Wisconsin, families like mine could be seen dragging luggage into the airport wearing nothing but shorts and T-shirts, their warm winter jackets left in their cars in the parking lot. It was as though they were already in Florida.

But we were leaving behind much more than our bulky winter clothing. We were also leaving behind a quintessential American family experience. We were leaving behind all the curious sights and amazing views, the unexpected delights and unanticipated dangers, the colorful characters and unforgettable people who could only be encountered when traveling the highways of America. We were leaving behind so many of the ingredients that made family vacations truly memorable.

That's not to say that the family road trip has entirely gone the way of the eight-track player or the fake wood-paneled station wagon. Road trips enjoyed a brief but robust renaissance in the wake of the terrorist attacks of September 11, 2001. While the threat of additional hijackings caused flights to be grounded across the nation for weeks, the attacks instilled a fear of flying in Americans that lasted far longer. What's more, the tragedy forced workaholic parents to take stock of their overscheduled lives. Many questioned why they were running themselves ragged to provide better lives for their kids when the extra income came at the expense of having no quality time to spend with them. Rather than canceling vacations, many families planned new ones. Only instead of taking to the skies, families once again took to the highways. For a while, many American families reacquainted themselves with the simple joys of heading out together on the open road.

In an article published in the *New York Times* on November 11, 2001—just two months after the 9/11 attacks—writer Julia Chaplin deftly captured the country's mood:

> For years now, the pleasures of the road trip have palled. Driving long distances became a time-guzzling burden, and interstates seemed more often linked with road rage and bad French fries. But then came an overnight fear of air travel and a yearning for escape from new urban anxiet-

ies, especially in New York. Suddenly, the open road holds a fresh appeal for those who have single-mindedly pursued big-city lives and ambitions.

The revival would be short-lived. By 2004, the cost of oil had surged, boosting prices at the pump. At the same time, the absence of further hijackings reassured Americans that it was once again safe to fly. Gradually American families returned to parking their cars and booking flights. By 2007, more Americans were flying than ever before. After a sharp decline due to the recession that began in 2008, the number of Americans traveling by air continues to rise steadily. Today, more than 750 million airline tickets are sold each year.

Of course, the decision to drive rather than fly to distant destinations will likely always make sense financially, especially for larger families. As of this writing, the cost of a round-trip coach airline ticket from Milwaukee to Fort Lauderdale during spring break costs $342. For a family of six, like mine when I was growing up, that comes to $2,052. Include a midsize rental car for an eight-day stay, and the cost swells another $750. That's $2,800 for transportation before laying out a single dollar for hotel, food, attractions, or other expenses. Now consider the cost to drive the same 2,902-mile distance in a minivan, which, when packed with six passengers and luggage, can struggle to achieve 22 miles per gallon. Using the current average gas price of $2.25 per gallon, that same trip would cost around $297. That's a difference of almost $2,500 in favor of driving versus flying. Without any pressure applied by my mom, I know what decision my dad would have made.

Yet many families today choose otherwise. The reason is simple: the world has sped up since the 1970s. We live in an era of instant gratification—of instant text messaging, overnight package delivery, and movies on demand. When we want something, we want it *now*. At the same time, we spend our lives rushing to meet impossible deadlines, making ourselves available by phone and e-mail around the clock, and putting in extra hours to get ahead in our careers. When we manage to work in a getaway, we want to make the most of it. For many of us, time has become far more precious than money, a priceless commodity not to be squandered lumbering along endless miles of highway and waiting in drive-through lines. We want to be there now, wherever the *there* is we're headed. We want to be on a beach under a hot sun, enjoying the view from the top of the Washington Monument, or taking smartphone snapshots of our kids with Mickey in front of the Princess Castle, *right now*. And until that teleporter from *Star Trek* is available, the quickest way to do that is by boarding an airplane.

For those of us who do decide to drive, the experience of taking a long family road trip together isn't the same now. For one thing, families no longer really experience a long car ride "together." In fact, for people sitting so close to one another, we've never been farther apart. In the backseats, where we as kids once sprawled out across our siblings, or constantly changed seat positions depending on who was annoying whom, today each child must be rigidly buckled into his or her own child seat. Securely strapped into their padded cocoons, our kids can barely lift a sippy cup to their mouths, much less exchange noogies with their siblings. To keep them entertained, we put headphones on their ears and place tablet screens in front of their eyes and allow each child to enjoy his or her own movie or game without even having to debate the choice with siblings. Meanwhile, in the front seat, Mom slips on her own headphones to retreat into her audiobook or podcast.

Behind the wheel, Dad turns up the satellite radio and drifts off into his own private world, singing along to his favorite songs—perhaps even the same seventies and eighties tunes he sang when he cruised the interstates with his parents. Largely gone are the days of family singalongs, playing the license plate game, or—God forbid—just talking to one another.

At the same time, the country we live in has become far smaller. On today's interstates, it's difficult to travel more than a few dozen miles without passing an exit with a gas station and fast-food restaurant, usually in the same building. Apps on our smartphones keep us updated regarding detours and traffic alerts and ensure that roadside assistance is always just a phone call away. Today's cars have also become so reliable and worry-free that few of us even check our oil, much less pack a tool kit before departing on a long trip. Even if things do go wrong, safety features like advance warning alerts and run-flat tires allow drivers to travel for miles to find help.

Yet those of us a certain age will recall that it wasn't so long ago that beginning a family road trip felt a lot like setting off into the wild frontier. True, the roads were paved and the route was marked (and we were unlikely to encounter any bears or bands of outlaws), but the journey ahead was still fraught with unknown perils. Before us lay hundreds of miles of open road, and anything could happen. We might run out of gas along a lonely stretch of interstate on a rainy night in Arkansas. We might take a shortcut only to find ourselves being chased by a pack of wild dogs on a back road in Louisiana. Or we could be turned away from a full motel after a long day's drive, the next motel with vacancy still hours of dark highway down the road. And when things did go wrong, we'd be on our own.

On our own but *together*. As a family. Ready to face whatever the coming miles and passing hours brought our way. More than anything else, that's what made a family road trip so special: the feeling of being inextricably bound together in a great adventure. An adventure based less on where we were headed, and more in the moments we shared along the way.

In the end, it never really mattered where we traveled in our car on all those great family road trips. In simply making the drive together, we were already in the best place of all.

ACKNOWLEDGMENTS

The process of writing a book, especially a first book, is a lot like taking a cross-country road trip: the journey is frightfully long and challenging, the experience is filled with countless highs and lows, and you often find yourself wondering why the heck you ever set out. The only way you eventually reach the final destination is with the support and encouragement of those who joined you for the ride (without ever being given the choice) and countless people who so kindly offered their assistance along the way.

For their generosity in sharing memories of road trips with their own families, I thank Dr. Philip Munschauer, Andy Smith, Scott and Bob Goehner, Alan Udell, Tracy Laine, Jason Ells, and I'm sure a few other folks I inadvertently left behind like a distracted dad exiting a rest area.

For boldly venturing out into pothole-riddled early drafts of my manuscript and providing desperately needed feedback, I owe my eternal gratitude (along with a souvenir T-shirt) to Judy Stowell, Anna Eherenman, Karen Ratay, Kelly Simmons, and all of my siblings. Extra special thanks goes out to my longtime creative partner and friend Gary Haas, for assistance with the art direction of the book's cover and my personal website, and for always providing helpful directions when I got lost.

Of course, the only reason I was even able to write this book is because I was blessed to be born to two loving parents courageous (some might say "foolhardy") enough to head out on the highways to show their four kids the wonders of America when, clearly, staying home would have been much more sensible and far less maddening. In so many ways, writing this book was really my way of expressing my eternal gratitude to them since they're no longer around for me to thank in person. In that same vein, I also need to salute my other travel companions on all those trips, my brothers, Mark and Bruce Ratay, and my sister, Leslie O'Connell, both for tolerating their obnoxious youngest sibling then and allowing him to divulge our family's private escapades to the world now.

I'd still be stranded beside the highway if not for my agent, Jennifer Weltz of the Jean V. Naggar Literary Agency, who graciously pulled over, got behind my work, and pushed (and pushed) me along to help. Even then, it took some skillful wrenching by master mechanic/editor Rick Horgan and keen-eyed copy editor Beverly H. Miller to get the book road ready. For that matter, I was unbelievably fortunate to have so many wonderful folks at Scribner willing to lend their talents and enthusiasm and tinker around on my humble little vehicle.

Finally, my sons, Rainer and Reed, deserve medals for coming home far too often to an ornery dad grumbling about rejections and rewrites. And I could never thank my amazing wife, Terri, enough for her limitless belief in me (despite so little evidence to support such faith) and for riding shotgun with me on so many unforgettable adventures together.

INDEX